Skills and Strategies for Coaching Soccer

Alan Hargreaves, MEd

Leisure Press
Champaign, Illinois

Library of Congress Cataloging-in-Publication Data

Hargreaves, Alan, 1933-
    Skills and strategies for coaching soccer / by Alan Hargreaves.
        p. cm.
    ISBN 0-88011-328-6
    1. Soccer--Coaching. I. Title.
    GV943.8.H37   1990
    796.334′07′7--dc20

                                                            89-35783
                                                                 CIP

ISBN: 0-88011-328-6

Developmental Editor: June I. Decker, PhD
Assistant Editor: Timothy Ryan, Robert King
Copyeditor: Julie Anderson
Proofreader: Dianna Matlosz
Production Director: Ernie Noa
Typesetter: Brad Colson
Text Design: Keith Blomberg
Text Layout: Kimberlie Henris
Cover Design: Jack Davis
Cover Photo: Will Zehr
Illustrations: Tim Birkin, John Hartshorn, David Hassall, and Elizabeth Salt
Graphic Services: Tim Offenstein and Kimberlie Henris
Printer: Versa Press

Printed in the United States of America

10 9 8 7 6 5 4 3 2

Leisure Press
A Division of Human Kinetics Publishers, Inc.
Box 5076, Champaign, IL 61825-5076
1-800-747-4457

Canada Office:
Human Kinetics Publishers, Inc.
P.O. Box 2503, Windsor, ON N8Y 4S2
1-800-465-7301 (in Canada only)

UK Office:
Human Kinetics Publishers (UK) Ltd.
P.O. Box 18
Rawdon, Leeds LS19 6TG
England
(0532) 504211

To my wife, Janet.

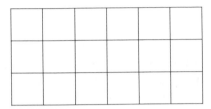

CONTENTS

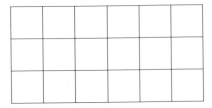

Preface

This is meant to be a friendly book, in which I have endeavored to share with readers some of the approaches, ideas, and methods I have found useful during many years of experience. The book is particularly designed to help men and women coaching youth soccer teams, and college and university students who intend to specialize in soccer coaching. For most of my professional life I have conducted courses and clinics for exactly such audiences; I have coached players ranging from 5-year-olds in California to seasoned professionals in the English League.

Few books start with the beginner and then provide, in a progressive sequence, practices suitable for professional players. Also, few if any books on soccer coaching invite the reader to consider a coaching style that is not only practical but also philosophical. This style combines a concern for the dignity of the individual with a love for the manner in which the game is played. Experience has proven this style to be effective in producing winning teams.

Readers of this book, whatever their experience, will find something of value to share and to use in their teaching of soccer.

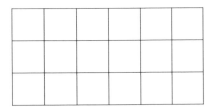

Acknowledgments

In England, thanks go to the following:

Allen Wade, former Director of Coaching of the Football Association, for reading the manuscript and for permission to reproduce his original work on the principles of play; Kevin Verity, Football Association Regional Coach and coauthor of an earlier college publication; Charles Hughes, Assistant National Coach of the Football Association, for his many publications and for his influence on English coaching; Basil Ashford (Staffordshire Polytechnic) and Dennis Wilshaw (formerly of Wolverhampton Wanderers Football Club of England) for advice on sports and educational psychology; Bill Harvey for help with the development of systems of play; and Tony Waddington (Stoke City Football Club) and Ernie Tagg (Crewe Alexandra Football Club) for giving me the opportunity to enter professional league soccer.

For the illustrations and artwork I thank Tim Birkin (Project Advertising, Stoke), John Hartshorn, David Hassall, and Elizabeth Salt; photographer Richard Biedrycki; David Thompson and players from Sneyd High School; and Eric Hassall, Pat Calvert, and colleagues at Wardell Armstrong.

In the United States, thanks to the following: John App, Ben Bushman, John Curtis, Paige Hartley, Norm Jackson, Derek Lawther, Alan Lewis, Margaret Miller, Rudi Rosier, Roger Thomas, and Fern Wender for their coaching and organizational ability; and Martha and Peter Schraml, who also codirected our Professional Soccer Academy, Simi, California.

Most importantly thanks to Dan and Marty Campbell, without whose lasting friendship the opportunity to visit and coach in America would never have arisen.

PART I

PREPARING
TO COACH

In Part I, I explain my views on some important ethical questions in coaching and outline some strategies that I have found useful when dealing with both individuals and groups of players. The ideas introduced in this section should help the reader understand the following chapters on the coaching of skills, tactics, and team management. Even if the reader is entirely familiar with everything in this section, he or she should gain something from it; I have found that having one's own ideas confirmed by someone else can be an encouraging experience.

CHAPTER 1

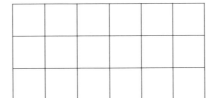

Ethics and Coaching Philosophy

In a soccer career extending over 20 or 30 years, a player will work with many different coaches who have their own ideas and personal coaching styles. While coaches will always differ in their approaches to tactics and teamwork, I hope they share a common view about sportsmanship and the manner in which the game should be played.

This chapter discusses three considerations that constitute, in my opinion, the basis of a code of soccer ethics. The first consideration deals with why so many people throughout the world are attracted to soccer as a lifetime sport—that is, first as a player and then as a coach, administrator, or spectator. The second consideration concerns the characteristics of what I call good play, by which I mean skillful and fair play. The third involves your own personal coaching philosophy. You may not agree with all my views, but the following material should help you clarify your own ideas about the satisfactions and achievements you personally expect to gain from coaching soccer.

Soccer as a Lifetime Sport

Those who are attracted to soccer as a lifetime sport are usually not motivated simply by keeping fit or meeting people, important though these objectives are. People play and watch soccer because they love the game itself and because they experience inner feelings of enjoyment, satisfaction, and achievement through playing soccer. They find soccer a game

3

that is worth playing for its own sake. People play soccer because they enjoy it.

Every coach is responsible for creating an atmosphere that safeguards this enjoyment factor, especially for younger players. Yet coaches cannot force players to enjoy the game, which is why personal coaching ethics are so important. The art of coaching is getting players to enjoy soccer because they want to, not because a coach tells them to. A love for soccer has to be nurtured and encouraged; achieving this leads directly to the second major consideration of soccer ethics. The link between all who love soccer is the ability to recognize and appreciate the meaning and importance of good play.

The Meaning and Importance of Good Play

Good play means play that is skillful. People who enjoy soccer as a lifetime sport do so because either they are or were skillful players or because they are intelligent spectators who can appreciate skillful play by others, including team tactics as well as individual skill.

The development and appreciation of skill is of paramount importance in coaching. The level of skill that can be achieved will vary according to the age and experience of the player; thus skillful play is a matter of judgment and intention as well as of execution. With all players, but especially with younger players, the coach must work hard to promote the desire or intention to play skillfully.

A useful example, which also demonstrates the importance of intelligent observation of the game, is the ill-informed coach who tells players to kick the ball whenever it comes to them. The informed coach, in exactly the same situation, may urge players to control the ball rather than kick it. The difference between the two sets of advice lies in the greater knowledge of the informed coach, who appreciates the more advantageous moves that result from a controlled, composed mastery of the ball. I believe that the player who continually tries to exercise control is more likely to develop into a skillful player. Similarly, the coach who appreciates and rewards the intention to play skillfully is more likely to be successful in the long run. He or she will certainly gain immense satisfaction when players improve as a direct result of good coaching.

The second criterion of good play is that it be fair play. Soccer was designed to be played according to a set of rules. More importantly, it was meant to be played by players who respect not only the letter of the law but also the spirit of the law. For example, tackling a player hard and tackling a player so hard and in such a manner that he or she cannot take any further part in the game are fundamentally different actions. The difference between a hard but fair tackle and a dangerous or vicious one lies in the intention of the player executing the tackle and not in the referee's judgment, which is always retrospective. Soccer was designed as a game of skill, not a game of brute force, and the game of soccer will only thrive in an atmosphere in which skillful, intelligent sporting play is appreciated by all who play, watch, and coach. To a person who really loves soccer, what matters most is not who wins the game but the manner in which the game is won. Wanting to win is important, but if to win players have to commit fouls, argue, or make obscene gestures, then although those players may have won the match, to a much greater extent the game itself has lost. A typical example of such undesirable play is the so-called professional foul.

The Professional Foul

A new kind of foul has crept into soccer called the professional foul. It occurs mainly when a defender deliberately catches a ball or body checks an opponent. In most cases the foul is committed to prevent the opposition from scoring; it is called a professional foul because although the individual is penalized, the team benefits.

If nobody gets hurt, why is the professional foul considered to be such a negative influence in the game? The professional foul is wrong because it spoils the game; allowing such fouls to occur destroys the game of soccer. Soccer was designed to be played according to certain rules and in a spirit of fair play. If these rules are deliberately violated, then the game as it was meant to be played no longer exists. Coaches and players must accept their responsibility to the game and must work together to eliminate any form of behavior that weakens the game. Such a stance is clearly an ethical one and as such embraces the personal philosophy of each individual coach.

What Is Your Philosophy?

Consider to what extent you agree with my philosophy that the main responsibility of every coach is to develop a love for the game by encouraging play that is skillful and fair and that takes place in an enjoyable sporting environment. In considering this, you must also examine the importance of winning.

A Winning Coach

Nothing is wrong with wanting to win. The whole purpose of coaching is to improve performance and, ultimately, to improve the chances of winning.

My experience—which includes professional clubs in which winning and job security go hand in hand and Olympic competition in which winning is a matter of fierce national pride—has shown that a coach who continually encourages and emphasizes good play is actually more likely to be a winning coach. That coach's team will be better coached, better organized, more skillful and, most of all, more resilient in times of stress because players are happier and enjoy a better team spirit.

Anyone engaged in competition will benefit from striving to win until the last possible moment. Not to try one's best is insulting to one's opponent and diminishes or even destroys the game as a spectacle.

My philosophy, therefore, certainly embraces the desire to win. Indeed, it emphasizes that players should strive to win until the very last moment of the game. This philosophy does draw a very clear line between wanting to win and wanting to win at any cost. For example, I reject the behavior of a coach who, in seeking to win, advocates dangerous tackling, verbally abuses players or officials, keeps a badly injured player in the game, or deliberately cheats on a player's eligibility. Such acts could never be admissible in my philosophy because they put winning the game before a concern for the well-being of the players and the spirit of fair play.

At this point I invite you to consider your own position. What is your philosophy? What kind of coach are you? What kind of coach would you like to be? To what extent, if at all, do you share my philosophy? What you think and how you feel should have a direct bearing upon how you actually behave.

A Soccer Code of Ethics

In ethics, what matters is what one does, not what one thinks or says. An ideal has little value until it is put into practice, and for this reason I now outline my personal code of ethics which I hope can be followed by everyone involved in soccer—players, spectators, and coaches.

- Certain fundamental concepts must be taught; the most important of these is an appreciation of what is meant by good play.
- Good play is skillful, fair, and sporting play that does not include foul or abusive language.
- The attitude of the players toward the match officials is vital. The referees' job is to ensure that skillful soccer prevails. They may make mistakes, but players must be encouraged to accept decisions without rancor, as dissent quickly destroys the atmosphere of any game.
- A game played in a fair, sporting manner will be more enjoyable for all concerned.

- Nothing is wrong with wanting to win; what is wrong is wanting to win at any cost. A person who really loves soccer cares less about who wins the game than the manner in which it is won.
- An important task for any coach is to encourage a love for the game in all who come into his or her sphere of influence.
- The coach must educate parents and spectators to acknowledge good play by both sides and to allow for mistakes, especially by younger players.
- The coach must always put the welfare of players before the result of a game.
- The coach is a model figure and should behave accordingly. The coach should not shout at players or officials.

In following chapters I show how this philosophy influences how we relate to and communicate with our players; I also show what kinds of coaching styles are most effective in developing a love for the game and in encouraging players to enjoy both practice and playing.

CHAPTER 2

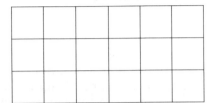

Individual Coaching Strategies

This chapter provides an insight into coaching strategies that have been helpful to me, especially when dealing with individual players.

Coaching Follows Observation

My first strategy is that coaching follows observation. Coaching is always retrospective; it is the exchange that takes place between you and your players after you have seen them perform. Of course, you may introduce a topic verbally or demonstrate what you want players to learn, but this is not coaching. Coaching only begins when you attempt to change or develop what the players are doing.

If you start by telling players what you want them to do, you run the risk of underestimating their ability and wasting their time. It is very embarrassing to give a lengthy introduction only to find that some, if not all, are already expert at the skill. It is much better to see players in action before you attempt to coach them. Only after you have seen players in action are you able to gauge your starting level according to their ability. For this reason, this book provides many examples of warm-up activities and small-team games that will enable you to watch your players in action before you start to coach them.

The same advice holds true for coaching team tactics. The work that you do in preparing your team will be based largely upon your observation of the previous game or your observation of your opponents. In both cases, you are coaching after observation. The best way to start a coaching session is to say, ''In last week's game I noticed that. . . .''

Good Diagnosis

My second strategy is concerned with good diagnosis. Like a doctor, the coach has to be able to diagnose correctly before prescribing a cure. Soccer coaches often say: If you can't see it, you can't coach it.

This means that you must have the knowledge and experience to diagnose a problem in order to improve performance. Furthermore, you also have to know when to offer a physical cure and when to offer a psychological one. Because good diagnosis is so important, the nine chapters in this book on the coaching of skills all carefully explain the key points of each of the basic skills. In addition, the principles of team play by which you can diagnose how well your team is playing are covered in chapter 15.

Coach the Players, Not the Drill

Clearly, good diagnosis depends upon your personal knowledge and experience, but it also depends upon your observations of what another person is actually doing. In soccer you never just coach a skill; you always coach a player how to perform the skill. There is always another person involved, and this is my third strategy—the recognition that you coach the player, not the drill.

Some coaches think they can produce a successful coaching session simply by running players through a conglomeration of drills. Good drills are important because they help to isolate a particular skill, but by themselves drills never produce or guarantee success. Drills provide a starting point, but what matters more is how you progress the drill according to the ability and response of the players. This leads to my fourth strategy.

Progressive Practices

The ability to start with a simple practice and gradually develop it into a realistic game situation is one of the hallmarks of a good coach. Drills must be progressed (and sometimes this means simplified) according to how the players respond. Throughout this book, I show how each drill can be progressed according to the response of the players. The ability to develop progressive coaching situations also leads to my next strategy, which is concerned with the ability to open the mind of the player through good communication.

Good Communication

Communication is a field of knowledge in its own right, one that has produced much valuable advice. For example, we all have the ability to receive as well as transmit messages, but many coaches are more skilled at transmitting their ideas than receiving other ideas. We might improve ourselves as coaches simply by becoming better listeners! Also, we know that body language, posture, and gestures (nonverbal communication) are all very important in transmitting messages to others. Finally, and most importantly, what we say or do often carries with it an emotional message. For example, some people can convey intense anger with a softly spoken word or inject humor into the most violent-looking gestures. I want to highlight three types of communication that are especially important and that all have one thing in common. They all require the coach to gain access to the minds of the players. I call this opening the mind of the player. The three main approaches, which are often combined, are physical, visual, and verbal communication.

Physical Communication

Shaping, which involves guiding players' limbs through the correct movement, is more important with younger players. Young children must discover how to perform new skills, and they learn more by doing and feeling the correct pattern or shape of the movement than by listening. Giving a player the feel of a movement can be a very productive approach, and sometimes it is the only approach! It is particularly valuable, for example, when teaching the correct positions for the foot and knee in the push pass, especially in the follow-through (chapter 5). Similarly, it is invaluable when teaching players to relax the foot or thigh when controlling the ball (chapter 4) or to tense the muscles in the neck and shoulders when heading the ball (chapter 11).

Using this technique affords a special advantage when coaching smaller children. In order to shape a movement, you often have to kneel in front of the pupil with your eyes on the same level as the player. Youngsters really do respond to being coached by someone who is literally on their own level rather than by someone towering above them and, perhaps, talking down to them in more ways than one.

Visual Communication–Good Demonstration

The ability to demonstrate well is a priceless gift. Not only does a good demonstration provide a picture for the watching players, it adds to your charisma and prevents the boredom of long verbal explanations. The important considerations for a good demonstration include the following:

- Simplicity. Emphasize only one major point and perhaps one minor point each time you demonstrate. Bring out additional features in the next demonstration.
- Reasonable goals. Your demonstration should always set goals that are within the ability of the players.
- Use of body language. If you want players to move quickly and urgently, demonstrate the correct pace and tempo of the movement. If you want to stress calmness and composure, let your body movements and your voice convey these qualities.
- Ability to talk while demonstrating. This enables you to draw attention to key points while you are actually demonstrating them.
- Appropriate amount of demonstration. Restrict demonstrations to one or two repetitions. You may get away with demonstrating a skill three times, but four or more demonstrations will usually bore your audience.

What If My Demonstration Goes Wrong?

You cannot afford to continually make errors in front of your students. How, then, do you handle a mistake when demonstrating? Following are three useful strategies:

1. Always try to rehearse in private. If you need a server, practice with him or her. If the server makes a mistake in the actual demonstration, don't try to compensate; stop and try again.
2. Before you demonstrate, say to the group, "I may need two or three attempts to get this demonstration right." If you alert the group to the possibility of failure, you don't have a disaster if you fail. Furthermore, this implies that the players too must be prepared for failure and that failure is not necessarily a bad thing. Of course, succeeding the first time is a bonus.
3. Whether your demonstration is successful or not, stop after the third attempt. Don't keep on failing! If you are not successful by the third attempt, start the players working with a comment such as, "Sorry, it's not going well for me today, but you can see what is needed!" No one is perfect, and the players would rather practice themselves than watch you fail. A sincere coach will have nothing to fear from an occasional failure.

What Do I Do If I Simply Can't Demonstrate?

The ability to give good demonstrations is a priceless asset. There are limits, however, and no one who is seriously interested in coaching soccer should be discouraged because he or she cannot demonstrate. You would not, for example, expect every track coach to sprint 100 meters in under 10 seconds! What matters most is that the coach knows what should be done and why.

A coach who does not feel confident enough to demonstrate can employ a number of strategies. These include a preselected demonstrator, the discovery approach, a group challenge, and visual aids.

The Preselected Demonstrator.   Select a good performer, take him or her to one side, and rehearse the skill or movement several times. Then let this player demonstrate for the entire group.

The Discovery Approach.   With this method you introduce the topic and start the group without an introductory demonstration. For example, to coach accuracy in passing you might start with the players in pairs passing to each other, or you might organize minigames of 3 vs. 3. Then you watch for players who perform the skill well. When these players identify themselves, stop the practice and allow them to demonstrate for the others.

Group Challenge.   This method is very useful when coaching restarts such as free kicks and corners. Give small groups of players the same task, for example, working out an attacking free kick. After a set period of time let each group demonstrate in turn. In this way you will produce a number of different tactical moves to discuss with the players. Further, you will have challenged their initiative.

Visual Aids.   Coaching videos and wall charts are useful but must be used with care. Examine films in advance, and show only the section you want students to see. Showing a complete film can be a waste of time.

Verbal Communication

Coaches probably use verbal communication more than any other method, and I believe that strategic feedback really can contribute dramatically to your coaching effectiveness. When you tell players what to do, always try to consider how they will receive your message; try to anticipate their reactions. For example, imagine that your players are involved in a practice. After watching them, you know what you want to say to them, but they are completely unaware of the kind of news they are about to receive. For the players, it could be good or bad news; they are either going to be praised or corrected. This presents you, the coach, with the opportunity to develop a very special coaching technique, which I call the double positive approach.

The Double Positive Approach

For the player, receiving good news is always pleasant. We all enjoy being praised, providing we know that it is sincere praise. Therefore, when you see a successful performance, stop the practice and explain and demonstrate why the performance is successful. I call this kind of motivation a double positive because the player is positively reinforced for good play and you simultaneously establish the correct points of technique for the benefit of all engaged in the practice.

However, players do make mistakes. When coaching young, sensitive players, you must try to correct mistakes without discouraging players. If you go directly to the negative—the failure or mistake—you can very easily make a player feel insecure to such an extent that he or she may avoid taking the responsibility to try again. Fortunately, you can always make a positive opening remark before you correct what the player is doing wrong. For example, "Good try, but . . ." or "Yes, that move was OK, but. . . ."

By giving an encouraging opening comment, you make the player feel secure and thus receptive. To be really effective, you must open the player's mind to advice. In this way you avoid creating the closed mind of the irritated or reluctant player whose negative emotions might momentarily interfere with cooperation and reason. In my view, the double positive approach is the most important of all of the strategies. If you can spend most of your coaching life looking for and positively reinforcing what is right, good, and correct, then you are much more likely to be a happy, successful, and respected coach.

The Question-and-Answer Technique

I believe it is a mistake for any coach to continually tell players what they should be doing. You can often achieve far more by asking players rather than telling. I recommend what is known as the question-and-answer technique. For example, if you ask your players a question like "Who can tell me why that was such a good pass?" or "What defensive system are our opponents using?" you will achieve two objectives. First, you will elicit the correct technical diagnosis; second, by involving the players in the discussion, you will encourage them to develop their own powers of observation and critical analysis. Getting players to appreciate and develop their own knowledge of the game is surely at the heart of good coaching, and the question-and-answer technique enhances this process.

CHAPTER 3

Group Coaching Strategies

Chapter 2 discussed the encouragement of successful relationships between individuals. Chapter 3 is concerned with some of the problems involved in coaching a larger group. This chapter presents a number of strategies for group coaching that I have found useful; they include good organization, the coaching grid system, methods of selection, accommodating different levels of ability, keeping momentum in a lesson, getting the group started, and planning a coaching session.

Good Organization

Good organization operates at two levels. First, it operates at a conceptual or team management level and includes functions such as preparing a syllabus for school or college; establishing a code of conduct for the team; having a long-term plan for systems of play; developing a policy for helping with the team chores; and determining a policy for including and dealing with parents and spectators.

Second, good organization operates at a specific level in each coaching session and includes functions such as preparing written notes; ensuring that the necessary equipment is both available and suitable; using the correct part of the field for the practice; organizing the practice in accordance with the number, ability, and development of the players; grouping the players according to ability; developing the practice to the best use of the available time; and modifying the activities in relation to the mental and physical states of the players. The coach who takes the time and trouble to organize in advance is much more likely to be successful. A well-organized group session will have a clear objective; will be well-timed, progressive, and demanding; and will involve every player for the maximum possible time.

It follows that, because good organization is both general and specific, examples are best considered in relation to specific objectives and practices. For this reason, every practice in this book includes detailed advice on organization. However, I do recommend one general system of organizing large numbers of players into manageable groups. This is called *the grid system* or *the coaching grid* and is worth examining in detail.

The Grid System of Coaching

One of the most useful strategies for dealing with a large class is to subdivide the group into smaller, more manageable coaching units, ideally of equal ability. One of the best ways to achieve this in a soccer lesson is by using a coaching grid.

A coaching grid is an area on the field that is divided into squares that are usually of 10 yards but can vary according to the age of the players and the available space. On school fields, the grids should be permanently marked with chalk lines, but flags, cones, or other markers provide effective substitutes (Figures 3.1a and b). Grids can be of any shape depending upon the available area. One-yard circles at intersections make useful targets.

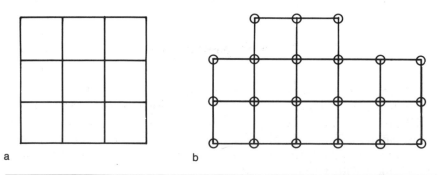

a   b

Figure 3.1
Typical layouts for coaching grids.

As a general rule, minigames require grids of approximately 10 square yards for each player; thus a 3 vs. 3 game would be played on six grids comprising an area 30 × 20 yards.

Features of the Grid System

The grid system has several interesting features; understanding them will help you gain maximum benefit from your practices.

Maximum Ball-Contact Time

In a full 11 vs. 11 game, playing time is reduced by stoppages from 90 to 60 minutes (or a 2:3 ratio to the length of the game being played), and this does not include the time lost when the ball is traveling between players. If every player were to have a fair share of the ball during the game, he or she would get a maximum of 3 minutes contact. We know that such a distribution is impossible because some players monopolize the ball and others touch it rarely, such as the goalkeeper. By using the grid to produce minigames and by arranging two or three players in each game, this automatically improves the ball-contact time. Because children learn largely by doing, the wisdom of this method is evident.

Easy Control of the Time-Space Variables

The numbers of players and the amount of space they require can be easily controlled—the less able the player, the more time and space he or she needs to execute the practice (chapter 5).

Progressive Decision Making

Closely allied to time-space variables is the advantage of progressive decision making. We do not take a novice driver on the freeway; similarly, we do not throw a young player directly into a full-game situation, especially if we want that player to learn how to make intelligent, composed decisions. To foster good decision making we start players off in simple situations and in a friendly environment.

The coaching grid provides this environment. For example, a player starts to learn passing in a simple 2 vs. 1 situation on two grids. Then, by putting several adjacent grids together and playing 3 vs. 3, the player graduates to a more difficult situation.

In the hands of the skillful coach, the grid system provides an excellent opportunity to develop the skills of players in a controlled manner.

Easily Identified Targets for Players

The lines restrict the area of play, and they can also provide targets and encourage positive attitudes in the players. A simple example is a 1 vs. 1 dribbling practice in which one player defends one of the lines of the square while a partner tries to reach, or cross, the line.

Better Use of Space

Finally, the coaching grid enables players to utilize the areas of grass that are away from the main playing field. In this way the match surface is protected against excessive wear and full use is made of the whole field. Note: The coaching grid can be overused and can prevent the players from becoming familiar with the larger team environment. A good coach will know how to achieve a balance between the grid system and other systems such as the wave attack system (p. 305), shadow soccer (p. 307), and coaching in the game (p. 297).

Good Selection Within Groups

It's always difficult to accommodate the varying levels of ability that exist within a group. In soccer, you will need to consider at least two different situations: how to accommodate players of different ability for skill practices and how to select teams for small-team scrimmages that will all have a reasonable chance of winning.

Selecting for Skill Practices

In an ideal world, the strong would help the weak to improve. However, pairing a good player with a weak player and expecting the one to help the other is usually a mistake. In reality, neither will derive much pleasure or make much progress. When coaching skills, try to match players or groups for ability so that you encourage fair competition.

Selecting for Team Games

Conversely, to encourage fair competition between miniteams (e.g., 5 vs. 5), you must distribute your strong players and weaker players evenly to foster equal competition.

When selecting teams, never bring the best players to the front of the group and let them select team players in sequence. Those who are among the last to be selected are terribly embarrassed and even humiliated. No youngster wants to be labeled a less able player, and you as the coach must ensure that no one is placed in this kind of situation. This situation is easy to avoid; simply select teams in advance and read them off your notes, or select randomly and rely on your experience to enable you to select balanced teams.

Getting the Group Started

Whenever a coach is faced with wet, cold, or inclement field conditions, he or she can do much useful preparatory work while the group is changing indoors. For example, the coach can tell the students who they are working with and how to start their first practice before they go out to the field. In normal conditions, however, the coach, after preparing the field and equipment in advance, begins coaching when the group is assembled. In these circumstances, I recommend three useful strategies.

Position the Group Properly

Ensure that the players are grouped so they can see and hear you. Remember, you should face the sun and keep their backs toward any distraction (e.g., another game).

Gain Attention Quickly

Don't start until everyone is listening. If players are not paying attention, don't wait for them to become quiet because this wastes valuable time. Take the initiative. Bring them to attention by using any of the following techniques, which are listed in order of severity: a glance (eye contact is a marvelous thing); a raised finger; a quiet word (perhaps "thank you"); a spoken name; a firm command. Don't shout or blow your whistle. Shouting can destroy your charisma and may give the impression that you are uncertain of your authority. Save your shout and your whistle for emergencies.

Keep Your Introduction Short

Keep your opening remarks as short as possible—two sentences if you can. For example, "I want to help you develop more accuracy in passing. Watch as I demonstrate."

Certainly you must tell the players what you intend to coach, but showing them is far more important (as discussed in chapter 2).

Keeping Momentum in Your Lesson

When handling a large group, you can easily lose momentum and interest when you have to stop one practice and move to another progression. To avoid long delays, I employ what I call the one-step-ahead technique.

While the class is working on the given topic, take a small group or even one individual aside and rehearse the next skill. Then you can stop the main group and let the small group or individual demonstrate the new task.

Obviously, this method helps you avoid wasting time between activities and causing problems of class control. By thinking "one move ahead" like a chess player, you save time between practices and achieve pace and momentum in your coaching. This is one of the hallmarks of a good coach.

Accommodating Different Rates of Progress

One way to achieve a reasonable balance of progress between the more and less able in a group is to use what I call the five-stage strategy. The best way to explain this approach is by using a flowchart diagram (Figure 3.2), from which you will see how you might progress your coaching according to the presence or absence of a common fault or ability. The model may look complicated, but in fact it is a very simple concept to grasp and use. You will quickly appreciate how this strategy fits in with the other recommendations I have made, such as preparing your next coaching point or demonstration in advance of stopping the group. The method also follows my general advice that coaching follows observation.

This method will help you to achieve an optimum rate of progress for the group based upon the ability of the average members. By ensuring that the majority can execute the skill reasonably well, you avoid going too fast or too slow.

Planning Your Coaching Session

Starting with a blank sheet of paper, draw three boxes horizontally connected by a line.

Ask yourself, "What is the main skill or theme I want to coach in this session?" Suppose that you want to coach the skill of supporting the player with the ball. You must now think of the best possible practice situation for developing this ability, and write the situation in Box 2.

In the case of support play, you will need a practice that involves both supporting and opposing players; a good example is 3 vs. 2 (or 4 vs. 1 for less able players).

Now ask yourself, "How can I best develop the 3 vs. 2 situation into a larger game-like practice?" and write the answer in Box 3 (chapter 5).

In our example the answer might be 5 vs. 5 on a half-sized field, but it could also be a game such as "floater" (chapter 6).

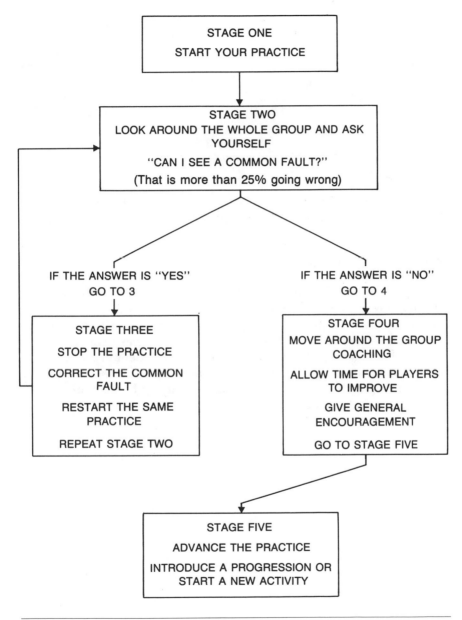

Figure 3.2
The five-stage strategy for group coaching.

Finally, ask yourself, "What activities can I use to start the session?" Write the answer in Box 1. In our case, this might be 4 vs. 1 passing outside the square (p. 63). Your diagram now looks like Figure 3.3.

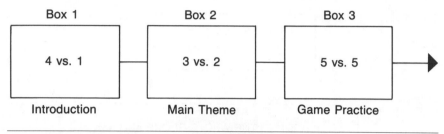

Figure 3.3
A coach's custom-made practice plan.

The number of players in each activity depends upon the size of your class. In the example, we have assumed the number is divisible by 5.

Organizing a Time Scale

In general, allow 1/6 of the available time for Box 1, 2/6 of the available time for Box 2, and 3/6 of the available time for Box 3.

This approach helps you plan your coaching session to achieve the maximum related skill practice in the theme you have chosen, and it ensures that at least half the available time will be spent in active, game-like situations in which the players apply the skills you have taught them. The combination of these two elements—activity and coaching—is at the heart of successful group coaching.

PART II

SKILLS AND TECHNIQUES

In Part II, I offer you my ideas on coaching the eight basic skills that, with goalkeeping, constitute the fundamentals of soccer. Some of the skills are well-known standards; some I have discovered for myself. I hope you will find of particular value the way I have presented the skills in a progressive sequence. I start with beginning skills and move to the intermediate stage and then to advanced practices that have been used with professional players. Once you have determined the starting ability of your own players, you will be able to select skills according to their ages, aptitudes, and abilities.

I hope that you will also appreciate my ideas on how to coach the mind of the player. Being able to execute a skill in isolation is one thing; being able to execute the same skill in a game situation is another. The key is knowing how to coach the basic skills in realistic, game situations—this is something I hope to share with you.

CHAPTER 4

Coaching Collecting and Controlling

The most important skill in soccer is the ability to control the ball. All players must be encouraged to develop this ability because it leads to confidence, satisfaction, and the freedom to execute the other skills of soccer more effectively. All players must also be taught to appreciate that good control means *one-touch control*—whichever part of the body is used, one touch should be sufficient to control the ball.

Pelé, the greatest of ball players, described collecting or controlling the ball as "the gentle art." I agree with Pelé; control is all about gentleness. To keep the ball close you have to absorb its force, and the key to this is relaxation. Tension and tense limbs repel the ball; relaxation brings success.

Basic Techniques

There are almost as many ways of controlling a ball as there are parts of the body; however, not all of these ways are consistently effective. The basic techniques can be divided into three categories or methods. Selecting which method to use is a matter of judgment by the player, but it is also largely determined by the manner in which the ball comes at the player, and the time and space in which the player must complete the move. For example, to control a high, dropping ball the player should use a part of the body such as the instep or thigh as a platform upon which to catch the ball. With a flat, driven ball or hard ground pass, the player should use a part of the body such as the chest or the inside of the foot as a cushion. When a ball is bouncing on the fly, the player should use a wedge or angle, usually made by the foot or ankle and the ground, into which the ball falls.

The Platform

The three most common platforms are the instep, the top of the thigh, and the forehead. By presenting a flat surface underneath the ball and withdrawing the surface on impact, the player takes speed or momentum off the ball. This is usually called "taking the pace off the ball."

The Instep

Here the raised instep receives or catches the dropping ball. Ideally, the ball remains in contact with the instep throughout; at worst the ball stays within easy reach. Because the player must balance on one leg to execute the move, his or her arms should be held out wide to improve this balance (Figure 4.1).

Figure 4.1
Control with the instep.

The Thigh

Depending upon how vertically the ball is dropping, the platform of the thigh is raised between 40° and 90° to receive the ball. Again, the arms are held sideways for balance but because the chest is tilted slightly forward, the whole body position is more compact and stable than with the instep method. Because of this stability and the much larger platform involved, the thigh trap is both easier and safer to perform. Done well, the ball drops straight from the thigh to the ground; a bounce off or upward from the thigh indicates poor execution (Figure 4.2).

Figure 4.2
Control with the thigh.

The Forehead

Catching or controlling a dropping ball with the forehead is a more difficult skill. The key is focusing the eyes under the ball, which almost gives the feeling that the eyes, not the forehead, catch the ball. This ensures that the head is tilted back, thus presenting the forehead as a better platform to receive the ball.

The knees can also help the head and shoulders cushion the ball by bobbing down at the moment of impact. The feet should be spread wide to allow the whole body to act like a shock absorber. When this skill is executed properly, the ball drops to the ground or can be controlled again on the thigh (Figure 4.3).

The Cushion

One-touch control of a ball driven hard on a flat trajectory or along the ground is good play. It is achieved by positioning a part of the body in the ball's path and cushioning the impact as the ball strikes. Obviously, the larger the cushion presented as a target, the easier the control factor.

Figure 4.3
Control with the forehead.

For this reason the chest (which can also be used as a platform) and stomach are two good areas to use (Figure 4.4).

The other areas that can be used as a cushion are the inside of the thigh when the knee is raised sideways (Figure 4.5) and the inside of the ankle when the foot is square to the line of flight (Figure 4.6).

Figure 4.4
Control with the chest.

Figure 4.5
Control with the inside of the thigh.

Figure 4.6
Control with the inside of the ankle.

The Wedge

With this technique the player makes an angle or wedge between the ground and the foot and lets the ball drop into this space. The most effective wedges are made with the sole of the foot or the inside or outside of the ankle.

The Sole of the Foot

Here the toes are raised but the heel is held low to produce the angle of the sloping wedge shape. The arms are usually held wide for balance, and the body is crouched or in a sitting position (Figure 4.7).

Figure 4.7
Control with the sole of the foot.

With this skill, the beginner must be taught to gently control the ball with the underneath of the toes. Performed correctly, this skill imparts a backspin on the ball, which brings it closer to the receiver (Figure 4.8).

Figure 4.8
Finesse the ball gently to get back spin.

Beginners must not be allowed to stamp on the ball; this is unnatural and ineffective.

The Inside and Outside of the Ankle

When the receiver is faced with a dropping ball and an onrushing opponent, he or she must be able to control the ball and move away from danger in the same movement. To do this, the player must control the ball with either the inside (the most popular) or the outside of the foot. In both cases, the movement requires a body lean in the direction in which the ball is to be controlled (Figure 4.9).

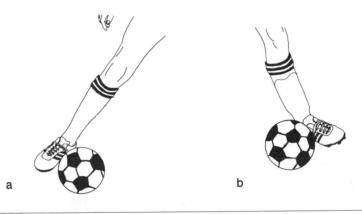

a   b

Figure 4.9
*Body lean is necessary when controlling the ball with a) the inside of the
foot/ankle, or b) the outside of the foot/ankle.*

Drills for Beginners

I recommend four drills for teaching beginners how to control the ball. The first drill involves controlling the ball with the thigh, the easiest method to learn, and the second involves controlling the ball with the instep. (Both drills involve platform techniques and are ideal confidence builders.) For teaching beginners how to control with the inside and outside of the foot and to use different parts of the body to cushion the ball, I recommend self-serve practices. Self-serve practices are useful because beginners can set their own targets; however, these practices don't sustain motivation in students. The answer is limited use; 3 to 5 minutes is long enough. That is not to say, however, that a dedicated youngster will not spend hours playing against the garage wall at home! These practices soon develop into the partner activities recommended for intermediates.

CONTROL WITH THE THIGH—THE THREE-HANDS METHOD

Figure 4.10

Equipment

1 ball for each 2 players.

Organization

Players are in pairs (1 server, 1 receiver).

Instructions

The server stands 2 yards from the receiver, and using both hands, serves a gentle, underarm lob directly onto the thigh of the receiver.

The receiver tries to catch the ball on the thigh, let the ball fall directly to the ground, and then push pass it back to the server (Figure 4.10).

Coaching Points

The ball should fall directly to the ground. If the ball bounces upward off the top of the thigh, then the force has not been absorbed correctly. Players should watch for this key point.

Coaching Progressions

The receiver initially catches the ball and then raises the knee up to it.

Next, the receiver catches the ball with thigh and hands together (i.e., the three-hands method).

The receiver uses the thigh only.

The receiver uses both left and right thighs in turn.

The server increases the distance of the throw to 3 yards and the height to just under head height.

The receiver returns the ball to the server with an accurate push pass.

CONTROL WITH THE INSTEP

Figure 4.11

Equipment
   1 ball for each 3 players.

Organization
   Players are in teams of 3 (1 server, 1 receiver, 1 supporter).

Instructions
   The server executes a gentle, underhand throw using both hands, aiming directly at the receiver's instep.

   The receiver tries to keep the ball "tied" onto his or her instep while leaning on the supporter for balance (Figure 4.11).

Coaching Points
   The receiver can relax the foot by shaking it.

   The receiver should feel that he or she is hanging the foot about 4 inches above the ground.

   The receiver should toe down.

   If the ball bounces forward off the receiver's foot, that player's ankle and foot are not relaxed sufficiently or the ball has hit the lower leg, not the relaxed foot.

   If the throw is accurate and the foot is relaxed, the ball remains on the foot as if by magic.

Coaching Progressions
   The server moves further and further back, up to 5 to 10 yards depending on the skill of the receiver. The ball is thrown on a higher trajectory, 6 to 10 feet.

The receiver no longer leans on the supporter.

The receiver tries to control the ball with alternate feet.

The receiver catches the ball on the instep and in the same movement turns around with the ball. (Only skillful players should attempt this.) This skill can be used for advanced shooting practices in which the player stands on the penalty area with his or her back toward the goal, catches the ball, turns, and shoots (chapter 10).

CONTROL WITH THE INSIDE AND OUTSIDE OF THE FOOT

Figure 4.12

This practice is excellent for learning how to use the wedge method of controlling the bouncing ball.

Equipment

1 ball for each player.

Organization

Individual players stand in free space but must beware of others.

Instructions

Players throw the ball into the air, move to the point at which it lands (the *pitch* of the ball), and control it using the inside or the outside of the foot.

Coaching Points

Players must move quickly to the pitch of the ball.

Players must achieve the correct angle with the foot and ankle to control the ball.

Players must lean in the direction in which they intend to move the ball.

Players must control the ball at the moment it first touches the ground, not after it has bounced or on the second bounce (Figure 4.12).

Coaching Progressions

Players throw the ball at different heights and in different directions but never so far or so high that they cannot reasonably get to the pitch of the ball. Players should set realistic goals.

Players decide which part of the ankle—inside or outside—to use and try to stick to this decision.

Players try not only to control the ball but also to move or sweep it away in different directions as if beating an opponent.

The player starts at a fixed point and sees how far he or she can throw the ball and still reach and control it.

WALL AS A PARTNER

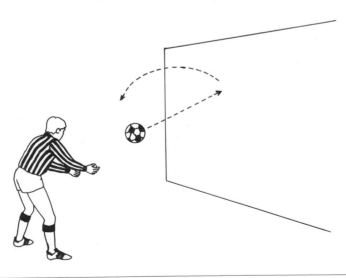

Figure 4.13

This practice is very useful in teaching players how to learn the cushion method of controlling the driven ball and also how to use the forehead.

Equipment
1 ball for each player, plus a large vertical surface.

Organization
Individual players stand in free space.

Instructions
Players throw the ball at the wall and try to control the ball after it rebounds (Figure 4.13).

Coaching Points
Select the part of the body to control the ball as early as possible.

Coaching Progressions
Players increase the force of the rebound.

Players decrease the distance from the wall, thus reducing the time available to execute control.

Players preselect which part of the body should be used.

Players control the ball and turn away from the wall in one move.

Players move up and down alongside the wall, controlling the rebound at an angle—just like the wall pass (p. 57).

Drills for Intermediates

Partner practices are excellent for developing all the different methods of ball control. These practices permit the service to be varied according to the ability of the receiver, and they also provide a very effective activity-to-rest ratio. They do require players to recognize two different attitudes—cooperation and competition. First, players are responsible for serving the ball to their partners in a cooperative manner; players have a duty to provide a careful, accurate service to help their partners improve. Only when partners are ready should they begin to compete with each other; this should not be done too soon. The coach is responsible for the change of attitude from cooperation to competition between the two players. I always direct when this change should take place.

PARTNER PRACTICE 1—ALTERNATING TARGETS

Equipment
1 ball for each 2 players; 2 markers.

Figure 4.14

Organization

Players are in pairs of equal ability (1 server, 1 receiver). Markers are placed 5 yards apart.

Instructions

The server throws the ball underhand alternately to the two markers.

The receiver moves sideways and controls the ball using any suitable method, or in response to a predetermined method, and plays the ball back to the server (Figure 4.14).

Coaching Points

The ball must be absolutely stationary before it is returned to the server. It must not be played back directly.

Coaching Progressions

Players start with a simple, underhand throw.

Players increase the speed and difficulty of the serve (e.g., using a spin).

Players serve the ball in the air so it bounces at the point of control.

Players change to a one-handed (javelin type) throw service to increase realism.

Players progress to pressure training (p. 356).

Players set targets (e.g., how many perfect controls can be achieved in 1 minute).

PARTNER PRACTICE 2—GOALKEEPER

Figure 4.15

Equipment

1 ball for each 2 players; 2 markers.

Organization

Players are in pairs of equal ability (1 server who stands 7 to 10 yards from the goal, 1 receiver). Markers are placed 5 yards apart (Figure 4.15).

Instructions

The receiver is a goalkeeper and must defend goals without using his or her hands.

The server tries to score.

Coaching Points

The receiver should select the controlling method early.

The receiver should position as much of his or her body into the path of the ball as possible to reduce errors.

The receiver should try to achieve one-touch control.

Coaching Progressions

Players cooperate before competing.

The server starts with a thrown ball before progressing to a volley or half-volley serve from the hand.

The receiver rolls the ball to the server who shoots. The first-time shot produces a very demanding challenge for the receiver.

PARTNER PRACTICE 3—REBOUND

Figure 4.16

Equipment

1 ball for each 2 players; 2 markers.

Organization

Players are in pairs of equal ability (1 server, 1 receiver). Markers are placed 5 yards apart (Figure 4.16).

Instructions

The receiver stands 2 to 3 feet behind the goal line and controls the ball to prevent it from bouncing forward through the goalposts and across the goal line.

The server plays the ball on the ground or as close as possible to the ground.

Coaching Points

Players should use the cushion method, especially with the inside of the ankle.

Players should select the controlling surface early.

Players should relax and withdraw the controlling surface on impact.

Coaching Progressions

The server starts with a push pass directly at the receiver.

The server plays the ball to the left and right of the receiver.

The server increases the speed and height of the service according to ability.

The receiver stands 1 to 2 feet behind the goal line, the reduced space making control more difficult.

Players see how many successful controls they can achieve in a set number of serves.

Drills for Advanced Players

Advanced drills require active opposition to generate the realism of the game. This does not necessarily mean that the opposing player must be 100% aggressive from the start of the practice, but while early opposition might be passive, the later stages of advanced practices will always involve a high degree of healthy competition. For this reason players must be matched according to their abilities.

1 VS. 1

Figure 4.17

Equipment

1 ball for each 2 players.

Organization

Players are in pairs, 5 yards apart.

Instructions

The server throws the ball underhand to the receiver. The server becomes the opponent and tries to dispossess the receiver.

The receiver controls the ball and must either keep possession for 5 to 10 seconds or must beat the opponent (Figure 4.17).

Coaching Points

The receiver can make the control factor easier by moving the ball away from the incoming opponent (Figure 4.18a) or harder by faking and disguising the move when the opponent rushes in (Figure 4.18b).

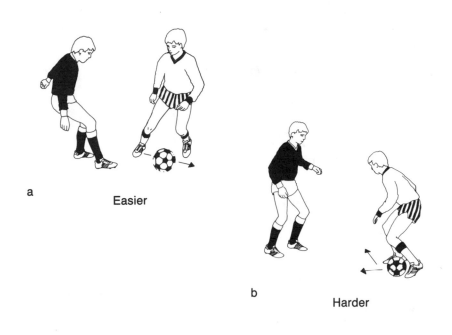

a   Easier

b

Harder

Figure 4.18

Coaching Progressions

The server waits until the receiver actually touches the ball before moving in.

The server moves in while the ball is still in the air.

The server varies the speed and flight of the service.

3 VS. 1 IN A CIRCLE

In the previous drills, the receiver has been able to see where the opponents are positioned. In this practice, the defenders can come from behind the receiver, which creates an exciting progression.

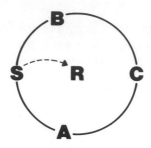

Figure 4.19

Equipment

1 ball for each 5 players.

Organization

Players are in groups of 5 (1 receiver, 1 server, 3 defenders). The defenders and server form a 5-yard radius circle around the receiver (Figure 4.19).

Instructions

The server serves underhand to the receiver. The defender who is to tackle, or put pressure on the receiver, is nominated by the server at the moment the ball is thrown. The server can nominate more than one defender as the practice develops. The server may also elect to be a defender.

The receiver gains and keeps possession of the ball for a given period (e.g., 10 seconds) or controls the ball and breaks out of the circle by dribbling.

Coaching Points

The receiver should try to control and shield the ball from all incoming opponents.

Coaching Progressions

The practice can be made easier or harder for the receiver if the server identifies defenders who are out of the receiver's sight. For example, consider the starting positions for the defenders shown in Figure 4.19:

• Position A is easy because the receiver can see the defender and move both ways to avoid him or her.
• Position C is hard because the receiver cannot see the defender and does not know which way to move.

The coach, or server, can instruct up to 3 defenders to try to dispossess the receiver.

The coach can also make things easier for the defender by allowing the server to help the receiver, thus making the practice 2 vs. 1, 2 vs. 2, or 2 vs. 3.

This practice is especially good for attackers who frequently have to play, often with their backs toward the goal, against 2 or more defenders.

GAME PRACTICE—THROW–CONTROL–PASS–PICK UP–THROW

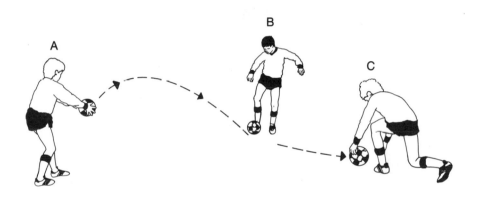

Figure 4.20

The 2 vs. 1 practice can easily be developed in a small-team game.

Equipment
   1 ball for each 3 players; 4 flags or cones.

Organization
   Players are in teams of 3 (or 4) on a 30 × 20 yard (or 40 × 30 yard) minifield marked by flags or cones.

Instructions
   The aim of the game is to keep possession and to develop control skills. Player A throws to Player B, who controls and passes to Player C. Player C picks up the ball and starts the sequence with a throw to Player A or B (Figure 4.20).

The players must keep the sequence: throw–control–pass–pick up–throw.

The player who picks the ball up may run with it before throwing. This opens up the game by increasing space and time.

Turning With the Ball

All players, especially attackers, must be able to turn 180° with the ball. This is one of the most important control skills. It is important in midfield, and it becomes crucial in attack. The sequence of movements used when turning with the ball is shown in Figure 4.21.

Figure 4.21
The proper sequence for turning with the ball is to a) turn sideways to receive the ball and offer a welcoming foot, b) cushion the ball on impact and let it run on, and c) take the ball with the other foot.

THE BASIC PRACTICE

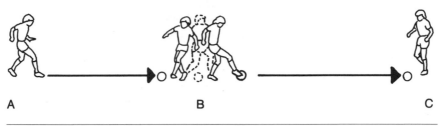

A   B   C

Figure 4.22

Equipment
   1 ball for each 3 players.

Organization
   Players are in teams of 3, standing in line at least 5 yards apart.

Instructions
   Player A push passes to the central receiver, Player B, who controls the ball, turns in one move, and passes the ball to Player C. Player C returns the pass and the practice continues (Figure 4.22).

Coaching Points
   Players should turn sideways to receive the ball and extend a welcoming foot to the ball.

   Players should cushion the ball and withdraw the foot—this maintains the momentum on the ball—and take the ball on with the other foot.

Coaching Progressions
   Players turn and pass the ball to the receiver.

   Players turn and drive with the instep to the receiver.

   Players turn with the ball going between the feet.

   Players develop the practice into shooting practices (chapter 10).

Ball Juggling

Ball juggling is an excellent way to encourage players to develop and retain their feel for, and mastery over, the ball. The constant touching of the ball develops finesse and confidence and encourages the use of many different parts of the body, especially the platforms, which are so important in bringing the ball under control (Figure 4.23).

The secret of ball juggling is practice; because this is time consuming, players must practice on their own time. (An inspiring example is Pelé, who as a boy had to use a grapefruit or a ball of rags tied together with string.) To inspire additional practice, start every coaching practice with a 1-minute competition to see who can achieve the most touches.

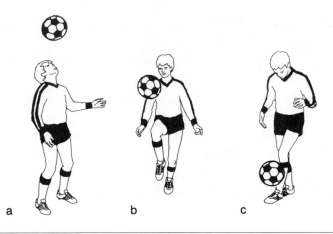

Figure 4.23
Ball juggling.

Drills for Beginners

Beginners do not have the ability to play the ball continuously; continued failure becomes depressing and inhibits progress. To encourage success, I recommend using a light ball, such as a volleyball, and a method that allows the ball to bounce on the floor while being played with the instep of the foot.

BASIC BALL JUGGLING

Equipment
1 light ball for each player (a volleyball or a soccer ball at a reduced pressure).

Organization
Individual players stand in free space.

Instructions

Players throw the ball into the air, let it bounce, and then play it once with the instep.

Players try to keep the sequence going, that is, let the ball bounce, play it with the instep, let it bounce again, and so on.

Coaching Points

Players should use the instep as a platform to lift the ball into the air.

If the ball starts to spin, players should stop and start over. (Spin only complicates juggling for beginners.)

Players should hold arms out wide for balance.

Coaching Progressions

Players make two touches with the instep for every bounce—play, play, bounce, play, play, bounce, and so on.

Players make three touches for every bounce.

Players score 10 touches before the sequence breaks down (professional players can reach several hundred).

Players try to use different platforms (e.g., forehead, thigh).

Players try to use the platforms in a sequence (e.g., head, thigh, foot, thigh, head).

Players set self-targets and hold competitions.

Developing Ball Juggling Skills

Anyone who can consistently achieve 10 or more touches without losing control is ready to move into the intermediate class. However, I do not advocate simply achieving more and more touches or mastering the use of body parts such as the shoulder or the back of the neck to catch the ball. Such skills are fine for the circus performer, but the soccer player will benefit more from developing basic moves with the regular platforms of the instep, thigh, and forehead. These moves are best learned in partner activities and in moving situations. Such situations as these are realistic rather than contrived and encourage effective soccer skills.

Drills for Intermediates

Any player who can achieve 10 touches without losing control can attempt the following partner practices.

CONTINUOUS HEADING

Equipment
> 1 light ball for each 2 players (a volleyball or a soccer ball at a reduced pressure).

Organization
> Players are in pairs of equal ability, 3 yards apart.

Instructions
> Player A gently lobs the ball to Player B, who heads the ball back; the drill becomes continuous.

Coaching Points
> Players' eyes should focus underneath the ball.

> Players should hold arms outstretched to the side for balance.

> Players should head the ball upward back to their partners.

Coaching Progressions
> Players aim to reach 10 or more continuous plays.

THREE TOUCH

Equipment
> 1 light ball for each 2 players (a volleyball or a soccer ball at a reduced pressure).

Organizations
> Players are in pairs of equal ability, 3 yards apart.

Instructions
> Players must play the ball at least 3 times before returning it to their partners.

Coaching Points
> Players should achieve height on the ball between touches to increase the time for each play.

Coaching Progressions
> Players return the ball to their partners with either the foot or the forehead.

Drills for Advanced Players

In the previous drills, the players remained relatively stationary. For advanced juggling, the players have to move while they juggle. Players start with individual activities and then move into partner practices.

INDIVIDUAL ACTIVITIES

Equipment
> 1 ball for each player.

Organization
> Individual player stands in free space.

Instructions
> Keeping the ball off the ground, players see how many yards they can cover forward, backward, and sideways.

Coaching Points
> Players should try to achieve height on the ball each time it is played.
>
> Players should take plenty of time.

Coaching Progressions
> Players start from a basic position and see how far they can travel.
>
> Players set a given distance and see how quickly they can reach the target and get back again.

PARTNER ACTIVITIES

Equipment
> 1 ball for each 2 players.

Organization
> Players are in pairs of equal ability, 3 yards apart.

Instructions
> Partners juggle the ball between each other while moving in the same direction. Note that when one player advances, the other retreats.

Coaching Points
> Same as for individual juggling activities.

Coaching Progressions

Players touch the ball once only.

Players touch the ball at least twice before returning it to their partners.

Players do not use the same part of the body twice in succession.

For ball control, see football tennis (head tennis) on p. 196.

CHAPTER 5

Coaching Passing

The second most important skill in soccer is the ability to pass the ball successfully. Good passing is the foundation of any team strategy and always involves at least two players—the passer and the receiver. Soccer players must develop physical and mental abilities in order to pass successfully. They must possess basic techniques of how to pass the ball, plus they must be able to decide where and when to pass the ball and how and where to support the passer. You will see that there is an exciting difference between coaching physical skills and coaching the minds of your players.

Basic Techniques of Short Passing

This section deals with the three most common methods of short passing: the push pass, the outside of the foot pass, and the instep pass. The swerve pass is more advanced and is included in chapter 9.

The Push Pass

The push pass is the most frequently used and therefore the most important basic passing technique. It is also the easiest to learn, which is why we coach it first.

The push pass is a sideways movement in which the knee is bent and the kicking foot is turned outward at an angle of 90° so that it is square to the intended line of direction of the pass. As with many other side-ways striking skills, such as the golf swing or the drives in tennis, a good follow-through along the line of flight is essential. Unlike golf or tennis, the backlift is relatively short; the power of the pass comes from the muscles inside the thigh and from a firm, fixed ankle, which acts as a club or hammer. While the pass can be made in a variety of ways, it is best done with the player in a firm, compact stance with the center of gravity low and the arms held low. The stance has been aptly called the monkey stance to draw attention to the crouched body shape. The players need to acquire the slightly sitting down position of the monkey. Figure 5.1 illustrates the sequence in detail.

Figure 5.1
Sequence of proper body and foot positions for the push pass.

Faults

Four common faults in the basic technique are worth examining. With the first fault the passing leg is kept rigid, often with the toe pointed. This causes the leg to swing over and across the target line and slice the ball. With the second fault the foot is raised but not held square to the target line. This plays the ball wide of the target. With the third fault the foot strikes the ball below its midline and causes it to lift, often with side-spin. Such passes are really kicks and are difficult for the receiver to control. With the fourth fault there is no follow-through. This causes a stabbing action, which fails to produce the important top roll and causes the pass to lose power.

Corrections

To correct all four faults, kneel at the feet of the player and guide his or her foot through the correct pattern to give him or her the feel of the movement. This is called *shaping* (p. 196).

The Outside of the Foot Pass

This pass uses a different part of the foot than did the push pass and also results in a different body shape. When using the outside of the foot, the body is often tall and upright; indeed, it is almost stately as the ball is guided past an opponent. Because of this body stance, however, this pass is much less powerful than the push pass and is best used over short distances and in tightly marked situations. Very often the ball is almost flicked away, although always with a firm ankle (Figure 5.2).

Figure 5.2
Passing with the outside of the foot.

The Instep Pass

The instep pass is the most powerful of all the passes, as it uses the movement that produces the most powerful kick in soccer—the instep drive. The pass can be used over long distances, but because of the need for precise geometry between the instep and the ball, this pass is much more difficult to learn. When used by beginners, the instep pass can be inaccurate, especially when compared to the much safer push pass (Figure 5.3).

Figure 5.3
Passing with the instep.

Drills For Beginners

The following five drills are arranged in a progressive sequence. I recommend the first two drills for beginners; beginners can also progress further through the sequence and can be introduced to the small-team games presented in chapter 6. This will encourage the development of both the basic techniques and the mental ability to play in realistic situations against opposition, however simple these situations may be in the early stages.

STATIC PRACTICE

In the first drill the players are in a relatively static position. This simplifies matters for the players and makes coaching easier.

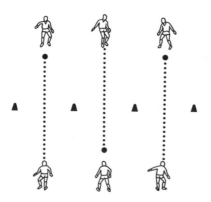

Figure 5.4

Equipment

1 ball for each 2 players; 1 marker for each pair plus 1 extra marker.

Organization

Players are in pairs, facing each other 8 to 10 yards apart.

Markers are set up about 6 feet apart to form passing lanes (Figure 5.4).

Instructions

Players pass the ball forward and backward to their partners using only the push pass.

Players try to keep the pass within their lanes.

Players stop the ball before passing it back.

Coaching Points

Check the basic techniques (p. 51).

Encourage accuracy; the pass should go between the feet of the static receiver.

Encourage a quality pass; the ball should hug the ground because it has top roll. It should not bounce or have sidespin.

Coaching Progressions

Players increase the speed of the pass.

Players reduce the distance between the cones.

Players return the ball without stopping it first (i.e., one-touch play).

Players increase the distance of the pass to 10 to 12 yards.

Players return to the basic starting situation but use the outside and instep techniques as variations.

PASSING ON THE MOVE—GIVE AND GO

Static practices help to introduce and develop the basic techniques, but moving practices add realism. They also demonstrate to players the need for accurate, properly weighted passes that hug the ground and have no sidespin.

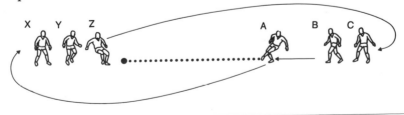

Figure 5.5

Equipment

1 ball for each 6 or 8 players.

Organization

Players are in 2 teams of 3 or 4, facing each other about 10 to 12 yards apart (Figure 5.5).

Instructions

Players use the push pass only.

Player A dribbles the ball forward a few feet, looks for Player Z, and passes to him or her.

Player A then follows the pass and runs to the back of the opposite team.

Meanwhile, Player Z dribbles forward, passes to Player B, and runs to the back of the opposite team.

The drill becomes continuous.

Coaching Points

In the early stages of the practice, the players should control the ball first, dribble a little, and then look before they pass.

As they become more proficient, players should develop the quality of passing in the following order: accuracy; proper weighting or force (not too hard or too soft); proper ball position (on the ground, top roll, no sidespin).

Coaching Progressions

Players progress to one-touch control.

Players decrease the distance between each other.

Players increase the speed of the practice.

Drills for Intermediates

As players improve, the emphasis of coaching changes from basic techniques to finesse and maintaining skill while moving. Often the ability to cope with an irregular bounce of the ball or an uneven surface is a sign of improvement.

GIVE AND MOVE BACK

Equipment

1 ball for each 6 players.

Figure 5.6

Organization

Players are in 2 teams of 3, facing each other 2 yards apart (Figure 5.6).

Instructions

Player A passes to Player Z but then quickly retires to the back of his or her own team.

Player Z passes to Player B and retires.

The drill becomes continuous.

Coaching Points

Players should develop one-touch passing as quickly as their ability permits. Don't let them become discouraged if their early attempts fail.

Insist on top roll; players will soon realize that sidespin makes control difficult.

Emphasize care and finesse; players should concentrate on and take pride in every pass.

Coaching Progressions

The teams move closer and closer together. This makes the practice really demanding and enjoyable.

WALL PASSING

Equipment

1 ball for each 6 or 8 players.

Organization

Players are in 2 teams of 3 or 4, facing each other at least 25 yards apart.

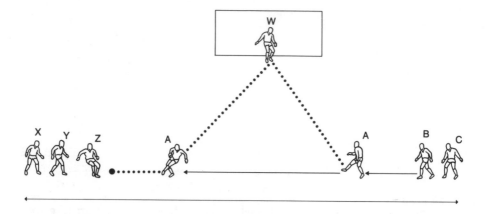

Figure 5.7

One player (Player W, who initially should be one of your better players) stands halfway between the teams and to the side by about 5 yards, to give a good passing angle (Figure 5.7).

Instructions

Player A dribbles a few yards, passes to Player W, keeps running to receive a return pass from Player W, collects the ball, dribbles, and then passes to Player Z. Player A follows the pass to the back of the opposite team.

Player Z repeats the sequence on the return. The drill becomes continuous.

Coaching Points

The sequence for the player with the ball is control, dribble, look, pass.

Each player should observe this sequence because this is the sequence that young players adopt in the game. You can encourage players to look before they pass by asking Player W to move his or her position.

Players should strive for accuracy and correct weighting.

Player W should try to give an effective lead pass.

Coaching Progressions

All players take a turn as Player W.

Players increase the speed of the practice while trying to retain accuracy and control. This is an excellent practice to develop into a shooting drill; the final pass becomes a shot on goal.

Drills for Advanced Players

The main objective is to keep both the passer and the receiver moving.
For this reason, most advanced practices involve active opposition; many
examples are included in this chapter and in chapter 6.

THE LAY-OFF OR ONE-TWO PASS

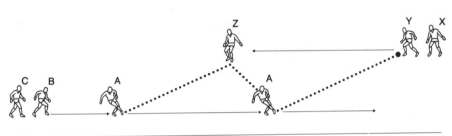

Figure 5.8

Equipment
> 1 ball for each 6 or 8 players.

Organization
> Players are in 2 teams of 3 or 4, at least 25 yards apart, slightly set
> off from the direct line (Figure 5.8).

Instructions
> Player A has the ball.
>
> On command, Players A and Z run toward each other.
>
> Player A passes to Player Z, who gives an immediate one-touch
> return to Player A.
>
> Player A controls and passes to Player Y.
>
> Players Y and B continue.
>
> The drill becomes continuous.

Coaching Points
> Players must realize that skillful cooperation is vital.
>
> Player A should pass the ball accurately and firmly.
>
> Player Z should move to meet the ball and should work to develop
> a high degree of finesse.

Coaching Progressions

This practice develops into a good shooting drill (chapter 10).

Players progress to one-touch control.

Basic Techniques of Long Passing

The techniques for long passing are identical to those for long kicking. See chapter 9 for a full explanation of the necessary technical details plus some coaching hints about the use of a kicking tee to help players kick under the ball without striking the ground. However, this chapter does include some advice on long passing plus two practices for intermediate and advanced players. (Beginners should concentrate on short passing and advance to long passing as their strength and technique improve.)

Drills for Intermediates

LONG PASSING

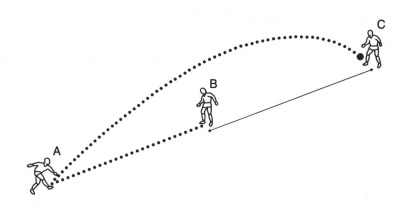

Figure 5.9

Equipment

1 ball for each 3 players.

Organization

Players are in teams of 3, in a line with at least 15 yards between players, or they are on a coaching grid (Figure 5.9).

Instructions

The central player (Player B) has the ball. Player B rolls the ball to one of the end players (Player A) who plays a long pass over the head (or past) Player B to the far receiving player (Player C).

Player C controls the ball and returns it to Player B. The practice is repeated, with each of the two end players practicing the long pass alternately.

Coaching Points

Player B must always give a quality pass to Players A and C. Such a pass requires a quality rolling ball with good top roll and no spinning or bouncing.

Players A and C should concentrate on playing an accurate long pass that will land at the feet of the receiving player.

Players A and C must use a long-leg swing and follow-through. They should kick under the ball to gain height and keep their heads down.

Coaching Progressions

Player B tries to intercept the pass.

Players A and C pass directly to each other without Player B playing the ball (i.e., 30-yard passing).

Players play the ball without stopping it first.

Passer tries to land the ball at the receiver's feet.

Players A and C use both feet. (The ability to play a long, accurate pass with the weaker foot is the sign of a good player.)

Drills for Advanced Players

For advanced players we progress to moving drills and practices.

LONG LOFTED PASSING—ON THE MOVE

Equipment

1 ball for each 3 players.

Organization

For groups of up to 12 players, players are in teams of 3 at one end of a soccer field (Figure 5.10).

Players use the full width of the field.

For groups larger than 12 (24 maximum), create two smaller areas by practicing across the field, allocating one group to each half.

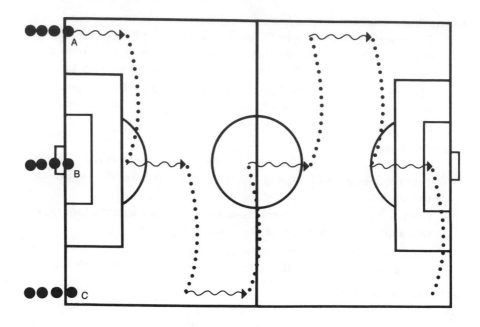

Figure 5.10

Instructions

Player A, with the ball, moves forward and then crosses or centers the ball to Player B.

Player B controls, moves the ball forward, and gives a long, lofted pass to Player C.

The drill becomes continuous as the players move along the field.

Coaching Points

Players should toe down and hit through the bottom half of the ball to make it rise.

Players should use a long swing of the kicking leg.

Players should develop high follow-through.

Players should lean away from the ball.

Players should keep the nonkicking foot well behind the ball.

Coaching Progressions

All 3 players move slowly up and down the field, controlling the ball carefully before making the pass. Initially, the pass is made with the stronger foot.

The player uses the foot that is farthest from the receiver (i.e., the left foot when passing to the right and vice versa).

The players move at high speed down the field.

Players pass the ball with a first-time kicking movement (i.e., no time is allowed to control and dribble before kicking).

Coaching the Mind of the Passer

Soccer players must think and act for themselves. In practices the coach directs the kind of pass to be made; but in a game the player must decide. To help players make correct decisions, create realistic game situations for players, starting with the passer.

Creating Realistic Situations

Coaches can create realistic game situations by providing two essential ingredients: opposition and supporting players.

We can then control these two ingredients according to the needs of our players. For the same reasons that we do not take novice drivers onto the freeway, we do not put beginning soccer players into situations that do not provide a reasonable chance of success. We have to introduce opposition gradually so the passer can develop the correct sequence of actions: control, look, and pass.

Drills for Beginners

The following is an excellent drill for coaching the beginner. It provides a *safety fence* behind which young players can develop their confidence.

4 VS. 1 OUTSIDE THE SQUARE

Equipment
　　1 ball for each 5 players; 4 flags or cones.

Organization
　　Players are in teams of 5, each team on a 10 × 10 yard square marked by flags or cones.

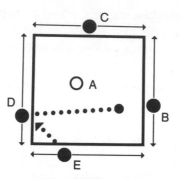

Figure 5.11

The defender (Player A) is in the square, with 1 attacker (Players B, C, D, and E) on each side (Figure 5.11).

The defender is changed at intervals in rotation.

Instructions

The defender must remain within the square at all times and try to intercept the pass.

The attackers may move sideways along their own lines, both with and without the ball, to support each other. They may not step inside the square.

The supporting attackers try to pass the ball across the square to each other without interception by the defender.

Coaching Points

Because the attackers cannot be tackled, they must be taught to show mastery over the ball and composure.

The attackers must lift their heads so they can read the situation.

The attackers must look for passing opportunities, or they must move the ball sideways to create passing opportunities.

The attackers must execute quality passes.

Coaching Progressions

The player with the ball has unlimited time to demonstrate control before making the pass.

Players waiting to receive a pass move sideways along their lines to create passing opportunities.

The player with the ball tries to feint or disguise a pass.

Players use one-touch passing across the square.

Players pass to the player opposite, not just to those on each side.

Drills for Intermediates

The next drill is an obvious and challenging progression from the previous drill.

2 VS. 4 OUTSIDE THE SQUARE

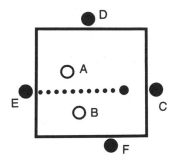

Figure 5.12

Equipment
    1 ball for six players; 4 flags or cones.

Organization
    Players are in teams of 6, each team on a 10 × 10 yard square marked by flags or cones.

    Two defenders (Players A and B) are in the square, with one attacker (Players C, D, E, and F) on each side (Figure 5.12). The defenders are changed at intervals in rotation.

Instructions
    Use the same instructions as for 4 vs. 1 outside the square.

    The objective is to deliver a killer pass (or through pass) between the two defenders.

Coaching Points
    The player in possession should try to fake or disguise the pass and dribble sideways to create a passing opportunity.

    All players should keep their heads up so they can look for the killer pass.

    The supporting attackers should try to make the killer pass possible by good movement.

Coaching Progressions

Players use one-touch passing.

Players use more advanced passes with the instep and outside of the foot; good players use swerve passes between and around defenders.

While the practice is developing, you must move around the outside of the square and coach from behind the players. In this way you can speak quietly to players, reinforce good decisions, and see the same situation as the player, thus sharing the experience with him or her. Keep repeating the key words: control, look, pass.

Drills for Advanced Players

The previous two drills aid in coaching the mind of the passer. For advanced players we must now remove the safety fence between the attacker and the defenders; this adds realism and demonstrates the difference between passing directly to the feet of a supporting player and passing into a space into which the receiver must move. Because we will become increasingly dependent upon our supporting players, we will next consider how to coach the receivers. We will return to the coaching of advanced players later in this chapter, in chapter 6, and in subsequent chapters.

Coaching the Mind of the Receiver

A pass that goes astray or causes the receiver to lose possession is useless. The coach's problem is determining which player, if any, is responsible for the mistake. Did the passer pass too hard, too soon, or too late, or did the receiver fail to anticipate the developing situation? We now consider coaching the mind of the receiver; we will start by considering an old soccer adage, "When not in possession, get into position."

Players who are not in possession of the ball should have only one thought in their minds—support. With younger players you might also use the word *help*. Help is a friendly term, and questions like, "Chris, where can you go to help?" get the message across. Impress upon players that willingness to help is essential for good teamwork. Often players have to make many unselfish runs without ever receiving a pass. The willingness to keep on running for the sake of the team is at the heart of every successful team; this spirit cannot be fostered too soon.

If players have the right attitude, how can coaches help them to make correct judgments about where to support, and show them how and when to move into position?

Where to Support

Basically, the supporting player can take only two positions: behind or in front of the player with the ball. To make the right decision between moving behind or going ahead of the player in possession of the ball, your player must *read* the situation. If the player with the ball is closely covered and does not have space to play the ball forward, then the supporting player should go behind. If the player with the ball does have space to play the ball forward, then the supporting player should run hard and go in front.

This is a relatively simple decision to make, providing players can recognize these situations.

Problem I

The attacker (Player Z) is prevented by the defenders (Players A, B, and C) from playing the ball forward. Player Z needs help.

The Solution—Go Behind

Support players need to help Player Z by moving into the shaded area shown (Figure 5.13). If Player Z then plays the ball back, the support players will be able to play the ball forward.

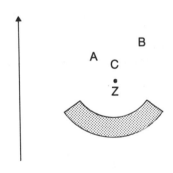

Figure 5.13
Support by going behind.

Problem II

The attacker (Player Z) has the ball with ample space to play the ball forward.

If Player Z dribbles the ball forward, he or she may commit the defender (Player A). But the longer Player Z dribbles, the longer the move is delayed and the more the ability to play the ball forward is lost. Player Z needs help.

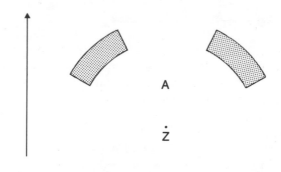

Figure 5.14
Support by going in front.

The Solution—Go In Front

Support players must, in this case, run toward and take up attacking positions behind Player A (e.g., into the shaded areas shown in Figure 5.14). Player Z can now play the ball forward into positions behind Player A.

Safe Passing Angles

All players must know what is meant by a *safe passing angle*. Basically, this is a matter of geometry. For example, if the attacker (Player A) is covered by the defender (Player Z) and does not have the space to play the ball forward, the safe passing angle is backward and away from the defender (Figure 5.15).

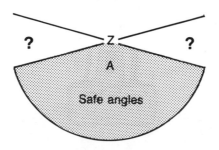

Figure 5.15
Safe passing angle for a tightly marked attacker.

Alternatively, if Player A is not tightly marked and does have space to play the ball forward, then the safest and best pass can be made forward, past the defender at a 45° angle (Figure 5.16).

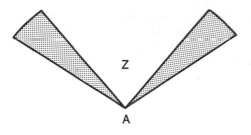

Figure 5.16
Safe passing angle for an open attacker.

The safest position of all is usually at an angle of about 45°. The *square* or sideways pass is always risky because if the defender intercepts it, then at least two players are caught out of position—the passer and the intended receiver. Consider the players in Figure 5.17.

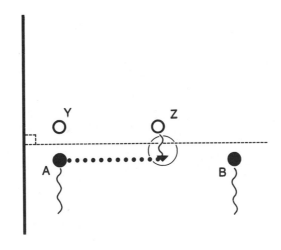

Figure 5.17
A square pass by A is intercepted by Z.

Player A has the ball, but because he or she is contained by the defender (Player Y), Player A tries to make a square pass to Player B.

Player Z moves forward quickly and intercepts the pass. At this moment, Players A and B are both caught out of position, and other team members, who should have been moving forward in support, are also likely caught out of position. Worse, the opposition has the initiative, and both Players Y and Z can move forward and attack with confidence.

In Figure 5.17, Player A has at least three safer alternatives: make a much more positive attempt to beat Player Y, play a killer pass between Players Y and Z for Player B, or receive support from behind Player B.

This final alternative requires Player B to know how and where to move, which concerns receiver strategies.

How and Where to Move

Always be prepared to spend time showing your players both how and where to move. Three basic moves are the curved run, diagonal run, and blindside run.

The Curved Run

Here the player moves on a wide, circular arc that takes him or her out of sight and away from the defender and also increases the target for the passer (Figure 5.18).

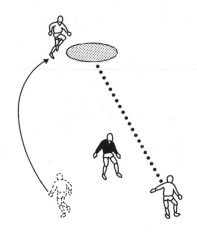

Figure 5.18
The curved run.

The Diagonal Run

With this run the player moves diagonally across the field of play. Such a movement, providing the player doesn't run offside, increases penetration and gives a better target for the passer (Figure 5.19).

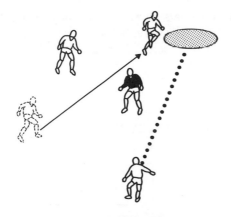

Figure 5.19
The diagonal run.

The Blindside Run

The other popular name for this move is the backdoor run. The object of the run is to take advantage of the unsighted defender by moving unseen behind his or her line of vision. Such a run increases penetration and provides the passer with an easier target (Figure 5.20).

Figure 5.20
The blindside run or backdoor run.

Drills for Beginners

For coaching receivers I recommend games that involve three attackers against one defender—even for beginners. The reason is that using 4 vs. 1

1 results in the four receivers standing statically in the four corners and simply passing the ball. This defeats the object of teaching the receivers to think and move for themselves in relation to the movement of other players.

3 VS. 1 PIGGY IN THE MIDDLE

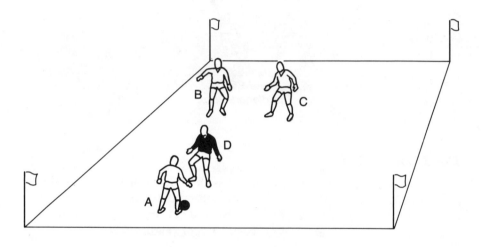

Figure 5.21a

Equipment

    1 ball for each 4 players; 4 flags or cones.

Organization

    Players are in groups of 4 (3 attackers, 1 defender), each group in a 15 × 15 yard square marked by flags or cones.

Instructions

    The attackers have to pass the ball and keep it away from the defender (Figure 5.21a). They are given a target (e.g., 10 passes).

    When the defender intercepts the ball, he or she changes place with one of the attackers, possibly in rotation.

Coaching Points

    Remember that you are coaching the receivers, not the passer.

    The receivers should look for and move into the spaces either behind or in front of the passer.

    The receivers should try to present safe passing angles.

The players should practice unselfish running.

Players should continually reassess their best supporting position in relation to the movements of the passer, the defender, the ball, and other supporting players. Each player's key thoughts should be, "Where, when, and how do I support?"

Coaching Progressions

To emphasize movement off the ball by the receivers, players start by playing basketball but quickly change to soccer.

Use the playback system to highlight a good move by a receiver (chapter 17).

If the players are not doing well, wait until one or both supporting players are caught in bad supporting positions and then, by using the double positive approach (chapter 2) and the playback system, explain the following: Player A has the ball. Players B and C are in bad positions because neither can receive a pass from Player A (Figure 5.21a).

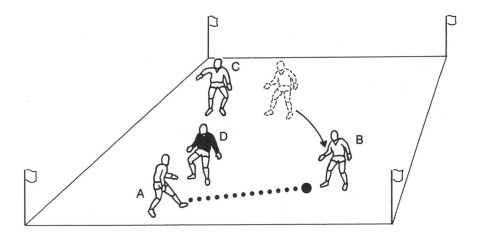

Figure 5.21b

Now using a positive opening comment, such as, "You are running hard but . . . ," show the players what is wrong, or let them tell you what is wrong, and restart the game with a correct move and pass. For example, Player B can make a simple blindside run to a position at a 45° angle to the passer (Figure 5.21b).

Let Player B move into his or her new and correct supporting position. Now let Player A make a correct pass to Player B; when the ball reaches Player B, the game restarts. I often use this method of

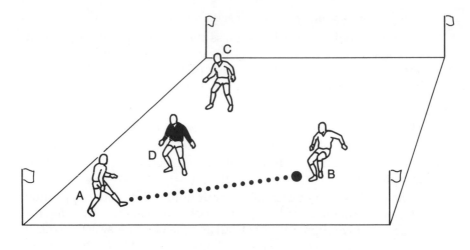

Figure 5.21c

restarting a practice—it helps reinforce the importance of the receiver moving into position (Figure 5.21c).

Players change to more advanced situations with more players (e.g., 3 vs. 2).

Drills for Intermediate and Advanced Players

Drills for intermediate and advanced players require either more players or a changed ratio between attackers and defenders. For example, you can increase the drill to 4 attackers versus 2 defenders or even 4 attackers versus 3 defenders; these situations make it much harder for the receivers to find space and support the passer. Outnumbering the attackers provides even more challenge (e.g., 4 defenders versus 3 attackers). In this situation the attackers really have to work hard to become good receivers. A whole range of small-team games are presented in chapter 6. This chapter presents one final activity for advanced players, which has proved very successful at the college level. It is a one-on-one situation in which the attacker tries to make and receive passes from four static passers.

CORNER-TO-CORNER PRACTICE

This practice is demanding, both physically and mentally.

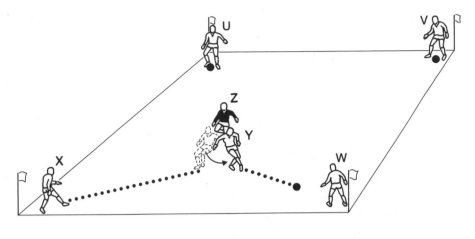

Figure 5.22

Equipment
3 balls for each 6 players; 4 flags or cones; pinnies.

Organization
Players are in teams of 6, each team in a 20 × 20 yard square marked by flags or cones (Figure 5.22).

Instructions
A player stands in each corner; 3 of these players have a ball. The fourth player does not have a ball and acts as the first receiver.

None of the corner players may move more than 2 yards in any direction from their corner.

Of the two players in the square, one is designated the attacker (Player Y) and one the defender (Player Z).

On command, Player Y has to move about the inside of the square, collect a pass from any of the 3 corner players with a ball, and then, by moving and dribbling, find a way of avoiding Player Z and delivering a successful pass to the corner player without a ball. If the pass reaches Player X successfully, then Player Y immediately moves back into the middle of the square and invites a pass from one of the two remaining players with a ball (he or she may not get a return pass from Player X). Having received this pass, Player Y must again try to avoid Player Z and deliver a successful pass to the player without a ball.

Coaching Points
Concentrate on the attacker, not the defender.

Show Player Y how to create space by moving away from the defender with sudden changes of speed or direction.

Receiving player should go to meet the ball.

Attackers should screen the ball to create time and space.

Players should show composure and avoid panic.

Attacker should see which corner is free before collecting the ball.

Having made one pass, attackers should move immediately and quickly to receive another.

Coaching Progressions

The defender assumes a passive role to allow the attacker to learn the drill.

The defender becomes more aggressive as the attacker improves.

The defender forces the attacker to receive a pass from the corner farthest from the open corner.

The attacker plays continuously for up to 2 minutes.

CHAPTER 6

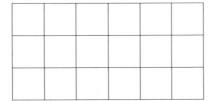

Passing Games

Previous chapters discussed the passer, the receiver, and the techniques of passing. In real games, the successful combination of all three of these elements is the hallmark of good play. An excellent way to combine these elements in practice is through use of small-team games, which involve both opposition and supporting players and which, when we want to focus on a particular skill, can be *conditioned* to highlight a desired outcome. (Conditioning means imposing rules to suit our own objectives. For example, we may require one-touch control, require all passes to be kept below knee height, or not allow players to tackle. The conditions we can impose are limitless; their usefulness lies in allowing us to focus attention on a specific skill or desired outcome.)

The Enjoyment Factor

The second advantage of using small-team games is what I call the enjoyment factor. I have learned through experience that in any sport, players enjoy practice more when it resembles a full-game situation that allows them to express their own skills and talents without the restriction of the coach. Conversely, the coach wants to influence the thoughts and actions of the players to ensure that they learn and improve. Small-team games offer a very useful compromise; they are an invaluable stepping stone between those twin objectives—learning and enjoyment. These games act as a bridge between learning skills and tactics and applying them in the full-game situation. Acquiring new skills can be physically demanding, repetitive, and exhausting. What really matters is that the players

experience a feeling of genuine satisfaction by the end of the session—
that they work toward an improvement, however small. Small-team
games provide a very useful vehicle to this objective.

Controlling Your Practices

The following games offer a variety of purposeful and enjoyable activities
from beginners to advanced players. However, remember my second
strategy—coach the players, not the drill. Always be prepared to modify
a game according to how well or how badly the players are responding.
If you make the game too easy you bore the players; if you make it too
hard the players won't improve. The following tips will help you control
your games.

If the practice is too hard (it keeps breaking down), increase the size
of the playing area, remove some of the players, change the balance of
the teams (e.g., change 3 vs. 3 to 4 vs. 2), or modify the rules.

If the practice is too easy, decrease the size of the playing area, introduce
more players, change the balance of the teams (e.g., change 3 vs. 3 to
4 vs. 2 but coach the 2 players), or modify the rules.

You can easily and effectively develop small-team games into attack
versus defense situations and advanced teamwork practices. For this
reason I consider these games important in providing stepping stones
to successful team play.

Games For Beginners

Small-team competitive games are the stepping stones to successful team
play. Frequent use of these games develops individual skills in realistic
situations. The games provide the basis for introducing the principles of
successful team play (chapter 14) and of improving tactics and teamwork
(chapters 17 and 18). The games in this section are appropriate for beginning players.

SOCCER BASEBALL

I designed soccer baseball for younger players to emphasize that a good
pass has to be both accurate and forceful. Soccer baseball is also enjoyable for older players.

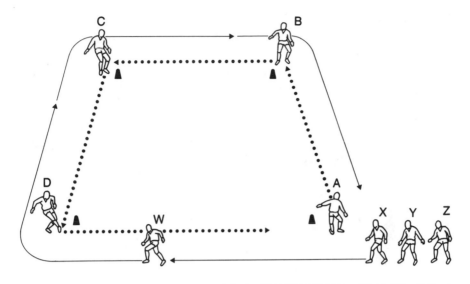

Figure 6.1

Equipment

1 ball for 8 players; 4 flags or cones.

Organization

Players of equal ability are in 2 teams of 4, each team on a 10 × 10 yard square marked by flags or cones.

Instructions

The fielding team places one player on each base (Players A, B, C, and D). On the command ''go,'' these players (starting with Player A) pass the ball around the outside of the bases and back to Player A. The batting team players (Players W, X, Y, and Z) stand at the corner of the square near Player A. On the command ''go,'' the batter (Player W in Figure 6.1) sprints around the square in the direction opposite the path of the ball. A run is scored if the batter gets back to the home base before the ball. Each player has one turn and then the teams change. Any number of innings can be played. If the batter touches the ball or a player when running, he or she is out.

Coaching Points

Batters should run quickly but also watch where the ball is. Fielders should pass carefully and accurately.

Fielders should aim at the feet of the receiver.

Fielders should try to give a quality pass—firm, fast, and with top roll to the feet of the receiver.

Coaching Progressions

The batters run around the square twice to score a home run. (This is good training!)

The batters run once around the bases while dribbling a soccer ball, and the fielding team passes the ball both clockwise and counterclockwise around the bases.

The batters, instead of dribbling around the bases, dribble in and out of 4 cones arranged as shown in Figure 6.2. The number of cones for the dribbling team varies according to the ability of the players.

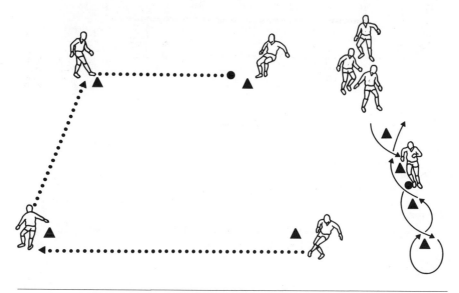

Figure 6.2

Games for Intermediates

The following small-team games progressively increase the physical and mental demands made upon the players.

5 VS. 2

Equipment

1 ball for 7 players; 4 flags or cones; pinnies.

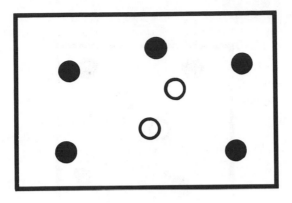

Figure 6.3

Organization

Players are in teams of 7 (5 attackers, 2 defenders), each team in a 30 × 20 yard rectangle marked by flags or cones or in of the penalty area (Figure 6.3).

Instructions

Defenders keep possession and make as many successful passes as possible.

Players change roles at intervals.

Coaching Points

This practice is an excellent starting point from which to develop team play. The generous ratio of attackers to defenders makes it fairly easy for players to combine successfully and produce effective passes. (With young players, you may have to make the practice even easier by changing to 6 vs. 1, thus giving even more time and space in which to think and act.)

It is also a good idea to act as one of the defenders yourself. Your joining in always stimulates players and ensures that the weaker players are helped even further. For example, you can control the situation in their favor by moving towards them, but not actually tackling—that is, offer passive resistance.

Coaching Progressions

Players must pass below knee height.

Players are limited to 3 touches before passing.

Players develop specific passes (e.g., a killer pass or one-touch passing).

4 VS. 2

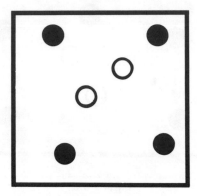

Figure 6.4

Equipment

1 ball for 6 players; 4 flags or cones; pinnies.

Organization

Players are in teams of 6 (4 attackers, 2 defenders), each team in a 20 × 20 yard square marked by flags or cones (Figure 6.4).

Instructions

Attackers try to retain possession of the ball and attempt to score a predetermined number of passes or hold the ball for a predetermined number of minutes.

Defenders try to win possession.

Players change roles at intervals.

Coaching Points

The passer should show composure and look for the opportunity to pass.

The receiver should make space to receive the pass.

The passer should have 2 players at good supporting angles. Weak passers should continue to serve as attackers until they improve.

Coaching Progressions

The player in possession screens the ball (chapter 7), and the players not in possession work hard mentally to give good support.

Players achieve longer and longer periods of interpassing without losing possession.

The passer uses a killer pass or screens the ball until passing opportunities arise.

Games for Advanced Players

In all small-team games it is important to demand high standards from your players. Insisting on a good response becomes increasingly important when coaching advanced players in small-team situations; realism and a competitive edge are vital ingredients.

3 VS. 2

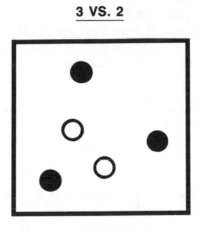

Figure 6.5

Equipment

    1 ball for 5 players; 4 flags or cones; pinnies.

Organization

    Players are in teams of 5 (3 attackers, 2 defenders), each team in a 20 × 20 yard square marked by flags or cones or in the center circle (Figure 6.5).

Instructions

    The game starts with the attackers in possession.

    The attackers try to retain possession or make a specified number of passes.

    The defenders try to win possession with, and without, tackling.

Coaching Points

    The passer should strive for increased control of the ball—encourage screening, feinting, and dribbling.

    Receivers should develop blindside moves.

Coaching Progressions

One of the 3 attackers is designated a floater. When the defenders win the ball, the floater moves over to their side and those 3 players then become the attackers. Each player is designated "floater" in sequence; in this way all players get to practice passing.

Players must use a specific type of pass (e.g., outside of the foot only, or two-touch control).

An Interesting Variation

To easily change from small-team practice to an advanced tactical or team practice, we simply move this activity to the area just outside the penalty area (Figure 6.6). The 3 attackers now must beat the 2 defenders by maneuvering the player with the ball into the penalty area; this player finishes with a shot at the goal.

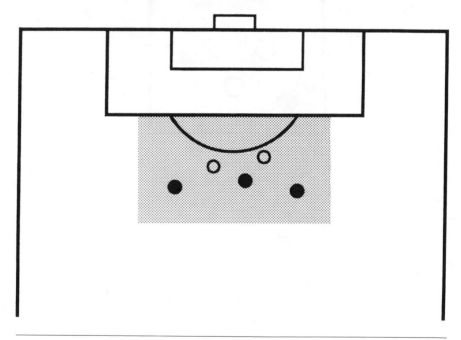

Figure 6.6

Coaching Points

Increase realism by introducing direction and a goal. This immediately highlights the importance of close control and the ability to turn with the ball, dribble past defenders, and shoot.

Coaching Progressions

After the attacker gets into the penalty area with the ball, he or she then moves into a 1 vs. 1 situation against the goalkeeper.

Players must observe the offside rule.

Coach starts the practice with different kinds of serves—lofted, ground pass, or volley pass.

Larger Game Situations

We now move into larger game situations, which require increasing mental and technical skills and, because they are played on a larger area, become more similar to the full-game situation. Larger game situations require individual responses from the players, who increasingly must think for themselves. A good example is the next game, called Goalkeeper (Figure 6.7).

GOALKEEPER

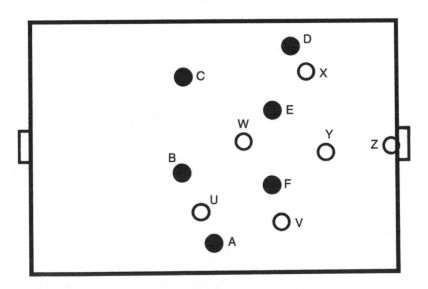

Figure 6.7

Equipment

1 ball for 12 players; pinnies.

Organization

Players are in 2 teams of equal number and ability (e.g., 6 vs. 6) on 1/2 of a soccer field.

Instructions

Start the game with a throw. The team that fails to gain possession must immediately put 1 player in their goal (usually the nearest player to goal). When ball possession changes, so does the goalkeeper. Thus the game always involves 1 goalkeeper plus 5 vs. 6. The team in possession always has the extra field player. In Figure 6.7, Players A to F have possession and Players U to Z have a goalkeeper.

Coaching Points

Teach the players to see the breakdown point (i.e., when the ball changes possession) and to react accordingly:

Attackers become defenders and have to close down quickly on their opponents or position themselves between the ball and their own goal.

Defenders become attackers and must move away from their opponents and look for spaces behind the defense or go wide.

Players should think for themselves.

Players should realize the importance of keeping possession.

Coaching Progressions

Players observe certain conditions, such as the offside rule or use of two touch control.

FOUR-GOALS GAME

Equipment

Four sets of small goals; ample soccer balls to aid continuous play.

Organization

Players are in small teams of equal size and ability (e.g., 7 vs. 7) on a half-sized soccer field with goals arranged as shown in Figure 6.8. Each team has 2 goalkeepers.

Instructions

Play progresses as for soccer, but players cannot be offside or score in the same goal twice in succession.

Players change roles at intervals.

Coaching Points

Do not overcoach.

Players should discover for themselves what to do when they have to defend 2 goals or attack 2 goals.

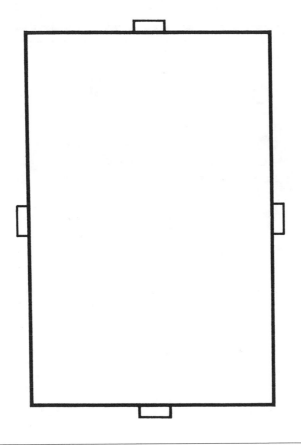

Figure 6.8

Coach individual players in mental skills and the art of reading the game.

Coaching Progressions

Attackers try to switch their attack quickly by using longer passes.

Defenders try to contain the attackers in a small area and prevent a direct shot at goal.

When the ball changes possession or is thrown into play by a goalkeeper, attackers try to look for open spaces while defenders move to cover and mark attackers in dangerous positions.

FLOATER

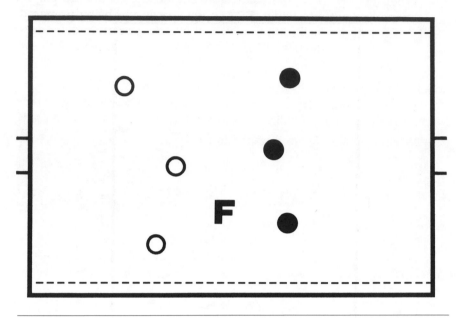

Figure 6.9

Equipment

Ample soccer balls; 4 flags or cones; pinnies, plus special colored pinny for the floater.

Organization

Players are in 2 teams of 2 to 7 players with 1 floater, in a square playing area marked by flags or cones (Figure 6.9). (Allow a minimum of 10 square yards for each player; for example, 7 players need 70 yards, or a 30 × 40 yard square.)

Instructions

The floater always plays for the team in possession of the ball. When the ball changes possession, the floater changes side.

Teams try to make use of the floater and benefit from the extra player.

No goalkeepers (players who can use their hands) are used in this game, but players can and should defend the goal.

Coaching Points

When players gain possession they should use their extra player by moving out into wider, more open spaces and being prepared to run with the ball until they attract at least 1 or more defenders and can release the pass. This should create more space for the new receiver of the ball.

Coaching Progressions

Introduce goals (e.g., corner posts 2 yards apart). This immediately adds the problem of direction to the game.

Players must observe the offside rule.

CHAPTER 7

Coaching Dribbling

Close dribbling to beat an opponent is probably the most exciting of all the skills of soccer. Like all skills it can be learned and improved, but dribbling is also an art, and players of outstanding ability always possess a natural flair or talent.

The best way to coach players to dribble is to present situations that teach the basics of dribbling but also create opportunities for the players to act and think for themselves. For this reason, this chapter contains four sections, each offering advice on the techniques of dribbling that are appropriate for beginning, intermediate, and advanced players. Each section recommends practices that allow players to demonstrate their own abilities and skills.

Coaching Beginners

Beginners have to develop a sense of touch and control. Often, beginners kick the ball forward and run after it. To correct this, they must learn how to play the ball forward gently with a relaxed foot.

Drills For Beginners

The next six practices encourage these skills and provide a rich variety of activities that will act as a springboard for many other games and activities of your own design.

MAKE FRIENDS WITH THE BALL

Figure 7.1

Equipment

1 ball for each player.

Organization

Players are in a group of unlimited number in a designated area (e.g., the center circle) (Figure 7.1).

Instructions

Players take the ball for a walk, jog, or run, keeping it as close to their feet as possible.

Coaching Points

Players should touch the ball gently. Using the big toe or little toe, players push the ball and relax the foot.

Coaching Progression

The players respond to the coach's whistle or call to start and stop the ball. Players increase the tempo of the game.

FOLLOW THE LEADER 1

Figure 7.2

Equipment
1 ball for each player.

Organization
Players face the coach (Figure 7.2).

Instructions
Players mimic the coach's moves.

Coaching Points
Players should achieve a low center of gravity, with the body slightly crouched and weight evenly balanced.

Players should use the inside and outside of the foot to change direction sideways.

Players should use the sole of the foot to pull the ball backwards.

Coaching Progressions
Coach increases the tempo of the movement.

Coach fakes moves by lifting the foot over the ball.

FOLLOW THE LEADER 2

Figure 7.3

Equipment
1 ball for each player.

Organization
Players stand in a line (Figure 7.3).

Instructions
Players mimic the actions and follow the pathways of the coach.

Coaching Points
Players should keep the ball close and hold their arms out sideways for balance.

Players should be alert to rapid changes of speed and direction.

Coaching Progressions

Players walk, then jog slowly, then move in different directions and at different speeds.

ZIG ZAG GAME 1

Figure 7.4

Equipment

1 ball for each player; up to 5 cones.

Organization

Players are in teams of 3. Cones are set at 5-yard intervals (Figure 7.4).

Instructions

Going one at a time, players use different methods of controlling the ball between and around the cones.

Coaching Points

Players should touch the ball as often as possible and avoid the kick-and-run.

Players should keep the ball close.

Coaching Progressions

Players increase the tempo of the dribbles.

Players engage in simple relays and competitions between players and between teams.

Coach reduces the gap between the cones, and players repeat progressions.

BALL DANCING

Figure 7.5

Equipment
1 ball for each player.

Organization
Players are in a designated area (e.g., the center circle).

Instructions
Using alternate feet, the player touches or taps the top of the ball with the underneath of his or her toes (Figure 7.5).

Coaching Points
Players should tap or touch the ball gently and continuously—like running in place—to develop a rhythm.

Players should hold their arms out for balance.

Coaching Progressions
Players apply pressure when touching the ball to make it roll gently backward.

Players make the ball go forward, sideways, or in the pattern of a square.

Players make other patterns, such as their initials.

SHIP AND LIFEBOAT

Ship

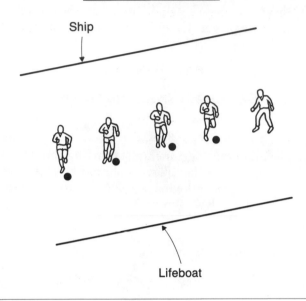

Lifeboat

Figure 7.6

Equipment

1 ball for each player; 4 flags or cones.

Organization

Players stand in a line with about 2 yards between each player. On either side of the line of players is a parallel line, marked by flags or cones; these 2 lines are about 10 yards apart. One is designated the ship; the other is the lifeboat. (Figure 7.6).

Instructions

On the command "ship" or "lifeboat," players dribble their balls to the correct line.

On the command "freeze," they put a foot on the ball and stop it.

On the command "goalkeeper," they fall on the ball and pull it toward their chests.

Coaching Points

Players should keep the ball close.

Players should stay alert and listen carefully to the calls.

Coaching Progressions

Coach sharpens players' wits by calling "ship" when players are already on the ship, or "freeze" when they are already still.

Coach changes calls with increasing rapidity.

Coach makes the game an elimination—the last to respond is out. (Don't eliminate players too quickly, as they won't enjoy the game and gain skills by watching!)

Coaching Intermediates

Thought processes are the main difference between the beginner and the intermediate player. For the beginner, just thinking about the ball is challenge enough, but intermediate players should be able to divide their attention between the ball and what is going on around them. This skill is further developed as players improve.

Drills for Intermediates

This section includes two drills for intermediate players.

THE DRIBBLING PEN

Figure 7.7

Equipment
    1 ball for each player.

Organization
    Players are divided into two groups—a working group and a resting and watching group. They are divided because, done properly, this

is a strenuous activity. (On cold days everyone works.)

Players move freely within a designated area (e.g., center circle) (Figure 7.7).

Instructions

Players keep the ball close to their feet; they don't kick and follow.

Players stay alert to commands and keep their heads up as much as possible.

Coaching Points—Control

In stop-start practices, players should use the sole of the foot to stop the ball.

Players should relax the foot that is playing the ball and develop gentle control.

Players should not kick and follow but should try to finesse the ball.

Players should use the sole of the foot to drag the ball backward to make space in front.

Players should develop combination moves and sequences.

Coaching Points—Peripheral Vision

Ask the players how far ahead they can look but still see the ball at their feet using peripheral vision.

Players should see the ball while staying aware of surrounding action, such as where the opponents are and how much space is between them.

Repeat all of the practices for control, emphasizing use of peripheral vision.

Increase the tempo of the practice, encouraging players to look for and move into open space.

Players should develop an awareness of how far ahead they can move the ball according to the proximity of other players.

Coaching Points—Change of Pace and Direction

Players should move freely about the zone in all directions, not just forward.

Players should change pace and direction when playing the ball with the front foot while driving off the rear; the inside and outside of the foot; and the sole of the foot while pulling the ball backward away from danger.

Players should use feints and fakes, exaggerating the fake by using the eyes, head, shoulders, and arms, by taking the body over the line of the ball, and by moving the foot over the ball.

Progress the practice by introducing opposition and developing confidence in the players.

5 VS. 2

Figure 7.8

Equipment
1 ball for each attacker; 1 pinny for each defender.

Organization
Players are in groups of 5 or 6, with 1 or 2 defenders according to ability of players. Players stand in the center circle (Figure 7.8). Defenders wear pinnies.

Instructions
Defenders try to win the ball or play it out of the circle.

Attackers try to keep possession.

Coaching Points
Players should be aware of the whole situation—the position of their ball, the other attackers, and the defender. Players should keep their heads up.

When confronted by a defender (who might be passive in the early stages), the attacker should try to beat him, not just turn away and screen the ball for safety.

Players should try to use and gain confidence in the techniques you have taught them previously.

Coaching Progressions
Each player has a ball. On command, players keep close control of their own ball while trying to cause other players to lose control of their ball. The last player in the circle is the winner, or players score a point each time they touch somebody else's ball, with the highest scorer the winner.

The Transition From Intermediate to Advanced

Real dribbling means taking on and beating an opponent, or better still several opponents! For this reason I base my advanced drills on 1 vs. 1 situations, but I believe there is a useful transition stage when introducing opposition.

For this transition, I recommend some drills that include a safety fence to allow players to develop the all-important qualities of composure and peripheral vision.

THE SAFETY FENCE

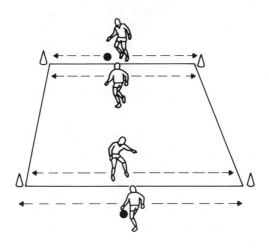

Figure 7.9

Equipment

1 ball for 2 players; 2 flags or cones.

Organization

Players are in evenly matched pairs (1 attacker, 1 defender), facing each other across a 10-yard line marked by flags or cones (a grid-system line is ideal) (Figure 7.9).

Instructions

The attacker has the ball and moves in different directions trying to avoid the defender. The defender has to react and keep his or her body directly opposite the attacker.

Neither the players nor the ball must cross the line. The attacker is successful when he or she can reach one end of the line after losing the defender.

Coaching Points

Players should try to drag the ball with the inside of the foot.

Players should lift the foot over the ball when faking moves and when changing direction with the outside of the foot.

Players should use vigorous body movements to fake changes of direction.

Players should practice faking by pointing in one direction but going the other.

Coaching Progressions

Players must work within a time limit. The attacker practices all the above moves with his or her back to the defender; this is also an introduction to screening (p. 110).

LONDON BRIDGE

This drill is a simple start to beating a defender that highlights the essential ingredients of successful dribbling.

Equipment

1 ball for each 2 players.

Organization

Players are in evenly matched pairs (1 bridge, 1 attacker).

Instructions

One player acts as the bridge, standing with feet wide apart.

The attacker dribbles the ball forward, slips it through the bridge's legs, and collects it on the other side (Figure 7.10).

Coaching Points

This practice ensures that the attacking players keep their heads up while approaching the bridge and develop a good sense of touch as the ball is played forward in small, controlled touches.

Players also develop a sense of timing and accuracy as they slip the ball through the bridge and learn how to accelerate past the defender once the ball has been played forward.

The attacker should not kick the ball through the bridge and chase after it. Try to get the player to collect the ball 2 to 3 feet behind the bridge.

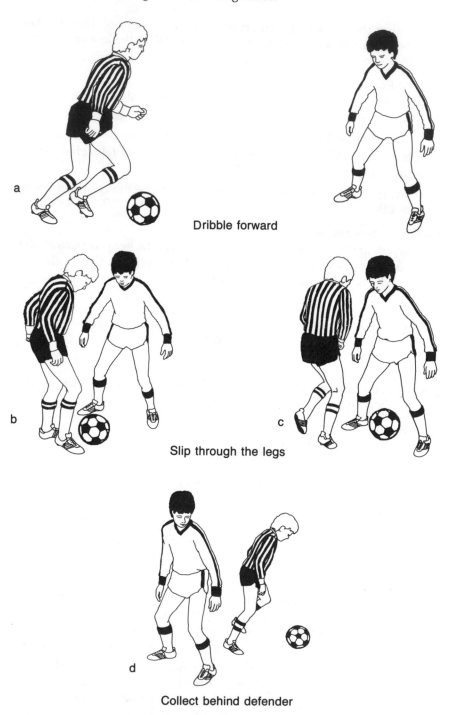

a

Dribble forward

b

Slip through the legs

c

d

Collect behind defender

Figure 7.10

Encourage approaching with the ball played with front foot, the ball dragged with rear foot, and the ball played with both feet.

Coaching Progressions

The player acting as the bridge does jumping jacks to open and close the gap. The attacker must time the move through the gap; this is both realistic and enjoyable.

The bridge backs off slowly as the attacker approaches, using the correct jockeying footwork (i.e., 1 foot forward and back, at an angle to the player).

When the bridge is ready, he or she uses a small jump to reposition the feet from the correct sideways jockeying position to the incorrect square position (jumps the feet square) and thus "invites" the attacker through (Figure 7.11). The bridge must help the attacker by making a definite jump square. This teaches the attacker to look and be patient and develops his or her confidence to hold the ball. This is very good practice for the attacker.

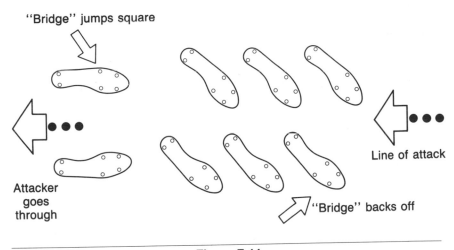

Figure 7.11

Coaching Advanced Dribbling

Skillful dribbling is a mixture of flair, composure, and practice; I feel that dribbling is really an art form. All good dribblers employ five basic moves at some stage; these are well worth examining in detail. The methods are showing the ball, pretending to kick, creating space with the ball, forcing the defender off balance, and screening around the defender.

SHOWING THE BALL

Figure 7.12

Equipment

1 ball for 2 players.

Organization

Players are in pairs of equal ability (1 attacker, 1 defender).

Instructions

Defender backs off as attacker brings the ball toward him or her using the foot (Figure 7.12).

Coaching Points

Attacker should present the ball to the defender in a manner that invites a tackle. As the defender lunges forward to strike, the attacker should play the ball past the defender or through his or her legs.

Coaching Progressions

Initially, the defender helps the attacker by making exaggerated, clumsy strikes. As the attacker improves, the defender becomes more controlled. Eventually the attacker takes the ball directly toward the defender so that he or she is committed to tackle.

PRETENDING TO KICK

Equipment

1 ball for 2 players.

Figure 7.13

Organization

Players are in pairs of equal ability (1 attacker, 1 defender).

Instructions

Attacker takes the ball directly toward the defender at a controlled speed and pretends to kick it hard at the defender (Figure 7.13).

Coaching Points

The attacker should make a vigorous fake kick at the ball with an upward lift of the head. This action must be sufficiently frightening to produce a reflex action in the defender, who should think that the ball is going to hit him or her. Few defenders will not rise up onto their toes away from the ball and shield their head. Some defenders will even jump up into the air!

Coaching Progressions

The attacker brings the ball in fairly quickly at the defender, fakes the kick, and then pushes forward and sideways off the rear foot.

The defender cooperates at first and gives the desired reaction. As the attacker improves, the defender reacts normally—he or she may still jump!

CREATING SPACE BY MOVING THE BALL

Equipment

1 ball for 2 players.

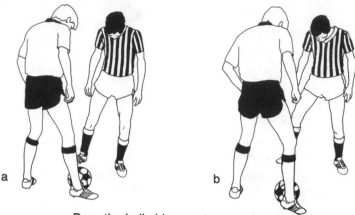

Drag the ball sideways to create space.

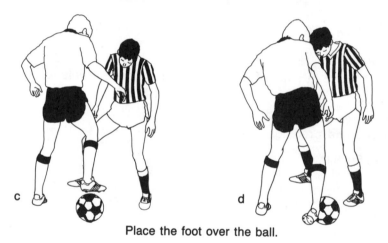

Place the foot over the ball.

Accelerate past the defender.

Figure 7.14

Organization

    Players are in pairs of equal ability (1 attacker, 1 defender).

Instructions

    Attackers cannot expect good defenders to jump out of the way, but the attacker can move the defender sideways out of position to create space through which to dribble. One way to do this is by moving the ball and making the defender follow.

    The defender has to move over as the attacker drags the ball to the left with the inside of the right foot (Figure 7.14a).

    The attacker draws the defender even further across and gets closer to him or her (Figure 7.14b).

    The attacker now lifts his or her right foot over the ball (Figure 7.14c).

    The attacker pushes the ball with the outside of the right foot past the defender and through the gap that has been created by moving the ball and the defender (Figure 7.14d and e).

FAKING AND MOVING THE BODY
TO GET THE DEFENDER OFF BALANCE

Equipment

    1 ball for 2 players.

Organization

    Players are in pairs of equal ability (1 attacker, 1 defender).

Instructions

    The attacker uses body feints and disguises his or her intentions so that the defender makes a wrong move and gets off balance. For example, the defender transfers his or her weight to the foot that is nearest to the ball, which should have been left free to tackle. Tennis players call this "having your foot in a hole."

Method 1.   The attacker fakes to go right, lifts his or her foot over the ball, and goes left by pushing the ball with the inside of the right foot (Figure 7.15).

Method 2.   The attacker drags the ball to the left, using his or her right foot. The attacker pretends to stop (as if to move in the opposite direction) but then continues left by dragging the ball with the inside of the right foot (Figure 7.16).

Method 3.   The attacker makes a bold feint by stepping completely over the top of the ball with the front foot and then plays the ball forward from behind with the back foot (Figure 7.17).

a   Fakes right

b   Foot over ball

c   Goes left

Figure 7.15
Method 1

a   Moves left

(Cont.)

Figure 7.16
Method 2

b   Fakes right

c   But goes left

Figure 7.16 (Continued)

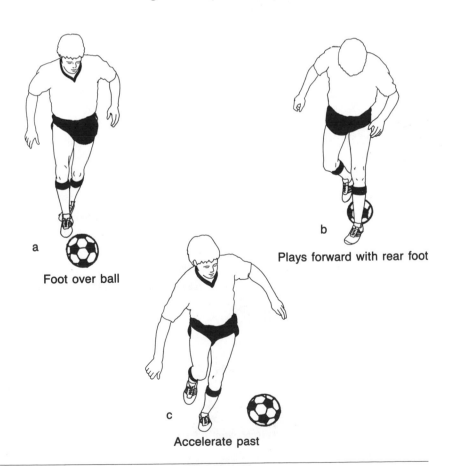

a

Foot over ball

b

Plays forward with rear foot

c

Accelerate past

Figure 7.17
Method 3

SCREENING AROUND OR ROLLING AROUND THE DEFENDER

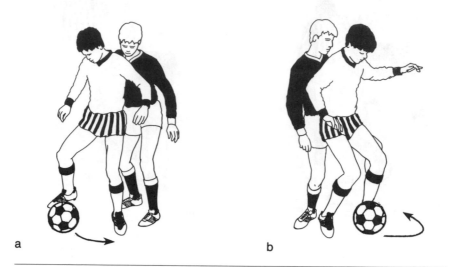

a

b

Figure 7.18

Equipment

1 ball for 2 players.

Organization

Players are in pairs of equal ability (1 attacker, 1 defender).

Instructions

The attacker moves the ball toward the defender and then turns his or her back to the defender and makes a wide screen (Figure 7.18a).

The attacker drags the ball around in a circle and uses the screen to roll around the defender. The attacker has now moved around the defender and can make progress or release a shot (Figure 7.18b).

Drills for Advanced Players

The following drills can be used to develop the five basic moves in dribbling. The drills should be used in conjunction with the small-team conditional games explained in chapter 6. Coaching points are not included in this section because the player chooses which method to try; the coach should advise after the attempt.

ATTACKING THE SQUARE

Figure 7.19

Equipment

    4 balls for 8 players; 4 flags or cones.

Organization

    Players are in pairs of equal ability (1 attacker, 1 defender). Each pair stands on 1 side of a 10 × 10 yard square marked by flags or cones (Figure 7.19).

Instructions

    Defenders stand 5 yards from the line. They may retreat as they are attacked but they must not move back over the line.

    Attackers start 10 yards away from defenders; to beat the defenders, attackers must keep possession of the ball and take it into the square. (This final point is critical; attackers must take the ball into the square.)

Coaching Progressions

    Players have a time limit.

    The attackers rotate clockwise to play against each defender in sequence.

    Players compete for greatest number of successes.

ATTACKING THE CORNERS

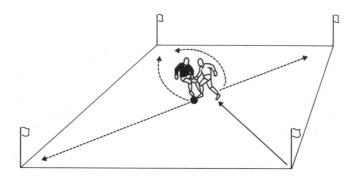

Figure 7.20

Equipment

1 ball for 2 players; 4 flags or cones.

Organization

Players are in pairs of equal ability (1 attacker, 1 defender), each pair in a 10 × 10 yard square marked by flags or cones (Figure 7.20).

Instructions

The attacker must control the ball and take it to any of the 3 corners. The attacker scores 1 point for reaching the corners to the left and right of the defender and 10 points for reaching the corner behind the defender.

The defender tackles and tries to move the ball out of the square.

Coaching Progressions

The attacker attempts to beat the defender by getting to any corner. The attacker must try, and keep on trying, to score 10 points.

Players have a time limit.

THE DRIBBLING PEN

Equipment

1 ball for 2 players; 4 flags and 4 cones.

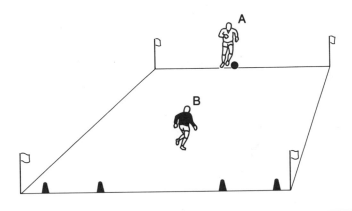

Figure 7.21

Organization
Players are in pairs of equal ability (1 attacker, 1 defender), each pair in a 10 × 10 yard square marked by flags.

Cones are set at 1-yard minigoals along 1 side of the square (Figure 7.21).

Instructions
Play begins with the attacker outside the square and the defender inside. The attacker tries to score by dribbling the ball through either of the minigoals.

The defender defends both goals and wins by tackling or playing the ball off the grid. The defender cannot tackle until the attacker enters the square.

The game continues until the attacker scores or loses possession.

Coaching Progressions
1 goal is assigned more points.

The attacker has 2 or 3 attempts before the players change roles.

The players compete for the highest score or the fastest goal.

The attacker is eliminated after 30 seconds.

CHALLENGE

Equipment
4 balls for 8 players; 8 to 10 flags or cones.

Figure 7.22

Organization

Players are in groups of 8 (1 goalkeeper, 3 defenders, 4 attackers) in 10 × 10 yard squares marked by flags or cones and arranged as shown in Figure 7.22.

One defender stands at the back of each square with the goalkeeper on his or her goal line.

Instructions

Attackers dribble toward each defender in turn and try to maneuver the ball past the defender into the next square and, if successful, into the penalty area for a shot at the goal. Defenders must wait until the attacker enters their square before they can move from the line, and they must offer only the degree of resistance specified by the coach.

Coaching Progressions

On the first attempt, the attacker is allowed to beat each defender in turn and shoot at the goal when he or she enters the penalty area. On the second attempt, the defenders are given a percentage resistance figure (e.g., first defender 10%; second defender 20%; and the third defender 30%). The aim is to provide the attacker token resistance to permit a second shot at the goal.

As the attackers improve, the degree of difficulty is increased. This can be done in one of two ways. Either the coach specifies the increased percentage resistance figure for each defender, or the attacker calls out this figure, thus specifying his or her level of opposition.

The ultimate challenge for the attacker is to defeat the defenders and score even when all defenders give 100% resistance.

Note: Percentage resistance by defenders is a subjective measure. The defenders must try to make a fair judgment, as they will soon be attackers themselves!

1 VS. 1

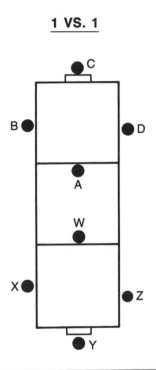

Figure 7.23

This is the final and most exacting of all dribbling practices. It is also physically demanding and requires you to act as a referee, as it can become very competitive.

Equipment

Ample balls; 4 flags; 8 cones.

Organization

Players are in pairs of equal ability (1 attacker, 1 defender) in a 30 × 10 yard minifield divided into 3 squares and marked by cones.

4-yard wide goals are marked by flags (Figure 7.23).

Instructions

Each pair plays for 2 minutes (or less for younger players). Goals can only be scored when the attacker is in the square nearest the goal (this encourages dribbling, not shooting).

When the ball goes out of play, the attacker takes possession at the point where the ball went out. The defender must retreat 4 yards to allow the attacker to restart play.

There is no goalkeeper; players defend the goal but they must not use their hands.

Those not playing stand around the playing area at regular intervals and retrieve the ball to encourage maximum continuous play.

Coaching Progressions

To introduce the games, always pair players according to ability.

If you play a tournament, use a round-robin or an all-play-all system rather than an elimination system, because those who are eliminated don't get any more practice and they are probably the ones who need it most. You may need more than 1 field of play.

If you do hold a straight elimination tournament, arrange a first-time losers competition on an adjacent area.

If you hold an elimination competition, use a handicapping system to encourage the less able players; do this by handicapping the better players (e.g., Player X starts minus 1 goal).

Note: This activity is a very useful way of handling the "ball hog" (chapter 20).

CHAPTER 8

Coaching Tackling and Defensive Skills

All players must develop good defensive skills, which includes more than being able to tackle correctly. Good defenders are able to outthink their opponents and can often win the ball or force an error without coming into contact with the attacker. Defenders must be able to anticipate plays, play aggressively, and position themselves correctly. When these mental skills are combined with courage and determination, we have a real defender. Chapter 8 begins with mental strategies for advanced players who already know how to tackle. If you coach beginners, you may want to start at p. 137, which deals with coaching the basic tackles.

Every defender must be able to recognize whether he or she is the first or the second defender. The first defender is the player who is nearest the opponent with the ball and whose main duty is to stop the attacker from advancing unchecked, playing the ball forward, and shooting a goal. The second defender must support the first defender but must also think about the developing tactical situation.

When defenders are confused about which roles they should be playing, they are most vulnerable. Players cannot be taught too soon that the nearest player goes to meet the ball. That is, the nearest defender is always the first defender.

The First Defender

The first defender must know how to

1. close down on an attacker and jockey,
2. win the ball by good positioning and interception,
3. stop the attacker from turning with the ball,
4. force an attacker one way, and
5. recover when beaten.

How to Close Down on an Attacker

The first defender must always go forward toward the attacker with the ball. If the attacker is close, the first defender has only a short distance to cover. However, when the attacker is some yards away, the defender must move quickly yet cautiously; to rush at an attacker who is in full possession of the ball is asking for trouble! You can coach players to close down on attackers in four stages:

Approach

The defender runs quickly and with a normal running action while the ball is traveling toward the attacker but is not yet under his or her control (Figure 8.1).

Figure 8.1
Approach.

Split Step

To halt the running action, the defender executes a split step by stopping sharply with one foot forward and one backward, the body in a crouched position to aid balance. This should be done about 3 yards from the attacker if he or she has full control over the ball (Figure 8.2).

Figure 8.2
Split step.

Close In

The defender now closes in on the attacker cautiously and in a threatening manner, edging forward step by step, front leg leading. The intention is to force the attacker to look down at the ball to see where it is. At the moment the attacker's eyes go down, he or she is no longer a direct threat (Figure 8.3).

Figure 8.3
Close in.

Jockey

Having contained the attacker and prevented a penetrating move, the defender should jockey and try to win the ball or force the attacker away from the danger zone (Figure 8.4).

Figure 8.4
Jockey.

How to Jockey.   Jockeying, the skill of keeping between the attacker and his or her intended target (usually the goal) requires the defender to slow down or delay the attacker by backing off slowly while at the same time trying to force an error or make a successful tackle. The jockeying stance is similar to that of a boxer; the body is held sideways, the feet are apart, and the weight is on the toes to allow quick movement in any direction. The eyes watch the ball and the midline of the attacker's body, not the head or shoulders of the attacker. In this way, sudden upper body movements do not throw the defender off balance.

The key to good jockeying is footwork. The defender's feet move like the boxer's (Figure 8.5) but must never be caught square to the line of attack (Figure 8.6).

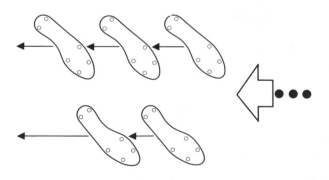

Figure 8.5
The proper foot position for jockeying.

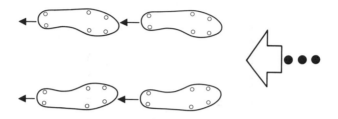

Figure 8.6
The improper foot position for jockeying.

Drills for Intermediates

The following drills are appropriate to use when coaching intermediate defensive skills.

LONDON BRIDGE (P. 101)

1 VS. 1

Equipment
    1 ball for each 2 players; 4 flags or cones.

Organization
    Players are in pairs of equal ability (1 attacker, 1 defender), each pair in a 10 × 15 yard coaching grid marked by flags or cones (Figure 8.7).

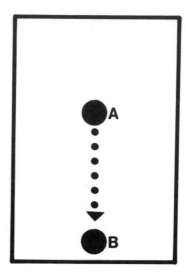

Figure 8.7

Instructions

The defender (Player A) plays ball to the attacker (Player B), then tries to prevent Player B getting past but without executing a tackle (i.e., jockey only).

Coaching Points

The defender should keep his or her body crouched, in a sideways position, with one foot forward and weight on the toes.

The defender should look at the midline of the attacker's body.

The defender should threaten to tackle and strike with the leading foot and steal the ball.

The defender should back off slowly.

Coaching Progressions

Players observe normal rules for tackling.

Introduce a second attacker as shown in Figure 8.8. Player A now plays the ball to either Player B or Player C and has to stop either of them from getting through (Players B and C may interpass).

Drills for Advanced Players

The following drills are appropriate to use when coaching advanced defensive skills.

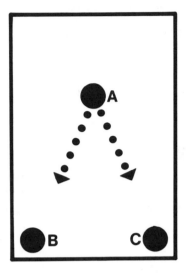

Figure 8.8

1 VS. 1

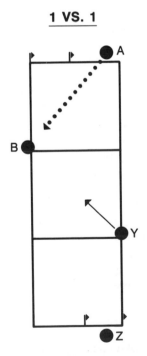

Figure 8.9

Equipment

1 ball for each 4 players; 4 flags; 8 cones.

Organization

Players are in groups of 4, each group on a 30 × 10 yard minifield divided into 3 squares and marked by cones. Goals are marked by flags (Figure 8.9).

Instructions

Player Z acts as goalkeeper.

Player A plays the ball to Player B, who controls the ball, turns, and tries to get past Players Y and Z to make a goal.

Player Y cannot start play until Player A actually passes the ball to Player B.

Coaching Points

The coach can emphasize any of the coaching points covered in this chapter as they arise. In particular the coach should encourage inventiveness and positive, aggressive play.

Coaching Progressions

Player A helps Player B maneuver around Players Y and Z.

Introduce the offside rule to help Player Y.

Winning the Ball by Good Positioning

Clearly, interception and good positioning go hand in hand; good positioning helps the defender to win the ball by interception. But I feel these elements have an important difference in the mind of the player. The decision to intercept comes at the moment the ball is actually played, while the thought processes that control good positioning occur over a period of time and in relation to the tactical movements of other players. This difference is worth developing with your advanced players, and you can start with the following two examples (Figure 8.10 and Figure 8.11).

Figure 8.10 shows the perfect example of how the defender (Player A) ensures winning the ball by good positioning. If the attacker (Player B) plays the ball over or past Player A, Player C loses in the race to the ball. If the ball is played to Player C's feet, Player A simply stops him or her from turning with the ball and in this way gains more time. This is good defending.

In Figure 8.11, the ball is played to the attacker (Player C) from midfield. The defender (Player A) is now in a position to win the ball by interception as a result of good positioning.

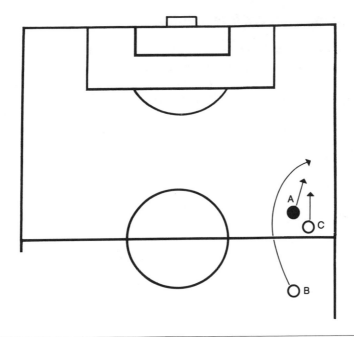

Figure 8.10
An example of good positioning by a defender.

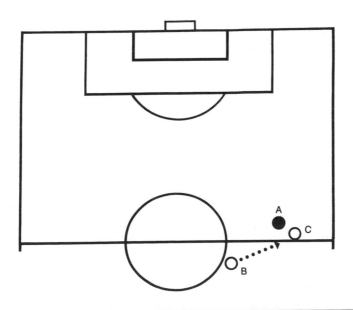

Figure 8.11
The defender positioned to intercept the ball.

Winning the Ball by Interception

Good positioning results from thought processes that occur over a period of time, while good interception requires a split-second decision and reaction. To coach interception you must coach the mind of the defender; the following practice is unique in its effectiveness for this purpose. You can use it with players of all ages and abilities and can very easily develop it into dribbling, screening, and tackling drills (Figure 8.12).

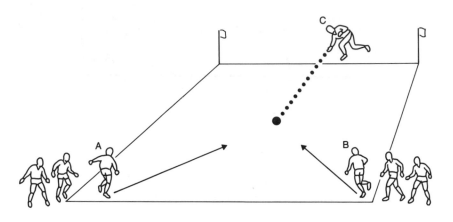

Figure 8.12

INTERCEPTING THE PASS

Equipment

1 ball for each 2 or more players; 4 flags or cones.

Organization

Players are in 2 groups of equal ability, each group in a corner of a 10 × 10 yard square marked by flags or cones (Figure 8.12).

Instructions

The coach serves the ball toward the players. Players A and B must both try to win the ball and play it back to the coach. After the play, the next players in line take a turn.

Coaching Points

The moment the ball is served, players must make instant judgments about whether or not they can get to the ball first. Some decisions are easy, as when the ball is directed in favor of a player. But sometimes players have an equal chance. In this situation, players should always go for the ball and hope they are quicker off the mark or a faster runner.

Players who quit in 50/50 situations will never win the ball.

Coaching Progressions

The coach serves several passes in such a way that it is absolutely clear which player will get the ball. This develops the confidence of the players to move forward and make successful, if easy, interceptions.

As the players gain confidence, the coach serves the ball in favor of one player as a 60/40 or 50/50 ball. Players have to develop much finer judgment, make their decisions early, and be determined.

The player who wins the ball becomes the attacker and has to turn with the ball and dribble it across the target line.

The player who does not win the ball becomes the defender and has 3 objectives: Stop the attacker from turning with the ball; jockey the attacker and force him or her sideways; and win possession of the ball and return it to the coach.

INTERCEPTING THE PASS (ADVANCED)

Equipment

1 ball for each 3 players.

Organization

Players are in a group of 3 (1 attacker, 1 defender, 1 server). Players are positioned as shown in Figures 8.10 and 8.11.

Instructions

The server plays a variety of balls to the attacker. The server may dribble the ball in different directions before making the pass—this changes the picture for the defender.

The attacker tries to gain possession and beat the defender. The attacker should keep moving to fool the defender.

While the server has the ball, the defender positions himself or herself to see the attacker and the server. The defender intercepts the pass if it is safe to do so. If not, the defender defends as appropriate.

Coaching Points

Remind defender that good positioning is a continuous process of decision making.

The defender should always be in a position to see the ball and the attacker. The defender should watch the tactical move develop without losing sight of the particular attacker that he or she is covering.

The defender should allow himself or herself a handicap start. If the ball is played toward the defender's goal, the defender should be able to win the race to the ball.

The defender should always position on the goal side of the attacker (or nearly always—there are some exceptions).

Coaching Progressions

The practice develops into a small-team game or a functional practice.

Stopping the Attacker From Turning With the Ball

Excellent defensive play will stop the attacker with the ball from turning and attacking the defender's goal. Such defensive play counters three potential dangers: the shot at goal, the pass forward, and the attacking dribble.

Stopping the turn is a hallmark of good defense by individuals and by the defense as a whole. It is an advanced skill, however, because it requires confidence plus the self-control not to tackle from behind and risk giving away a free kick or, worse, a penalty kick (Figure 8.13).

Figure 8.13
Stopping the turn.

STOPPING THE TURN

Equipment

1 ball for each 2 players.

Organization

Players are in pairs of equal ability, moving in free space.

Instructions

The attacker tries to turn with the ball and beat the defender.

The defender tries to stop the turn.

Coaching Points

The defender should stay about 3 feet behind the attacker.

The defender should stay on his or her toes and be patient.

The defender should not tackle through the legs—this may be a foul.

The defender should tackle when the attacker tries to turn.

Coaching Progressions

Play moves to situation shown in Figure 8.14.

See chapter 16 for more advanced drills.

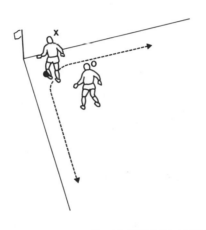

Figure 8.14

Forcing an Attacker One Way

In addition to slowing an attacker by jockeying and backing off, a good defender can often force the attacker one way. That is, by positioning to one side of the attacker, the defender can force the attacker away from the danger zone, toward other, supporting defenders, or onto the stronger tackling side of the defender.

Perhaps the best example of forcing an attacker to move in the least dangerous direction occurs when the fullback directs or "invites" the winger to play down the sideline, thus stopping the winger from attacking directly toward goal.

FORCING AN ATTACKER

Equipment
1 ball for each 2 players.

Organization
Players are in evenly matched pairs, facing each other 5 yards apart on any straight line on the soccer field.

Instructions
The attacker has the ball and tries to beat the defender by getting the ball onto the line behind the defender.

The defender tries to force the attacker away from the line in the direction the defender wants the attacker to go.

Coaching Points
The defender should use a technique similar to jockeying but with a much more definite body position that shows the attacker the open side.

Coaching Progressions
The defender forces the attacker in the direction the defender selects.

The defender identifies the weaker kicking foot of the attacker and forces the attacker that way.

Players use this technique in a 1 vs. 1 drill (p. 121).

Recovering From Being Beaten

What do I do if I'm beaten? This is not the kind of question a player is likely to ask a coach because the answer might be a rebuke: "Don't think about being beaten—think positive!" However, players do get beaten, and they must know what to do when it happens. Players should be taught the following.

Give Immediate Chase
Inexperienced or poor players often throw their heads up or cry out in anguish if they make a mistake; this wastes valuable time. The first thought in the player's mind must be to get back into the game.

Use the Recovery Line
Unless a player is the last defender, he or she seldom chases directly after the player who has the ball, because the cover defender will be chasing that player.

When beaten, defenders should run hard along their recovery line (Figure 8.15).

Get Goalside of the Ball

The player must continue to run hard along the recovery line until he or she is closer to the goal than the ball is.

Stop and Cover

Having reached this point, the player reassesses the situation and normally becomes the second defender (Figure 8.16).

Recovery Lines

All defenders have recovery lines. These are pathways along which players run if they are beaten. Players who are beaten on the sides of the field run back toward the nearest goalpost. Players beaten in the center of the field run back toward the penalty spot or the middle of the goal.

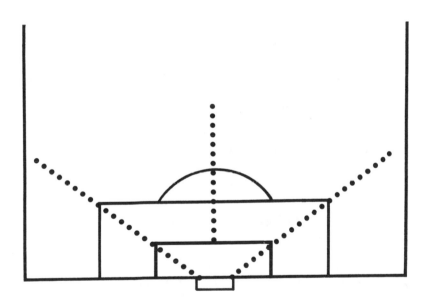

Figure 8.15
Recovery lines for a beaten defender.

The four stages of recovery are shown in Figure 8.16. In this diagram, the first defender (Player A) has been beaten by the attacker (Player C). The second defender (Player B) covers to prevent Player C from having a clear run at goal. Player A now goes through the recovery drill by turning quickly and sprinting back along the recovery line until goalside of the ball. Once Player A has recovered goalside of the ball, he or she acts as the second defender.

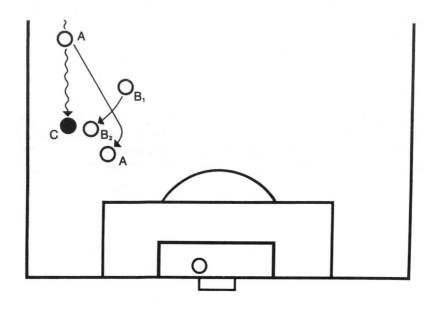

Figure 8.16
Four stages of recovery.

The Second Defender

The second defender must support the first defender who has gone to meet the attacker with the ball. The manner in which the second defender moves to give this support is vital to good defensive play; a player who moves too soon or too late can be easily bypassed. So how should the second defender cover and support, and what other tactics can he or she employ to foil an attack? This section deals with covering and supporting the first defender and setting the offside trap.

How to Cover and Support

The basic covering position for the second defender (Player B in Figure 8.17) is about 6 to 10 yards from the first defender (Player A), at an angle of 45° and on the most dangerous side (usually the goal side). Exact measures such as 6 to 10 yards or 45° can never be absolute, but they do provide a useful starting guide for the following reasons. A defender who stands square does not provide support because the attacker can beat both defenders in one move (Figure 8.18).

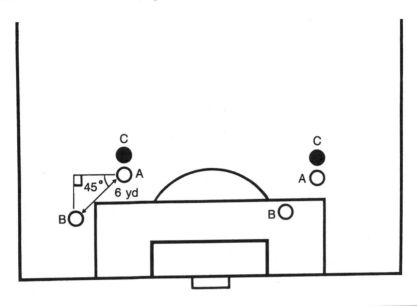

Figure 8.17
Basic covering position for the second defender.

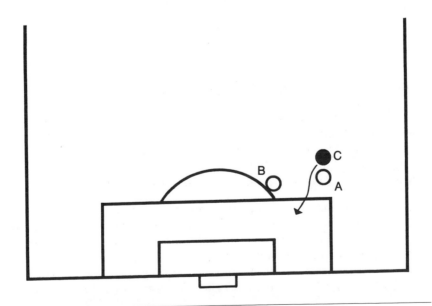

Figure 8.18.
The second defender should not stand square to the first defender.

If the second defender stands more than 8 to 10 yards behind the first defender, then the second defender is not providing sufficient cover. The attacker has ample room in which to play (Figure 8.19).

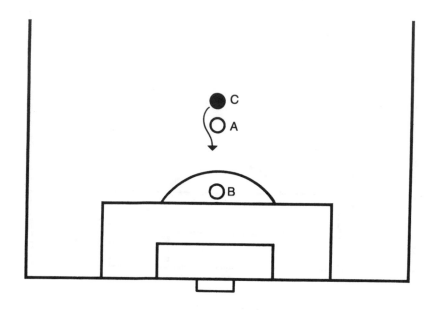

Figure 8.19
The second defender should not stand more than 8 or 10 yards behind the first defender.

How To Set the Offside Trap

Knowing how and when to catch opponents offside is an ability all players must acquire. Providing it is not overused (becoming a dangerous tactic for the defense to use and simultaneously destroying the character of a game), it is a legitimate and important part of defensive play. To use this technique your players must develop three fundamental skills.

1. A knowledge of the rules governing offside play.
2. The ability to simultaneously observe the player with the ball and the tactical situation that is developing. Such vision often begins with the simple instruction to players to keep their heads up.
3. The recognition by all defenders that only the player at the very back of the defense—usually called the rearmost defender—should

execute or spring the offside trap. The rearmost defender is the key player in executing the move personally and in controlling the actions of other defenders.

The following diagrams show how the offside trap can be used to stop an attack.

Stage 1—Identifying the Rearmost and Key Defender

In Figure 8.20, the defenders (Players X and Y) are outnumbered by 4 attackers, of whom Player B has the ball.

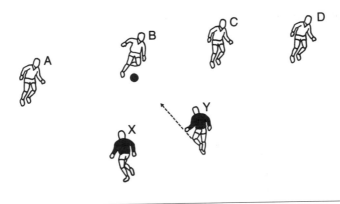

Figure 8.20
Identifying the rearmost and key defender.

Player Y goes forward to contain Player B. The nearest defender going to meet the ball is good play.

Player X is now the rearmost and therefore the key defender. Player X must first give cover to Player Y. (If Player B dribbles past Player Y, then Player X is the only defender who can prevent a direct attack on goal). However, while giving support, Player X must also recognize the possibility of playing the offside trap.

Stage 2—Prepare But Don't Act

While supporting Player Y, Player X must also watch the movements of all the attackers, including Player A who may be hoping to make a blind-side or backdoor run. This is the essential skill of the good defender—the art of being able to watch the ball and the developing situation at the same time (Figure 8.21).

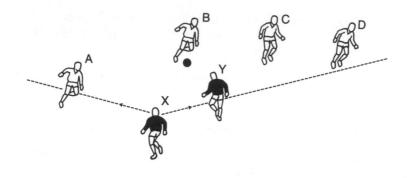

Figure 8.21
A defender must be able to watch the ball and the field at the same time.

Stage 3—Spring the Trap

The defenders hope that the attackers, in their haste to take advantage of the situation and before Player B releases the pass, will continue running forward and come square into line with Player X or even run goalside of Player X. (In either case they are offside, because to be in line is sufficient.) In this situation, Player X simply stands still and lets the attackers put themselves offside (Figure 8.22).

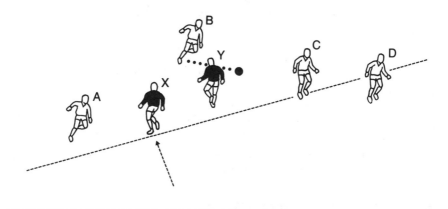

Figure 8.22
Spring the trap.

Against more experienced attackers, Player X can actually produce the offside situation by moving quickly upfield just before Player B releases the pass forward. This is a critical moment, and the decision and timing must be exact; if Player X makes the move too late, not only are the attackers not offside but they are in an even better position. Judging when to move requires practice in attack versus defense. The defender must watch both the player with the ball and the movements of the other attackers. One useful signal of when to move comes when Player B, with the ball, looks down at the ball to kick it. At this moment, Player X can often outwit the attackers.

Only the rearmost defender can set the offside trap. Because the second defender will often also be the rearmost defender, he or she must always be alert to the possibility of catching the attackers in an offside position. To set an effective offside trap, the rearmost defender must

- make sure he or she is the rearmost defender by looking both ways across the field,
- identify the attacker who is most easily caught,
- split his or her attention between this attacker and the attacker who has the ball and who will usually be covered by the first defender, and
- be patient, watching and waiting until he or she anticipates that the attacker with the ball will actually make a pass forward.

Remember, the attacker must pass because dribbling does not breach the offside rules. Just before the pass is made, the defender should move quickly upfield leaving the chosen attacker as the only player between the ball and the goalkeeper at the moment the ball is played. This is the critical move.

The Basic Tackles

This section examines the techniques of the three basic tackles in soccer: the block tackle, the side tackle, and the sliding tackle.

I always coach the block tackle first because it introduces the idea of hard but safe body contact, which can help some beginners overcome a natural aversion to hard physical contact. Be careful when coaching this tackle; a player who becomes overcompetitive can cause an accident. For this reason keep strict discipline and match your players for weight as well as height and ability whenever possible.

The Block Tackle

This tackle is very effective when the attacker comes directly toward the defender, especially when space is limited as in a crowded penalty area. This tackle is a powerful movement, which if done well not only stops the attacker but gives the defender a reasonable chance of winning possession. To generate sufficient force to overcome the momentum of the attacker, the defender's body has to be crouched to lower the center of gravity, the instep of the striking foot has to move as if to go "through" the ball rather than to stop at it, and the leading shoulder has to move powerfully forward as the foot strikes the ball.

The player whose body position is similar to that shown in Figure 8.23 will never win a tackle!

Figure 8.23
Poor body position for a tackle.

Drills for Beginners

BLOCK TACKLE DRILL

Because the block tackle can be dangerous if taught badly, I use a series of progressions into the full action. They work and are enjoyable, and I recommend them to you.

Equipment
   1 ball for each 2 players.

Organization
   Players are in pairs of equal size, weight, and ability.

Instructions
   Follow the sequence under Coaching Progressions.

Coaching Points

Players should keep their bodies crouched with a low center of gravity.

Players should use their insteps and keep their knees over the ball.

Players should put their weight into the tackle, shoulder forward.

Players should strike through the ball, not at it.

Coaching Progressions

Players place their hands on each other's shoulders, keeping their arms straight (Figure 8.24a).

Both players tackle gently so that their feet come into simultaneous contact with the ball (Figure 8.24b).

Players drop their arms. This is the same tackle but the shoulder now comes into play. Players increase force and realism, but the ball should not move (Figure 8.24c).

a   b

c

(Cont.)

Figure 8.24

Figure 8.24 (Continued)

Players take one short step backward. On command, they step in with the left foot and tackle with the right. Both players should tackle simultaneously; this is most important.

Players move to active but not 100% effort. They progress to live competition but limit the number of practices to 5 (Figure 8.24d).

Drills for Intermediates

CORNER AND LINE ATTACK

Equipment

1 ball for each 2 players; 4 flags or cones.

Organization

Players are in pairs (1 attacker, 1 defender), each pair in a 10 × 10 yard square marked by flags or cones (Figure 8.25a).

Instructions

The attacker (Player A) has the ball and tries to attack the defender's (Player B's) corner.

Player B tries to win the ball. Player B must stay on his or her feet, using no sliding tackles.

Coaching Points

Same as for jockeying and block tackles.

Coaching Progressions

Player A tries to attack Player B's line (Figure 8.25b), which makes defending harder because of the wider target line.

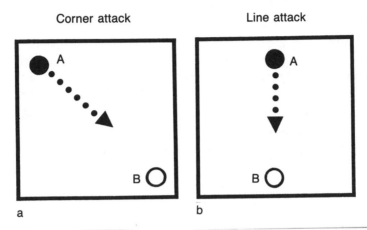

Figure 8.25

Drills for Advanced Players

For advanced players I recommend a tackling pen system, in which two players act as defenders and the remaining players bring the ball toward them one at a time.

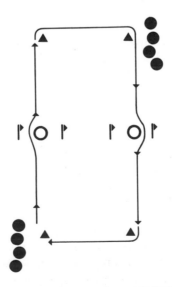

Figure 8.26

TACKLING PEN

Equipment
> 1 ball for each attacking player; 4 cones; 4 flags.

Organization
> Players are in a group of unlimited number (2 defenders, the rest attackers) in a 30 × 20 yard minifield marked by cones, with 5-yard wide goals marked by flags (Figure 8.26).

Instructions
> Defenders remain between their goals and do not move more than 2 yards from this area. Defenders try to stop the attackers.
>
> Attackers use continuous, single file approach, giving the defenders time to recover position between tackles. Attackers beat the defenders by dribbling through the goals.

Coaching Points
> Same as for Block Tackle Drill.

Coaching Progressions
> Players compete to see how few attackers beat the defenders.
>
> The defenders change at regular intervals, because this is a very demanding drill.

The Side Block Tackle

Using the front block tackle is one way of dealing with an attacker who brings the ball directly toward a defender. To stop the player who is moving past the defender diagonally or who is already past, there are two main techniques—the sliding tackle and the side block tackle. I teach the side block tackle first because it allows the defender to stay on his or her feet and also provides a very useful introduction to the sliding tackle.

The tackle is best considered in four stages. First, the defender runs hard to draw alongside the attacker (Figure 8.27a). Next, the defender turns inward at the attacker using the foot nearest the attacker (Figure 8.27b). The defender then crouches down and hooks the tackling foot around the ball using the side of the instep (Figure 8.27c) and completes the turn while hooking the ball until it breaks clear from the attacker's foot (Figure 8.27d). Ideally the defender gains possession of the ball; in reality the defender often stops the attacker while the ball bounces free. At the beginning stage, it's most important that the defender is still standing upright after the tackle and at least has a chance to continue to pressure the attacker.

a

b

c

d

Figure 8.27
The side block tackling sequence.

Drills for Intermediates

SIDE BLOCK TACKLE

Equipment
    1 ball for each 2 players.

Organization
    Players are in pairs of equal ability, size, and weight (1 attacker, 1 defender).

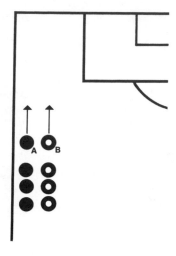

Figure 8.28

Both players stand facing the same direction along the sideline (Figure 8.28).

Instructions

The attacker (Player A) has the ball and dribbles it forward at a steady pace and in a straight line.

The defender (Player B) executes the tackle.

Coaching Points

The defender should run hard to get level, turn on the nearside foot, and crouch down as he or she turns to get a lower center of gravity.

The defender should hook the tackling foot around the ball and complete the turn, hooking the ball hard until it breaks clear.

Coaching Progressions

The attacker increases the pace of the dribble.

The defender tries to actually win possession of the ball rather than just force it away.

Drills for Advanced Players

Use the previous drill for intermediates but require the defender, after he or she completes the first tackle, to immediately chase and tackle a second attacker, who waits for the first challenge to finish and then moves off in another direction.

Use the tackling pen (p. 141).

The Sliding Tackle

A good defender will stay on his or her feet as long as possible and only use the sliding tackle as a last resort, because if it fails, that defender is out of the game. Nevertheless, on many occasions the sliding tackle is the only way to stop an attacker who has broken through; it is an essential skill for every player. Moreover, because this tackle is a spectacular and exciting achievement when executed successfully, all players enjoy practicing it, providing the ground is soft and the players wear protective clothing. Never have your players practice on hard, dry ground without protection; you will do more harm than good.

The tackle contains three stages: the chase, the slide, and the sweep. The tackling player chases the ball until confident that his or her leading foot will overtake the ball (Figure 8.29a).

The near leg (the left leg in the figure) leads, allowing the player to sink down onto the left leg, which curls beneath the seat. The far leg (the right leg in the figure) swings around in a wide sweep, with the foot hooked, toward the ball (Figure 8.29b).

a

b

(Cont.)

Figure 8.29

c

Figure 8.29 (Continued)
Slide tackle sequence.

The tackling leg sweeps through the ball and either traps it with the hooked foot or, more usually, plays the ball away (Figure 8.29c). As a fullback I used to love the sliding tackle, especially when I came out of it with the ball!

Drills for Advanced Players

SLIDING TACKLE DRILL

Equipment
    1 ball for each 2 players; defenders wear sweatpants.

Organization
    Players are in pairs of equal ability and speed (1 attacker, 1 defender). Both players stand facing the same direction along the sideline (Figure 8.28).

Instructions
    The attacker (Player A) has the ball and dribbles it forward at a steady pace and in a straight line. The defender (Player B) executes the tackle.

Coaching Points
    The defender should not jump in—this is a foul.

The defender should watch the ball and strike through it.

The defender should always tackle with the outside leg, the one farthest from the attacker at the start of the tackle.

The defender should use the nearside hand to cushion the fall and make sure he or she can reach the ball before attempting the tackle.

The defender should sprint hard to catch up with the attacker but should not get too close behind the attacker. The defender will need room to execute the slide.

Coaching Progressions

The tackling player sits on the ground in the correct position while the coach explains the position.

Players practice gently lowering down into this sitting position, learning how to take the weight on the nearside hand.

Players practice moving and tackling a stationary ball, emphasizing playing through the ball.

The player with the ball dribbles in a straight line at an easy pace inviting the tackle and keeps going until tackled. The speed increases as the players progress.

The coach rolls the ball for the 2 players to chase. The tackle must be made within 20 yards by the designated tackler.

Determination

No chapter on tackling is complete without a word about determination. Without a wholehearted, fearless commitment to the tackle, a player is likely to be beaten and is also likely to get hurt. There is no substitute for a hard but fairly executed tackle, and the key coaching point is always determination.

CHAPTER 9

Coaching Kicking

Unfortunately, many young players find learning how to kick a painful experience because they stub their toes on the ground. As a result, they often develop two bad habits: Either they use a toe punt or they curve their foot across the ball.

Teaching Beginners

The easiest ball to kick is one that is airborne and captive. For absolute beginners use a captive ball held in a string bag or placed on a tee. Do not use fast, awkward, spinning serves with novice players. A rolling ball is easier to kick than a stationary ball because it has less inertia, and a spinning ball is always difficult to kick because the contact zone is moving.

Do give your players time to prepare, to "balance" themselves before kicking.

For beginners and shooting practices use the following sequence:

- A ball that is rolled gently toward the player with no sidespin
- A ball that is rolled gently away from the player (a lead pass) with no sidespin
- A ball that is bouncing gently but not spinning

How Soccer Cleats Should Be Laced

Many young players have large, loosely tied bows that interfere with the contact on the ball and may come loose during the game. The correct method of lacing provides a neat, flat kicking surface and is securely tied off with a flat knot on the outside of the cleat.

To lace cleats correctly, first remove the lace completely. Using one end of the lace only in a surgeon's stitching action:

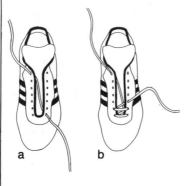

Go down into the top right hole and up out of the bottom left hole (Figure 9.1a).

Continue stitching with the left end of the lace by going down into the holes on the right side and up out of the holes on the left side until fully laced (Figure 9.1b).

Tie off on the outside using a flat knot (Figures 9.1c and d).

Figure 9.1
Proper method of lacing cleats.

The length of the ends can be adjusted very easily and the lace tightened by pulling with the fingers on the next to the bottom loop and working upward.

How to Make and Use A Kicking Tee

When teaching a novice player how to kick correctly, or teaching an experienced player how to kick with his or her weaker foot or to swerve the ball, use a kicking tee. To make a tee, take a medium-sized plastic-coated cup and cut the bottom half away as shown in Figure 9.2. The top half of the cup is inverted to make the tee upon which the ball is placed.

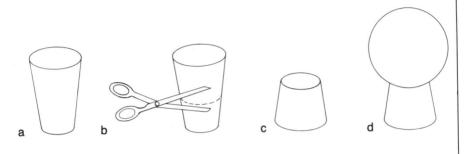

a   b   c   d

Figure 9.2
Making a kicking tee.

Because the ball is now raised off the ground, the player can kick it correctly with the instep (the laces) without the fear of stubbing his or her toe. As the player improves, cut the tee down lower and lower until it is no longer needed.

You can also use the tee when teaching advanced players how to swerve a ball or how to gain height and distance from a corner kick or goal kick.

The Instep Drive

The instep drive is one of the most powerful kicks in soccer; because it keeps the ball low, the instep drive is most effective when shooting at the goal. Using this drive, the player kicks the ball with the instep, which fits comfortably and almost vertically into the back of the ball. If this part of the geometry is correct, the rest of the body position is of secondary importance; however, several factors can improve the player's chance of success. For example, the toe must be down; the knee should be placed over the ball; the body should be compact and over the ball, not open or leaning back; and the follow-through should be short and straight on line. All of these points can be achieved more easily if the nonkicking foot is placed alongside the ball, the head is kept down and still, and the body shape is compact (Figures 9.3a, b, and c).

Figure 9.3
The instep drive.

Drills for Beginners

I always use a kicking tee for beginners. It is a simple coaching aid, but it really does make learning to kick easier and safer.

KICKING TEE DRILL

Equipment
   1 ball for each player (ball must be of the correct size and pressure for the player); ample kicking tees (unless they are made of plastic, they are easily damaged).

Organization

Players are in groups of up to 6 players in a straight line with a minimum of 3 yards between players. The line should be parallel to and about 10 yards from the target goal.

For larger groups arrange a rotation system.

Instructions

One at a time, when called, players use the instep drive to play the ball toward the target.

Players must not lift the ball more than 3 to 4 feet off the ground.

Coaching Points

Players should approach the ball in a straight line with the toe down and with compact body shape.

Players should follow through in a straight line.

Coaching Progressions

Players increase power and distance by moving further away from the target.

Two Common Faults

Even at this early stage, you must watch for the two most common faults in beginners—the toe punt and slicing the ball (Figures 9.4a and b). To correct these faults, review the earlier stages of this drill.

Figure 9.4
The two most common errors in beginners are a) the toe punt and b) slicing across the ball.

Drills for Intermediates

Intermediate players should strike at a moving ball and increasingly generate power, accuracy, and distance.

MOVING BALL DRILL

Equipment
> 1 ball for each 2 players.

Organizations
> Players are in pairs 10 to 15 yards apart with a minimum of 10 yards between pairs.

Instructions
> Player plays the ball to his or her partner with the instep drive, keeping the ball below 3 to 4 feet in height.

Coaching Points
> Players should strive for accuracy and technique before power.
>
> Players should strike through the ball, not at it, and should generate power from the hips.

Coaching Progressions
> Players stop the ball and play it forward before kicking.
>
> Players drive the ball directly back to their partners (i.e., first-time kicking).
>
> Players increase the distance between each other.

Drills for Advanced Players

The best progressions for intermediate and advanced players are the shooting drills contained in chapter 10 and arranged in a progressive sequence. One additional and enjoyable drill is a penalty competition in which the players must use the instep drive. The usual variation is an elimination competition, but initially you can have a qualifying competition that allows every player to have 3 attempts at instep driving before being eliminated for missing.

The Long, Lofted Kick

This kick requires both height and distance. The player achieves height by leaning back, keeping behind the ball, and kicking underneath it. The player achieves distance through a combination of factors, such as a powerful swinging action with a high follow-through, a long lever (like a golf club), and an angled approach, approximately 45°, to the intended line of flight.

In preparing for a long, lofted kick, the player lengthens the final stride to give a long follow-through. Then, the player hits through the ball with a straight leg, striking for distance rather than height and aiming for a high follow-through.

Don't let the apparent ease with which professional players kick the ball fool you; like professional golfers, they have learned to time this action and produce what is called a kinetic chain (Figures 9.5a and b).

a   b

Figure 9.5
Sequence for the long, lofted kick.

Drills for Beginners

The secret to success with beginners is using a kicking tee and having the players kick into a net or a baseball cage. By using this method you can watch each player's technique closely and in complete safety, and nobody has to chase after the ball.

LOFTED KICK FROM A TEE

Equipment

1 ball for each player; ample kicking tees; regular goal net or base-ball cage.

Organization

Players are in a straight line 3 yards apart, not more than 5 yards from the target or net.

Instructions

One at a time, players kick into the net, aiming for height and distance.

Coaching Points

Players should lengthen the final stride to give a long follow-through.

Players should keep the toe down and strike through the bottom of the ball.

Players should approach at an angle of 45°.

Players should keep the nonkicking foot well behind and to the side of the ball.

Players should aim for a long, high follow-through.

Coaching Progressions

Players progress from using the kicking tee to kicking from the ground.

Players try with the nonpreferred foot kicking from a tee.

Drills for Intermediates

Intermediate players should first practice long kicking a ball that is gently rolled toward them, then try long kicking a ball that is rolling away from them, and finally practice kicking a stationary ball.

DISTANCE DRILL

Equipment

1 ball for each 4 players.

Organization

Players are in groups of 4, standing 20 yards apart in free space.

Instructions

Player A rolls the ball to Player B, who plays a long, lofted kick to Player C.

Player C rolls the ball to Player D, who kicks the ball back to Player A. The sequence continues with all players taking their turn to kick.

Coaching Points

Players should keep their heads down until after contact.

Players should go for a high follow-through and hit through the ball with a straight leg.

Players should increasingly aim for distance rather than height (e.g., trying to play the ball over the heads of the receiving players).

Drills for Advanced Players

Advanced players should engage in two kinds of drills—kicking a stationary ball in the goal kick, corner kick, or free kick situations, and practicing long kicking while moving.

The Volley

The volley kick has a number of variations which all have two things in common: The ball is completely airborne, and it is kicked with the instep. Because the ball is airborne it is light and responsive, making the volley a powerful kick. The problems of balancing on the nonkicking foot and making perfect contact with the instep make this a difficult kick. Three things are essential: keeping the toe down, the head still, and the arms out for balance (Figure 9.6).

Figure 9.6
Proper body position for the volley.

Drills for Beginners

STATIONARY VOLLEY

Again we start with a stationary, captive ball. (This is an ideal practice for teaching players to use their weaker foot.)

Equipment
   1 ball in a net bag for each player.

Organization
   Individual players work in free space.

Instructions
   Player rests the ball on the ground (to ensure it is both captive and still), raises it gently until it is at knee height, then volleys using the instep.

Coaching Points
   Players should use the instep and keep the toe down.

   Players should keep eyes on the ball and head still.

   Players should follow through in a straight line.

Coaching Progressions
   Players increase the force of the kick until the ball in the bag completes a full circle.

   Hold the ball for the player, who stands and volleys, then moves in and volleys.

Drills for Intermediates

BALANCE DRILL

Now the player has to learn how to balance on one foot while kicking with the other and how to develop finesse and timing.

Equipment
   1 ball for each 2 players.

Organization
   Players are in pairs, 2 to 3 yards apart.

Instructions

Player A gently tosses the ball to his or her partner, who volleys it back for the server to catch.

Players must be careful and gentle. The volley is a delicate skill—blasting off or not controlling strength can be dangerous for the server.

The server should always use two hands to serve.

Coaching Points

Players should keep the toe down and the head still.

Players should hold arms out for balance.

Players should finesse the ball.

Players should keep the foot, ankle, knee, and leg in a straight line.

Coaching Progressions

Players work to develop the skill in both feet.

Players should progress to volleying on the move: Player A moves gently backward while Player B follows, serving and catching the ball volleyed by Player A.

Then Player A moves forward and B moves backward, still serving and catching the volley.

Players change to a serve over the crossbar, which the receiver volleys into the goals.

Drills for Advanced Players

Soccer Tennis (p. 196) is one of the best ways to develop advanced volleying skills. Or, pairs of players can use chest control to catch a thrown ball, let it fall to knee height, and volley it back to the partner (see Ball Juggling, p. 47).

The Chip

The *chip* gets its name from the golf shot played with the wedge—it is a short, high, lofted kick with backspin. The player uses a sharp "stabbing" action, toes underneath the ball, with little or no follow-through. The ball is lifted almost vertically; when it lands, it remains almost stationary or, if very well played, spins backward (see Figure 9.7).

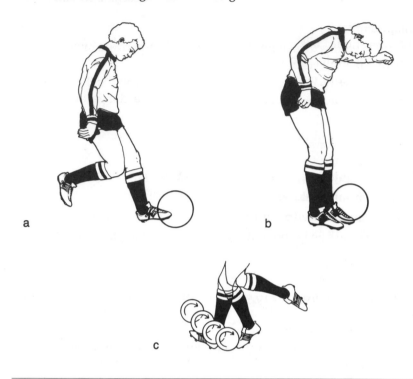

Figure 9.7
Sequence for the chip.

Drills for Intermediates

Because the chip is too difficult for beginners we begin with intermediate drills.

CHIP DRILL

Equipment
    1 ball for each 2 players.

Organization
    Players are in pairs, 5 to 8 yards apart.

Instructions
    Server rolls the ball gently to the kicker with no spin. Kicker chips the ball back to the server.

Coaching Points

Players should use a short back lift and a stabbing action, with the toe going under the ball.

Players should use a short follow-through or none at all.

Players should keep the head down over the ball.

The body should jackknife downward as the kick is executed.

Coaching Progressions

Players change to a stationary ball.

Players should work to chip for greater height (such as over the partner or an obstacle).

Players should try to get the ball to stop dead on landing or even to roll or spin backward.

Players can try to chip a ball moving away from them.

Drills for Advanced Players

Set plays provide effective chipping practice, but one of the best general drills for advanced players is the one attributed to the Dutch player Johanne Cruyff. He is reputed to have practiced the chip kick over an empty goal, chipping the ball over the crossbar so that it spun back into the goal (Figure 9.8).

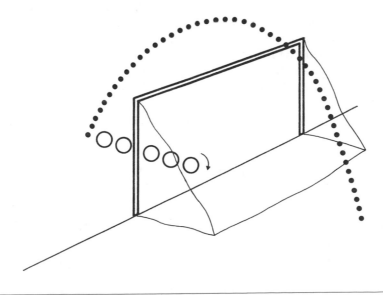

Figure 9.8
Stab foot under the ball to get backspin.

CRUYFF DRILL

Equipment

Ample soccer balls and a regular goal without a net.

Organization

Players face the goal, about 10 yards away.

Instructions

Players chip the ball over the crossbar in such a way that it spins back into the goal on landing (Figure 9.8).

Coaching Points

Same as for intermediate chipping.

Coaching Progressions

Server rolls the ball to the player who chips.

Players practice using a stationary ball.

Players hold competitions to see who can spin the ball back farthest or can make the most successful chips in a set number of attempts.

The Swerve or Banana Kick

No kick has had a more dynamic effect on modern soccer than the swerve or banana kick. It is now a priceless asset for attacking free kicks and is being used more and more in passing situations. It is an advanced skill, and even experienced professionals have difficulty controlling the amount and timing of the swerve. Nevertheless, the kick is impotant and is enjoyable to practice; even beginners can practice this kick if they use the kicking tee.

The laws of physics control the movement of the ball after impact (Figure 9.9).

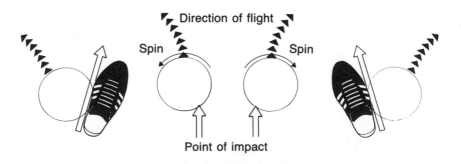

Figure 9.9
The banana kick.

Drills for Intermediates

BANANA DRILL

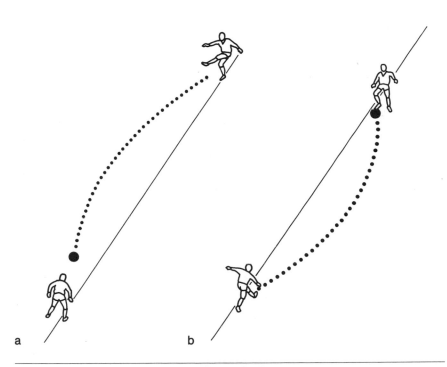

Figure 9.10

Equipment
   1 ball for each 2 players and ample kicking tees.

Organization
   Partners stand facing each other on a straight line, 15 to 20 yards apart.

Instructions
   Player swerve-kicks the ball so that it moves away from the line but lands at the partner's feet (Figure 9.10).

Coaching Points
   Players should select the direction and then *focus* on the point of contact on the ball.

   Players should remember to follow through.

Players should kick at the bottom of the ball to get a lofted swerve and at the midpoint of the ball to keep it low.

Coaching Progressions

Players should start with a kicking tee, then progress to a stationary ball.

Players should work to increase swerve and distance and should attempt both inswing and outswing kicks.

Drills for Advanced Players

Because the swerve kick is so effective for attacking free kicks, the best practice situations are set plays just outside the penalty area. Some excellent and safe drills are explained in chapter 16. The following drill is also good fun for general practice and can motivate players to work on their own.

CORNER DRILL

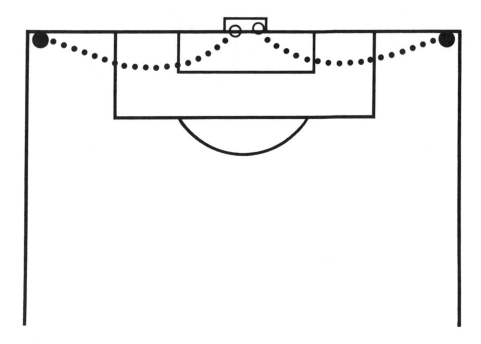

Figure 9.11

Equipment

Regular goals plus ample soccer balls.

Organization

Players line up on the goal line (Figure 9.11).

Instructions

Player swerve-kicks the ball into the goal.

Coaching Points

Same as for intermediate swerve kick.

Coaching Progressions

Players use tees placed at the 6-yard line, the penalty line, and the corner.

Players use a stationary ball.

Players should kick from both sides to develop using the inside and outside of the foot.

CHAPTER 10

Coaching Shooting

Chapter 10 shows you how to develop shooting practices using the techniques described in chapter 9. Chapter 10 also covers where to aim and how to encourage players to stay calm while shooting. This chapter shows you how to invent game-like practices that emphasize the importance of shooting at the earliest opportunity but also stress the need to remain calm and composed under pressure.

Where to Shoot

Research tells us that it is easier to score in the corners of the goal, and that low shots along the ground to the far post are the most difficult to save (Figure 10.1).

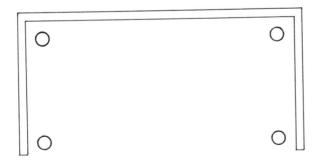

Figure 10.1
Difficult areas of the goal to defend.

Research also tells us that shots from a narrow angle are easier to save. Make sure that your players understand the difference between the shooting zone and the passing zone, and that they know that attempting a shot from the passing zone is seldom in the best interest of the team (Figure 10.2).

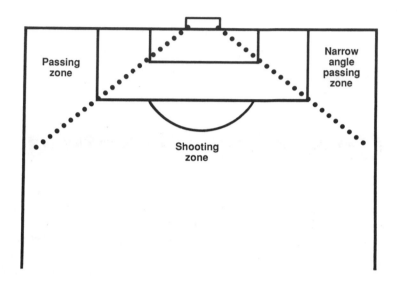

Figure 10.2
Avoid shooting from a narrow angle.

Drills for Beginners

The most exciting and the easiest shot at the goal is the instep drive when the ball is rolling gently toward the player. I recommend coaching this first so players will develop a powerful shot that keeps the ball below an 8-foot high cross bar.

The following drills are arranged in a progressive sequence.

INSTEP DRIVE 1

Equipment
Ample balls; goal with nets.

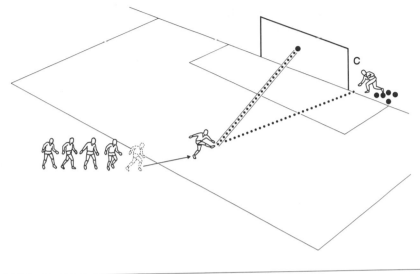

Figure 10.3

Organization

Players are divided into 2 groups of up to 10 players. One group stands behind and to the side of the goal to retrieve the balls; the other stands as shown in Figure 10.3.

Instructions

The coach rolls a ball gently forward toward the incoming player, who shoots at the goal (Figure 10.3).

Initially players do not have a goalkeeper. When a goalkeeper is used, players must not shoot from less than 15 yards (to protect the goalkeeper).

Coaching Points

Players should not rush but should stay calm as they move in. Players should use the instep drive and toe down. Players should try to place the ball into the corners of the goal.

Coaching Progressions

The coach serves from the other post to the left foot of the player.

A goalkeeper is used; players try to aim at the corners of the goal.

The coach keeps the serve simple and friendly to build up confidence.

INSTEP DRIVE 2

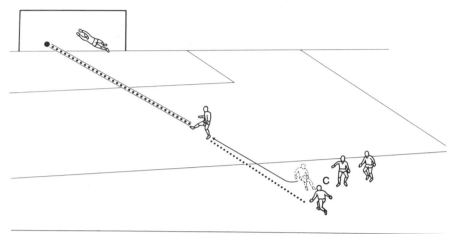

Figure 10.4

Equipment

Ample balls; a goal with nets.

Organization

Players are in a group of unlimited number on a standard soccer field.

Instructions

The coach stands about 25 yards from the goal. The player stands with his or her back to the goal, facing the coach.

The coach rolls the ball past the player toward the goal. The player spins, chases the ball, and shoots (Figure 10.4).

Coaching Points

Players should get the nonkicking foot alongside the ball.

Players should keep a compact body shape, stay down on the shot, and follow through on the target line.

Coaching Progressions

Coach serves the ball over the head of the player and then requires the student to shoot with the left foot.

Drills for Intermediates

Intermediates should be given a simple control factor before shooting to begin to achieve greater realism. Again, these drills are in a progressive sequence.

INSTEP DRIVE 3

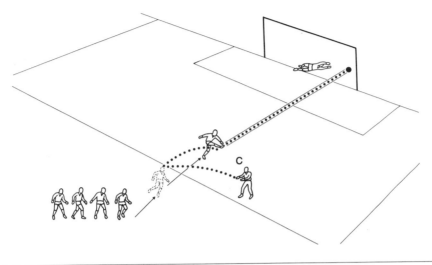

Figure 10.5

Equipment
Ample balls; a goal with nets.

Organization
The players are in a group of unlimited number on a standard soccer field. The coach stands on the penalty line; the players stand outside the D.

Instructions
The coach lobs an aerial ball to the player who heads it forward, follows in, and shoots (Figure 10.5).

Coaching Points
The simple act of heading the ball forward gives great realism to the practice.

Players should not head the ball too gently or too hard—it has to give them just enough time to release the shot.

Players should head toward their best foot and balance on their feet before shooting. That is, be light on the toes while moving in and adjust the feet to the movement of the ball.

Players should pick a spot and aim carefully.

Coaching Progressions
Players release the shot within 3 seconds of the first headed contact.

Players use the nonpreferred foot.

The coach sets the target area (e.g., low right) as the player moves into the shot.

INSTEP DRIVE 4

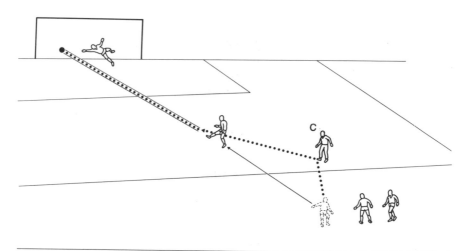

Figure 10.6

Equipment

Ample balls; a goal with nets.

Organization

Players are in a group of unlimited number on a standard soccer field. The coach stands on the D, back to the goal.

Instructions

Each player, with a ball, dribbles toward the coach in turn, then passes to him or her. The coach gives a return lead pass to the player to control and shoot (Figure 10.6).

Coaching Points

The pass to the coach must be firm and accurate; a sloppy pass is ignored. The player must accelerate when giving the pass, but must balance before shooting.

Shot must be the instep drive and should be controlled accordingly.

Coaching Progressions

The coach plays the ball to both sides.

Players who miss the target must retrieve the ball.

The coach plays the pass with some lift or spin to make the shot more difficult.

The coach designates the target area (e.g., high left).

INSTEP DRIVE 5

This next drill is fun and can be made into a competition. It also accustoms the players to dribbling the ball, at speed, immediately prior to a shot.

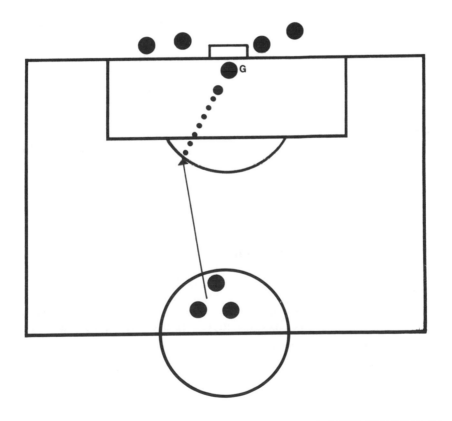

Figure 10.7

Equipment
>1 ball for each 2 players.

Organization
>Players are in 2 groups of equal number, with 1 goalkeeper, on a standard soccer field. Group 1 is in the center circle, each player holding a ball. Group 2 stands behind the goal. The goalkeeper stands in front of the goal (Figure 10.7).

Instructions
>A player from Group 1 dribbles at speed into the D and releases a shot at the goal on (or very close to) the penalty line.

>The goalkeeper stays on the line until the player enters the D, then works to defend the goal.

>Players from Group 2 retrieve the balls.

Coaching Points
>Players must select a target, watch the goalkeeper, and place the shot accordingly.

>Players should not lean back, but should have a compact body shape, with toe and head down.

>Players should strike through the ball, not at it, and follow through along the target line.

Coaching Progressions
>The time for the shot to be released is limited (e.g., shoot within 20 seconds).

>Teams compete.

>A defending player chases the shooter, who has a start of 8 yards.

Drills Without Regular Goals

The absence of regular goalposts does not eliminate the opportunity to organize shooting practices. You can have some excellent drills using corner flags as goals, especially when you are concentrating on low shots at goal or when you are teaching your players the art of 1 vs. the goalkeeper (when the attacker has broken through and has only the goalkeeper to beat). This is a drill that every attacker must practice.

INSTEP DRIVE 6

Equipment
>Ample balls; 2 flags.

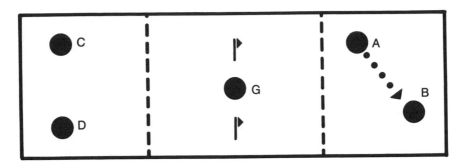

Figure 10.8

Organization

Players are in 1 team of 5, with 1 goalkeeper, on a 30 × 10 yard minifield with practice goals marked by flags as shown in Figure 10.8.

Instructions

Player A plays the ball to Player B, who shoots. If the goalkeeper saves, he or she returns the ball to Player A, turns around, and invites a shot from Players C and D

If the ball goes past the goalkeeper, Players C and D retrieve the ball and set up their own shot.

Coaching Points

Players should stay cool, select a target, and place the ball past the goalkeeper.

Players should not lean back but should maintain a compact shape.

Coaching Progressions

The shooting player plays the ball once before shooting and tries with one touch to set up a perfect feed.

The shooting player takes a first-time shot.

The serving player gives different passes (e.g., from the front, from behind, and as the players improve, from the side).

The server, after serving, becomes a defender.

Drills for Advanced Players

I feel the drills that follow are ideal for coaching advanced shooting technique because they can be used to coach the mind of the shooter. This is both a demanding and a very rewarding challenge.

When under pressure from defenders, the shooter is denied the most essential element—time. Not surprisingly, players under pressure become anxious and either take too long or shoot hastily. Superior players always know where the goal is and can see the target while preparing to shoot or when dribbling past defenders, but young players have to develop these skills.

The following practices are ideal because they develop the correct sequence of actions. That sequence includes maneuvering the ball into a realistic shooting position, glancing up at the target, and releasing the shot. These processes can be reduced to a familiar sequence—control, look, shoot. As players improve, they can look and then control and shoot in the same movement.

The drills are in a progressive sequence.

INSTEP DRIVE 7

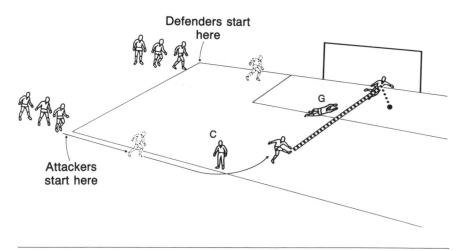

Figure 10.9

Equipment

    1 ball for each 2 players.

Organization

    Players are in 2 groups of equal number (1 group of attackers and 1 group of defenders), with 1 goalkeeper, on a standard soccer field.

    The coach stands on the penalty line opposite the center of the goal. The players stand in 2 lines as shown in Figure 10.9.

Instructions

On command, the first attacker dribbles forward, goes around the coach, and shoots for the goal.

The first defender sprints along the goal line and tries to stop any shot that gets past the goalkeeper. Defenders cannot use their hands.

The goalkeeper must remain on the goal line until the attacker has passed the coach.

After the play, the next players in line take a turn.

Coaching Points

Attackers should dribble quickly but avoid panic.

When attackers pass the coach, they should glance up and pick a target.

Attackers should concentrate on the correct instep drive technique, keep their eyes down, and follow the shot for a possible rebound.

Coaching Progressions

Players attack from the other side of the penalty area to develop left-foot shots.

INSTEP DRIVE 8

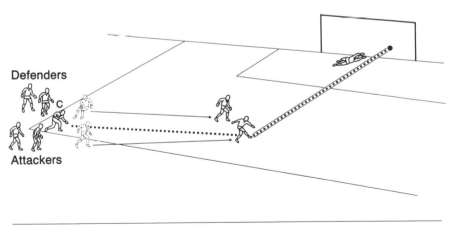

Figure 10.10

Equipment

Ample balls.

Organization

Players are in 2 groups of equal number (1 group of attackers and 1 group of defenders) on a standard soccer field.

The coach stands at the corner of the penalty area, facing the goal. The players stand in 2 lines as shown in Figure 10.10: Attacking players face the goal, and defending players face the coach.

Instructions

The coach serves the ball toward the area between the penalty spot and the 18-yard line and shouts ''go.''

The first attacker chases the ball and tries to score.

The first defender spins around and tries to stop the attacker. After the play, the next players in line take a turn.

Coaching Points

If the defender is too good or too quick for the attacker, the defender may be handicapped by 1 or 2 extra yards.

The attacker should control the ball (if necessary), look for the goal, keep the eyes down, place the shot, and stay cool.

Coaching Progressions

Change to the other side of the penalty area so players have to use their left foot.

INSTEP DRIVE 9

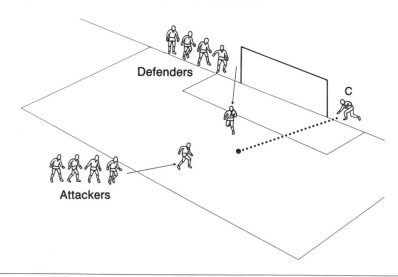

Figure 10.11

Equipment

1 ball for each 2 players.

Organization

Players are in 2 groups of equal number (1 group of attackers and 1 group of defenders) on a standard soccer field. Groups are organized so that players of equal ability compete with each other.

Defenders line up on the goal line outside the goal, and attackers line up outside the penalty area.

The coach stands on the side of the goal opposite the defenders (Figure 10.11).

Instructions

As the coach rolls the ball, the first attacker moves into the penalty area, controls the ball, and tries to score.

At the moment the coach releases the ball, the defender sprints to challenge the attacker. (The defender must not be allowed to move too soon.)

Coaching Points

Attacker should control, look, and shoot.

Coaching Progressions

Initially, the attacker has a clear advantage, which encourages shooting. The coach serves firmly and accurately.

As players improve, or with better players, the coach serves more balls that are bouncing and are more difficult for the attacker to control.

Two attackers and 2 defenders play at a time.

A goalkeeper is used.

Shooting Games

Players never seem to tire of shooting drills, so this section includes some additional shooting games for your coaching repertoire. You will need to use pinnies or regular team shirts to distinguish between the teams.

3 VS. 3 IN THE PENALTY AREA

Equipment

Ample balls; pinnies.

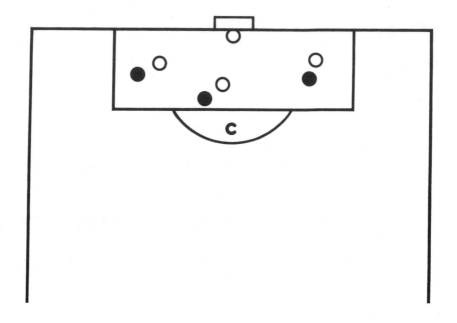

Figure 10.12

Organization
Players are in a group of 7 (3 attackers, 3 defenders, 1 goalkeeper) on a standard penalty area (Figure 10.12).

Instructions
The coach holds the ball until an attacker moves into an open situation. The coach then serves the ball and the game starts.

Defenders and attackers switch roles at regular intervals.

Coaching Points
Attacker should be positive in attacking the defender and take shooting opportunities early.

Players should aim for accuracy before power and should stay calm.

Coaching Progression
If attackers are unable to get shots on target, the number of defenders is reduced.

The player with the ball tries to turn and beat the defenders.

4 VS. 4

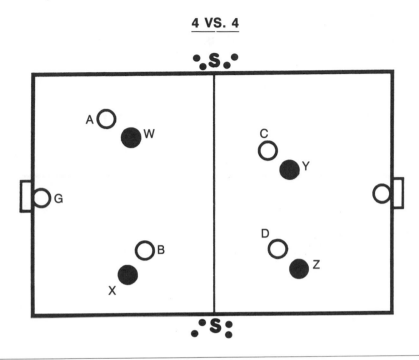

Figure 10.13

Equipment

Ample balls; portable goals or flags; pinnies.

Organization

Players are in 2 teams of 5 (4 players and 1 goalkeeper each), with 2 servers, on a 40 × 25 yard minifield (Figure 10.13). Teams are organized so that players of equal ability compete with each other.

Instructions

The servers, with a good supply of balls, alternately deliver balls using a variety of serves.

Goals may only be scored in the attacking half.

Coaching Points

All players should try to score when in the attacking half. Players should try not to shoot from the passing zone. When shooting, players should stay cool and take careful aim, using low shots if possible.

Coaching Progressions

Progress to one-on-one marking (e.g., only Player X can tackle Player B).

CONDITIONED GAME FOR THE WHOLE TEAM

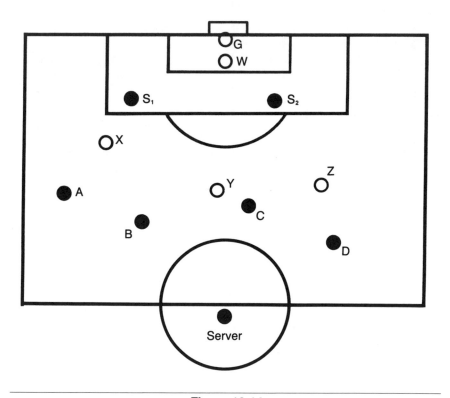

Figure 10.14

Equipment

Ample balls; pinnies.

Organization

Organize as shown in Figure 10.14. The goalkeeper and 7 outfield players adopt their regular positions (3 defenders—X, Y, Z; and 4 attackers—A, B, C, D).

The two strikers (S_1, S_2) are positioned in and restricted to playing in the penalty area.

The remaining defender (Player W) must stay in the goal area with the goalkeeper until the ball enters the penalty area. Defender W may then play as he or she feels is appropriate in defending against the two strikers.

Instructions

The server starts the game by passing to one of the attackers.

Players A, B, C, and D combine to get the ball into the penalty area (which they cannot enter).

Players X, Y, and Z defend as best they can outside the penalty area (which they cannot enter).

Player W stays in the goal area until the ball enters the penalty area; then Player W is free.

The strikers remain in the penalty area. When the ball arrives, they try to score or pass to colleagues who must shoot the first time.

Coaching Points

The players should think for themselves—don't overcoach.

Coaching Progressions

The players change positions to sustain interest.

CHAPTER 11

Coaching Heading

The keys to powerful heading are tensing the muscles of the neck and shoulders and striking the ball with the forehead like a hammer strikes a nail. The key to accurate heading is looking at the intended target with your eyes, which ensures that the ball goes where you intend it to go. Unfortunately, many beginners not only close their eyes on impact but also tilt their forehead downward and let the ball land on the top of their head, which can be very painful! Indeed, this combination of faults makes many learners frightened of heading the ball.

The fear of injury can be overcome several ways. Most methods make use of a light, soft ball such as a volleyball or a small, underinflated soccer ball. This chapter describes two methods; the one I recommend is based on a simple diving movement from the kneeling position. Remember to keep heading practices short so players don't get headaches.

In addition to beginning techniques, this chapter also deals with attacking and defensive heading for intermediate and advanced players and introduces the game of head tennis.

Drills for Beginners

THE DIVING TECHNIQUE

This is my favorite way of teaching beginners.

Equipment

1 volley ball or soft soccer ball for each 2 players.

Organization

Players are in pairs (1 header, 1 server) 3 yards apart.

Instructions

The header kneels, trunk upright and arms bent.

The server gently lobs the ball using both hands, so it lands 2 feet in front of the header.

The header must dive gently forward putting weight on his or her hands, with eyes open, and head the ball with the flat part of the forehead directly back to the hands of the server (Figure 11.1a, b, and c).

a

b

(Cont.)

Figure 11.1

c

Figure 11.1 (Continued)

Coaching Points

Header should keep his or her eyes open and head back, so the ball is struck with the flat part of the forehead.

The header should dive at the ball and remember the ball goes where the eyes direct it.

Because the server stands above the player, the forehead is correctly aligned; the dive of the player ensures that the head strikes the ball. When the ball is headed correctly it goes straight back to the hands of the server.

A ball that is headed too soon rises up in an arc. A ball headed with the eyes down simply hits the ground. Therefore, both the player and the coach get instant feedback about how well the ball was headed.

As the player gains confidence, the dive will become more adventurous; the server can develop this by serving to the side or conducting the practice in front of goal and developing the full diving header.

THE STANDING TECHNIQUE

This is the more common starting drill.

Equipment

1 volley ball or soft soccer ball for each 2 players.

Organization

Players are in pairs (1 header, 1 server) 3 yards apart.

Instructions

The server gently lobs the ball using both hands.

The header, standing, heads the ball on a flat trajectory back to the server (Figure 11.2).

Figure 11.2

Coaching Points

The header should stand with 1 foot forward, arms out to the sides.

The header should keep the eyes open, watching the ball as it comes toward the forehead.

The header should strike the ball with the forehead, keeping the neck muscles firm and using the upper body to add power.

Coaching Progressions

The header heads the ball toward the server's feet.

While the ball is in the air, the server names a target (e.g., high, low, left, right).

The server places the ball above head height and the header has to jump to head it back.

The header increases the power of the head.

Attacking Heading

Headers attacking the goal usually require the ball to be directed downward and away from the goalkeeper. Thus, the player has two problems of direction; a good way to coach both is to use a triangular system of serving and heading (Figure 11.3).

Drills for Beginners

HEADING IN 3S

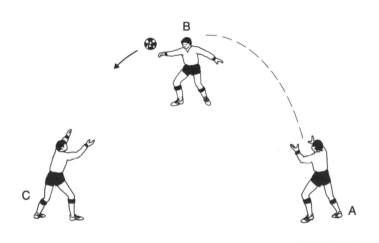

Figure 11.3

Equipment
    1 volleyball or soft soccer ball for each 3 players.

Organization
    Players are in groups of 3 in a triangle, about 4 yards apart.

Instructions
    Player A throws to Player B, who heads to Player C. Player C throws to Player A, who heads to Player B. The sequence continues with each player heading in turn. (This is the throw-head-catch sequence, which is used again later.)

Coaching Points

The server should serve in front of the header, who heads down.

Headers should strike the ball rather than letting it hit them.

Headers should place their feet apart to form a good base, let their eyes direct the ball to the target, keep their neck and body muscles firm, and use their arms to increase power.

Coaching Progressions

Players move about the field, slowly at first, continuing the sequence. This sequence develops into the throw-head-catch stance.

Throw–Head–Catch

Equipment

1 regular soccer ball per 6 players.

Organization

Players are in 2 teams of 3 on a 20 × 30 yard minifield with small goals.

Instructions

The team in possession can only score by heading a goal. They lose possession if the ball touches the ground, they miss the goal, or the opposition intercepts the ball.

Drills for Intermediates

This next activity is one of my favorite drills—players of all abilities find it very enjoyable (Figure 11.4).

2 VS. 2

Equipment

1 ball for each 4 players; 4 flags or cones.

Organization

Players are in 2 teams of 2, in an area 10 yards square with 8-foot wide goals.

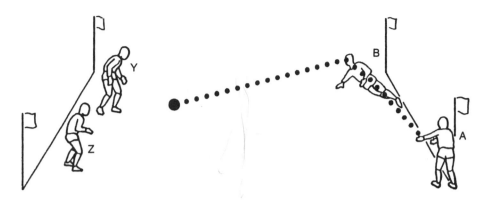

Figure 11.4

Instructions

Player A serves to Player B, who tries to head past Players Y and Z to score.

Players Y and Z act as goalkeepers. When they save or catch the ball, they become attackers.

The first team to score 10 goals wins.

Coaching Points

The serve must always be in front of the header.

The header should use the forehead, strike the ball hard, tense the neck and shoulder muscles, and direct the ball past the goalkeepers by looking at the ball's target.

Coaching Progressions

The header progresses to a diving header (which is made possible by a careful serve).

The header moves in and jumps up to head the ball at goal, as an incoming forward would in a game.

Drills for Advanced Players

Advanced players must have a proper goal to aim toward, must play with a goalkeeper, and must learn to contend with opposition and a ball played at varying heights and distances. Such drills are best built up in stages (chapter 17). A typical example is as follows.

HEADING AT GOAL

Figure 11.5

Equipment
Ample soccer balls of regular size and pressure.

Organization
Players are in groups of 5 (1 server, 1 goalkeeper, 3 headers) on a standard soccer field.

Instructions
The players form a line at the penalty spot. The server starts with gentle, helpful serves. Each header takes a turn, aiming for the corner of the goal (Figure 11.5).

Coaching Points
The header should start 5 yards from the point at which contact will be made.

The header should move in and jump or dive as appropriate.

The header should aim to generate power with direction.

Coaching Progression
Headers must dive at the ball.

The ball is served from the side or from a greater distance.

The ball is volleyed. Or, with good players, wingers dribble the ball and center or cross it (Figure 11.6).

Defenders try to stop goals.

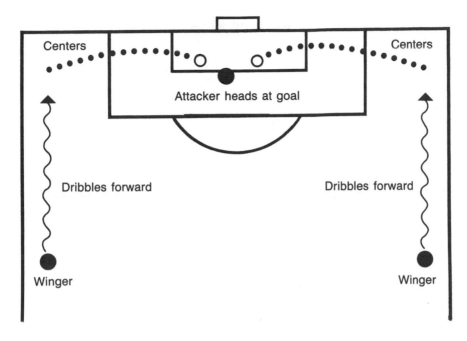

Centers   Centers

Attacker heads at goal

Dribbles forward   Dribbles forward

Winger   Winger

Figure 11.6

Defensive Heading

By the time you coach defensive heading, your players will have reached the intermediate stage and will know the basic techniques. What they now must develop are power and the courage to meet the ball regardless of the challenge from the attacker. Indeed, the courage to attack the ball is a characteristic of both attacking and defensive heading, and it cannot be emphasized too soon.

A good play by a defensive header has three qualities. The first is height; height gains time and safety and allows the defense to regroup. The second quality is distance; this really does clear the ball away from goal. The third quality is width; the ball must be directed out toward the wings and thus away from the shooting zone so it does not fall at the feet of an attacker.

Drills for Intermediates

Drills for intermediates are best taught without opposition.

HEADING IN 3S

Equipment
1 ball for each 3 players.

Organization
Players are in groups of 3, standing in a line with 5 yards between each player.

Instructions
Player A throws to Player B, who heads the ball over Player A to Player C (Figure 11.7).

Figure 11.7

Coaching Points
The header should stand with feet apart and use the ground for leverage.

The header should place the head at the bottom half of the ball to gain height and use the arms to pull the chest forward to gain power.

The header should keep the neck and body muscles firm and be aggressive.

Coaching Progressions
Players increase the distance between themselves.

The header increases the height of the clearance.

The header runs in, jumps, and heads.

The receiver becomes a moving target.

The server, having served, becomes an opponent.

Drills for Advanced Players

Advanced drills for heading must contain realistic ingredients— such as opposition and variety of service—that develop commitment and the courage to move in and attack the ball regardless of the challenging players. These elements are best introduced in stages.

HEADED CLEARANCES

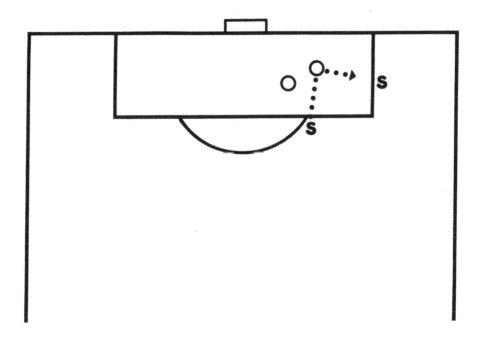

Figure 11.8

Equipment
    1 ball for each 4 players.

Organization

Players are in groups of 4 (2 headers, 2 servers) on 1/2 of a standard soccer field (Figure 11.8).

Instructions

The first server serves a high ball to a nominated header.

The header heads the ball to the second server, who stands outside the penalty area and at least 8 yards away. Having caught the ball, this player returns a throw to the second header who heads the ball back to the first server, making the drill continuous.

Coaching Points

The header should head the ball with both feet on the ground to generate power.

The header should time the jump to head the ball at the highest possible point.

The header should use the neck and shoulder muscles to generate force.

The header should strive for height, distance, and accuracy—in that order.

Coaching Progressions

Servers vary the height and trajectory of service. One player becomes a defender, opposing the other first passively, then actively. Transfer the practice into the area in front of the goal. Add a goalkeeper to develop a functional practice with a center half opposing a center forward.

Two defenders compete against each other to clear the danger.

Players have more opposition; 2 groups of 4, with a goalkeeper, compete in a realistic goal-attack situation.

Players practice full-scale defensive versus attacking corners. This is excellent practice for both attacking and defensive heading.

HEAD TENNIS

This game can be used with players of all abilities, if you modify the rules to suit their abilities. It is very popular with all levels of players and makes an enjoyable break from normal training (Figure 11.9).

Equipment

1 soft volleyball; 1 net approximately the height of the players.

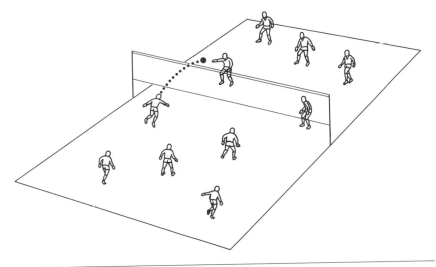

Figure 11.9

Organization

Players are in 2 teams of up to 8 on a volleyball or tennis court or in the center circle of a standard soccer field. If a net is not available, leave a central out-of-bounds zone between the teams.

Instructions

For beginners: Players head the ball directly back OR catch it and serve it to a team member who tries to head it over the net or zone.

For intermediates: Players head the ball directly back OR head it to a team member who heads it back over the net or zone.

For advanced players: Players head the ball directly back OR head it among team members no more than 3 times before heading it back over the net or zone.

Rules for all levels: The game is scored like table tennis. Each team has 5 serves. The first team to score 21 (or another number the coach chooses) wins.

A point is scored if the ball bounces on the opponents' side or if it is not returned properly.

A point is lost if the ball fails to clear the net or bounces out of court or if the ball is not played over the net according to the rules.

Final Point

Even with the best coaching, and especially if you use a regular soccer ball, players may still develop headaches if they practice too long. Therefore, heading practices should be frequent but short.

CHAPTER 12

Coaching Goalkeeping

The goalkeeper is the single most important position on the field. A good goalkeeper not only prevents the opposition from scoring but inspires the defense and by quick skillful distribution contributes to the attack. I feel that many coaches neglect the goalkeepers, partly because the position is sometimes difficult to coach and partly because coaches devote the majority of their time to the majority of their players, who are outfield players.

This chapter should provide you with a useful insight into the coaching of goalkeeping and persuade you that the best way to help your goalkeepers improve is to provide them with at least one special session a week. This session should be a 35-minute (or more) coaching session individually designed for goalkeepers, held before regular practice begins or at a separate time in the week. If you have an assistant coach you may be able to work with goalkeepers during regular practice, but if not, you may be surprised how willingly outfield players will attend special sessions for goalkeepers.

Selecting Your Goalkeepers

A well-organized squad should have two regular goalkeepers plus at least two other players who are capable of goalkeeping. Indeed, I believe that all players should try the goalkeeper position at some time. There are three reasons for this. First, by engaging everyone in goalkeeper practice, you are better able to identify natural talent. Second, you have a responsibility to give all your players a soccer education, and this includes goalkeeping. Third, this practice gives everyone personal knowledge of the position and thus encourages an appreciation of and respect for whoever plays in goal, especially if he or she makes a mistake.

Discovering natural goalkeeping ability can be very enjoyable for all concerned if you build a group session around the practice called High Hand/Low Hand (p. 208). In choosing a goalkeeper you will also look for desirable physical characteristics; there is no doubt that height is an advantage to a goalkeeper. Other qualities are also important, such as gymnastic agility, flexibility, speed of reaction, a sense of position, and courage. These are all desirable qualities and are essential for top-class players.

Goalkeeper Safety

The coach has a special duty to the goalkeeper. No goalkeeper should have to practice in a worn, rutted, perhaps muddy area in front of the goal. A good coach will provide the best possible practice surface for the goalkeeper; often this is found in the area under the goal net. To expose this area, simply reverse the goal net and shoot into the back of the goal. This means that you have both a goal and a net (which is realistic), and you have also provided a safe surface (Figure 12.1). Portable, tubular goals are ideal, and every school should have at least one pair.

The second way to ensure safety is through good player discipline in the penalty area. No player should be allowed to simply blast off at the goal, and two or more players should never shoot simultaneously.

Not all experienced goalkeepers like to wear protective clothing or devices such as knee and elbow protectors. Perhaps goalkeepers shouldn't be required to wear these during a match, but in practice sessions I always advise the use of protective clothing. Sweatpants, long-sleeved uniforms, and pads should all be a part of the team equipment and should be provided for the goalkeepers—prevention of injuries is always better than cure.

Goalkeeper Warm-Ups

Goalkeepers, like outfield players, should follow a careful, individually designed, and systematic warm-up program. Prior to a coaching session, I recommend the following sequence of activities.

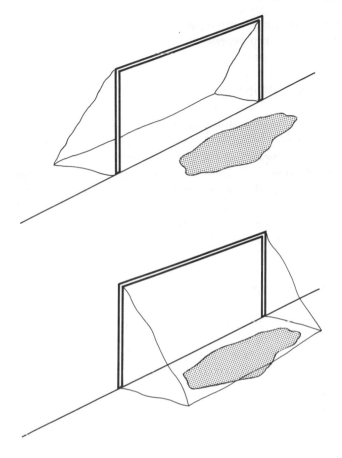

Figure 12.1
Provide a safe surface for the goalkeeper to practice on.

General Jogging

Goalkeepers can do this with the outfield players because the aim is the same—to increase heart rate, raise the body temperature, and stimulate the circulation prior to strenuous exercise.

Rolling

Next, goalkeepers roll on the ground in all directions mostly in the sitting or tuck position with the hands clasped around the knees and the chin down. In this safe sitting position, players can roll in different directions—forward, backward, and side to side.

Stretching and Mobilizing

Goalkeepers stay seated on the ground and use progressive *static stretching* to work on the groin, spine, neck, arms, and shoulders. Players should not use any bouncing or ballistic exercises at the start of the sequence.

Players stand up and continue working on the groin, hamstrings, and arms and shoulders and then gradually and very gently begin to flex and extend the spine. They gradually involve the arms and shoulders and begin swinging movements to extend the range and speed of the movements. At this point they are ready to begin more explosive moves.

Explosive and Jumping Movements

Powerful, explosive, springing movements are essential in goalkeeping for diving saves and for dealing with high balls. Players must therefore train for these movements but again should start gently with actions that employ perhaps 40% to 50% effort. Vertical jumping and one-footed take-offs with one or both arms raised simultaneously as if catching or punching a ball are ideal. Then players can work increasing on the power of the movements—jumping to block a ball thrown just over the cross bar (as in volleyball) is a good example. Also, the goalkeeper can practice pressure training to catch high balls thrown at short intervals toward different parts of the goal, perhaps by two or more servers. Catching a series of balls 2 feet above normal stretch height is good hard training and is very skill related.

Diving Movements

I always complete my warm-ups with simple diving movements to safely introduce the necessary body-to-ground contact, but I include more "falling on the ball" activities than actual diving. (Diving is included in skill training practices, which always include a ball.) The goalkeepers, fully protected, simply toss the ball into the air and fall on it when it lands, hugging it to the body. As the activity progresses, encourage them to throw the ball higher and farther away so that they have to move several yards to get to the bounce of the ball, always trying to fall down vertically upon it. Finally encourage them to roll after smothering the ball. The full sequence then becomes throw, move, fall, and roll; this provides a very demanding yet satisfying drill. At this stage no full sideways diving movements are made—these come later in the section dealing with skill and reaction drills.

Skills Practice

After completing all other warm-ups, goalkeepers should then practice game skills.

Dealing With Shots—The Basic Techniques

The goalkeeper spends the major part of the game dealing with shots at goal. This is certainly exciting to coach because it involves both diving and catching skills and intelligent decision making about positional play. The goalkeeper's work can also be risky, so good discipline in your shooting practices is essential.

The Basic Stance

Like the receiver in tennis, the goalkeeper must be able to react quickly in any direction. To achieve this, the body position is slightly crouched, with the feet shoulder-width apart, weight forward on the balls of the feet, and the hands held above waist height with palms forward and fingers spread (Figure 12.2). The goalkeeper's body should be still at the moment the attacker shoots, and the goalkeepers eyes should be fixed on the ball.

Figure 12.2
The goalkeeper's stance.

Catching the Ball

While the hands catch the ball first (later I include practices for catching the ball with the hands only), complete safety is ensured if the ball can also be clutched into the chest or the stomach as a second barrier. Teaching this method first highlights the vital skill of getting as much of the body into the path of the ball as possible, which requires good footwork. This double barrier, hands and body, can be emphasized by drawing attention to the two sounds made by a perfect execution. The first sound is the slap of the ball into the hands; the second is made when the ball is pulled into the body (Figures 12.3a and b).

a   b

Figure 12.3
Two-sound catching.

Catching the Ball Above Chest Height

A ball that arrives high up on the chest or just under the chin can be awkward to hold unless the goalkeeper uses an overhand grip, with one hand above and one below the ball (Figure 12.4).

Ground Shots

Shots along the ground range from those that roll gently toward the goalkeeper to those that are driven hard over a possibly bumpy, uneven surface. To collect the former, the goalkeeper simply bends from the waist, places the feet together just in case there is an awkward final bounce, and lets the ball roll up into his or her hands (Figure 12.5).

Figure 12.4
Proper hand position for catching a ball above chest height.

Figure 12.5
Fielding a weak ground shot.

Dealing with a hard driven shot is more serious. The goalkeeper should first turn sideways to the ball, drop down on one knee with the knee so close to the other foot that no space exists for the ball to run through, and make a wide cradle with the hands and arms (Figures 12.6a and b). Now if the ball comes awkwardly, the goalkeeper has at least two effective barriers against making a mistake.

Goalkeeping Drills

Drills for goalkeepers often serve a dual purpose; what is a learning experience for a beginner can be a warm-up drill for an experienced

a   b

Figure 12.6
Fielding a hard shot or a shot on uneven ground.

goalkeeper. Perhaps the best example of this is the very popular drill called Pingers, so named because of the sounds made when the server volleys the ball and when the goalkeeper takes the shot in the hands. When the drill is done well, the two ''pings'' are most impressive.

PINGERS

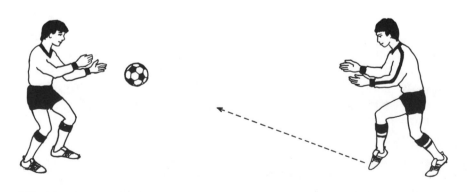

Figure 12.7

Equipment
1 ball for each 2 players.

Organization
Players are in pairs (1 server, 1 goalkeeper) in free space standing 8 to 4 yards apart—the closer the players, the more difficult the drill for the goalkeeper.

Instructions
The server volleys the ball to the goalkeeper. The goalkeeper takes the ball with the hands only, but with the body behind the line of flight (Figure 12.7).

Coaching Points
The goalkeeper should use good footwork, weight forward, and so on, and keep the hands in the W formation (fingers spread wide behind the ball, thumbs almost together).

The goalkeeper should receive the ball rather than snatch at it.

Even though the goalkeeper takes the ball with the hands, he or she should try to get the body into the line of flight.

Coaching Progressions
Progression with this practice depends upon service. To increase difficulty, decrease the distance, vary the height, and increase the force of the serve.

Advanced Drills

All goalkeeper drills, at an advanced level, require partner activity. The server can, from different ranges and at different speeds, roll, pass, throw, kick, volley, and dribble the ball to the goalkeeper, depending upon which technique the goalkeeper needs to improve. To progress such drills, change them into pressure training (chapter 21).

For advanced drills, refer also to the chapters on shooting and tactics at corners and free kicks (chapters 10 and 16), which contain many excellent situations for realistic goalkeeper training.

Diving and Punching Saves

"If you can, catch the ball; if you can't, punch it." This is a useful way to tell your goalkeepers that catching the ball is usually better than punching it away because the goalkeeper retains possession. However, to try to catch and to fail could be disastrous, so good judgment is essential and must be developed through realistic drills.

Diving Saves

Diving saves are the most spectacular and enjoyable of all the goalkeeper moves. When saves are taught properly, players love them. Diving saves do involve an element of danger, so please note the safety precautions given earlier and progress your players slowly through the following practices.

Sitting and Catching

The player sits with legs straight. When the ball is thrown, the player catches it and rolls sideways (Figure 12.8).

Figure 12.8
Sitting and catching.

Kneeling and Catching

The player, kneeling, stretches to the side, catches the ball, and rolls (Figure 12.9). The player should not land on the point of the elbow but should turn the shoulder underneath for safety (Figures 12.10a and b).

Punching—High Hand/Low Hand

Now the goalkeeper is ready to dive for balls that are beyond catching reach. He or she has to learn to punch with the hand and fist, which gives the greatest distance on the *stretch diagonal* (the line through the body from one foot to the opposite arm and hand). Goalkeepers can reach

Figure 12.9
Kneeling and catching.

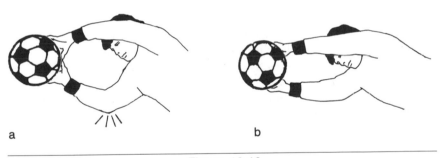

a   b

Figure 12.10
*When diving, the goalkeeper should not land on the point of the elbow (a)
but should turn the shoulder under (b).*

farther if they use the high hand for the aerial shot and the low hand
for the ground shot. The goalkeeper always starts in the kneeling position (Figure 12.11).

The ideal width of the goals for this practice is twice the height of the
goalkeeper. Players love this practice and usually forget that they are
diving on quite a hard surface. Further, they begin to make decisions for
themselves, which is what goalkeeping is all about.

Teaching the Full Dive

Only if goalkeepers enjoy the simple diving practices just described should
you teach the full dive. Find a soft surface and then follow these steps.

Figure 12.11
Use the top hand to defend against high shots.

Stage 1: The goalkeeper crouches, back to the coach. The coach stands at body length distance holding the ball (Figure 12.12a).

Stage 2: The coach makes a loud, sharp command, like ''Now!'' or ''Go!''

The goalkeeper turns and dives to take the ball from the coach's hands at full stretch (Figure 12.12b).

a

(Cont.)

Figure 12.12
Goalkeeper's diving practice.

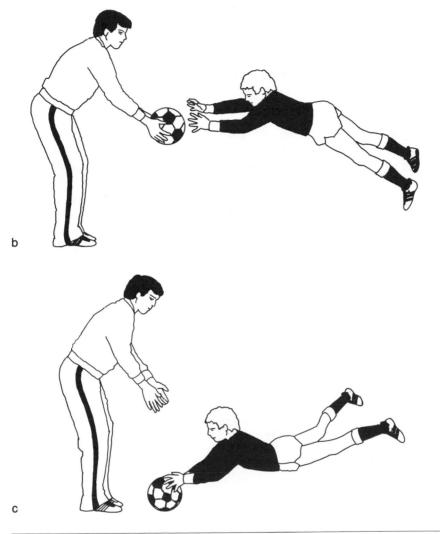

Figure 12.12 (Continued)
Goalkeeper's diving practice.

Stage 3: The goalkeeper takes the ball at full stretch and then hits the ball down onto the ground in order to cushion the landing (Figure 12.12c).

By using this method, the goalkeeper learns how to react to a sudden command; in the general excitement, thoughts of injury or discomfort when diving never occur. Also, the goalkeeper learns how to use the ball to break the fall. After this practice, put the goalkeeper back into goals, continue the normal shooting practices, and encourage the full dive whenever you can. Remember, however, that the goalkeeper enjoys the shots he or she saves, so control the service to benefit the goalkeeper, not the shooters.

Dealing With Crosses

All good goalkeepers love to demonstrate their skill at catching a high ball crossed in from the wings. This is a spectacular move, which requires a high degree of positional sense and perfect timing of the jump to ensure that the ball is taken at full strength and at the highest possible point in the air.

To gain maximum height, the player must make the jump off one foot ideally after a short run toward the ball, so that the nontake-off leg can also generate lift with a powerful, bent-knee action. As the player's arms and fingers reach upward, the eyes must be fixed on the ball. Indeed, fixing and keeping the eyes on the ball throughout the complete sequence is the key to success. Once the goalkeeper is committed to the move, he or she must not allow anything to distract the actions of looking at and catching (or punching) the ball (Figure 12.13).

Figure 12.13
Proper body position for fielding a cross shot.

Both hands should take the ball, with the fingers spread in the W formation around the back of the ball (Figure 12.14).

Figure 12.14
Proper hand and finger position for fielding a cross shot.

Drills for Beginners

The starting drills are very simple. The coach stands to one side of the goal and tosses the ball for the goalkeeper to catch as high as possible in the air. The coach checks the points of technique.

BASIC GOALKEEPING

Equipment
   1 ball for 1 player and the coach.

Organization
   1 player acts as goalkeeper and stands on the middle of the goal line.

Instructions
   The player is positioned so that he or she can see both the ball and the incoming attackers. The goalkeeper's stance is always slightly open to the field of play.

   The player moves toward the ball if possible and jumps off one foot, bringing the other knee up high to add vertical lift.

   The player takes the ball at the highest possible point, using both hands in the W formation.

   On landing, the player crouches down and protects both him- or herself and the ball.

Drills for Intermediates

These drills are similar to beginner drills, but the coach moves farther and farther away to increase the height and distance of the service. This leads to the ball being volleyed or kicked across to add to the realism. As the goalkeeper improves, opposing players are introduced, which leads to the next section for more advanced practices.

Drills for Advanced Goalkeepers

The introduction of more players, both attackers and defenders, into the drill makes the actual technique of catching the ball more difficult, because the goalkeeper is now in a crowded situation and may not have a clear route to the ball. It also requires the goalkeeper to make the same kinds of mental decisions as required in a game. The two most important decisions are (1) leaving the goal to try to reach the ball versus staying in the goal to see what happens and (2) catching the ball versus punching it away.

In this kind of drill, the goalkeeper has to make decisions about what to do, which requires the coach to coach the mind of the goalkeeper.

CROSSES AND SHOTS

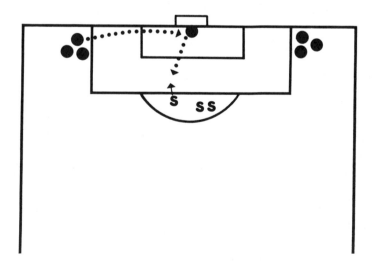

Figure 12.15

Equipment

Ample balls, at least 1 for each player.

Organization

Players are in groups of 10 (6 servers, 3 shooters, 1 goalkeeper) on a standard soccer field. Three servers are on each side of the penalty area and 3 shooters are in the D, as shown in Figure 12.15. The goalkeeper is in the goal.

Instructions

The goalkeeper collects a high cross from one of the servers and then rolls the ball to one of the shooters, who takes an immediate shot at goal.

Coaching Progressions

A shooter moves in to the cross, and the goalkeeper must decide whether to stay in the goal or leave it.

A player making a cross tries to float the ball into the goal and score.

A player making a cross aims for the farside servers, who become strikers.

The goalkeeper has defenders: initially a center half, then 2 backs, then full defense.

Players progress to wave attacks (chapters 17 and 18).

Players practice tactics at corners (chapter 16).

Diving at the Feet of an Attacker

This is the most difficult of the goalkeeper techniques; it requires skill, timing, and courage. This skill is for advanced players only and requires careful coaching to impress upon the attacker that he or she is there to help the goalkeeper, not to score at any cost.

This drill involves the goalkeeper moving out of goal and competing 1 vs. 1 against an attacker who has broken through the defense. The goalkeeper tries to jockey and position to force the attacker to move in a certain direction. (Players usually move toward their right side because they are more confident with their right foot, and this knowledge should help the goalkeeper.) Having made the attacker move in a sideways direction, the goalkeeper dives in at the feet of the attacker and smothers the ball. The drill has four stages, and the goalkeeper has four decisions to make.

First, the goalkeeper must determine the exact moment to start moving out of the goal toward the attacker. If the goalkeeper moves too soon, the attacker can simply chip the ball over the goalkeeper into an empty goal. If the goalkeeper moves too late, the angle is not reduced and the attacker has a very wide target at which to shoot. I tell the goalkeeper to stay back until the attacker crosses the penalty area line and then make a swift but balanced move forward (Figure 12.16a).

Second, the goalkeeper must try to force the attacker to move sideways away from the direct line toward the goal (Figure 12.16b).

Third, the goalkeeper must time the start of the dive by waiting until the ball is being played sideways by the attacker (Figure 12.16c).

Fourth, the goalkeeper must time the actual dive in such a way that the hands and arms gather the ball at the same time the body presents as long a barrier as possible to the attacker (Figure 12.16d).

a

b

(Cont.)

Figure 12.16
When defending an attack the goalkeeper a) moves forward and b) forces the attacker to move sideways.

c

d

Figure 12.16 (Continued)
The goalkeeper c) starts the dive and d) gathers the ball with the hands and arms.

Practice Drills

Attackers simply dribble the ball into the penalty area and try to score. The difficulty is increased for the goalkeeper by the speed and realism of the attack.

Narrowing the Angle and Judging Angles

When the goalkeeper moves off the line and goes to meet the attacker, we call this narrowing the angle. By moving forward, the goalkeeper reduces the target area (Figures 12.17 and 12.18).

Figure 12.17
Goalkeeper stays on the goal line and leaves space for the shooter.

Figure 12.18
Goalkeeper moves forward to narrow the angle and denies the shooter space to aim at.

Timing the Move

Timing relies on the goalkeeper's judgment, but the best general advice is for the goalkeeper to wait on the goal line until the attacker moves into the penalty area, then move forward.

Judging Angles

The goalkeeper always moves toward the player with the ball but must do so with regard to the position of the goals. In particular, the goalkeeper should always protect the near post (Figure 12.19).

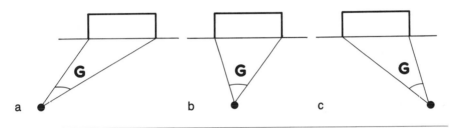

Figure 12.19
The goalkeeper always moves to protect the near post.

Note: The best way to teach your goalkeeper to find the correct angle is to use a piece of cord 20 yards long. Tie the ends to the bottom of each post and take the apex of the triangle to the ball; the resulting lines tell the goalkeeper exactly where to stand.

Drills for Beginners

A good way to teach the concept of positioning to a novice goalkeeper is to use the practice called clock shooting (Figure 12.20).

CLOCK SHOOTING

Equipment
　　1 ball for each player.

Organization
　　Players are in a group of unlimited number in a semicircle around the penalty area of a standard soccer field. The shooters are numbered as shown in Figure 12.20. The goalkeeper stands in front of the goal.

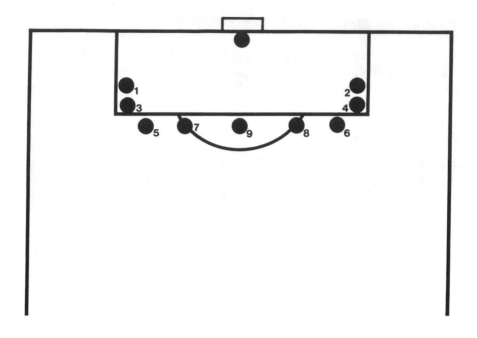

Figure 12.20

Instructions

The shooters shoot only when their numbers are called.

The goalkeeper positions himself or herself for each shot. The goalkeeper must be given time to position between each shot.

Coaching Points

Goalkeepers should protect the near post, narrow the angle, and be still at the moment the shot is released.

Coaching Progression

The shooters increase the speed at which they release their shots.

Drills for Intermediates

Clock shooting is fine for the novice but it takes time and is not sufficiently dynamic for improving goalkeepers—this next drill is (Figure 12.21).

ALTERNATE SHOTS

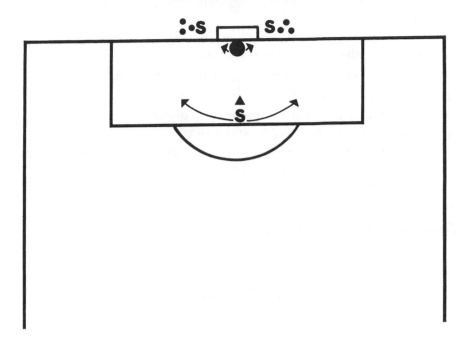

Figure 12.21

Equipment

Ample balls; 1 flag or cone.

Organization

Players are in teams of 4 (1 goalkeeper, 1 shooter, 2 servers) on a standard soccer field. The shooter operates from an area just inside the penalty area, from behind a central cone or flag (Figure 12.21). The servers, with ample soccer balls, stand by each goalpost.

Instructions

The shooter runs behind the cone, shoots, and runs to the opposite side of the penalty area.

The servers roll the ball so as to feed the shooter at a reasonable rate.

The goalkeeper positions correctly for each shot from left and right alternately.

Coaching Points

The goalkeeper should move quickly as the ball rolls toward the shooter.

The goalkeeper should orient himself or herself from the near post and remember to guard the near side first.

The goalkeeper should be still just before the shot is released.

Coaching Progressions

A second shooter, when called, has to dribble a ball into the area, dribble past the goalkeeper, and score.

This forces the goalkeeper into a 1 vs. 1 situation and calls for the ability not only to narrow the angle but to dive at the feet of the oncoming player.

Drills for Advanced Players

THREE-SIDED GOAL

Figure 12.22

Equipment

Ample balls; 3 corner flags.

Organization

Players are in teams of 4 (1 goalkeeper, 3 shooters), in a 3-sided goal, with flags about 8 yards apart (Figure 12.22).

Instructions

The goalkeeper moves to each goal in sequence and reacts according to each shooter, whose only instruction is to score. The shooters may elect to shoot or to dribble.

The shooters must realize that it is their aim to get the goalkeeper to make a good save. They are there to bring the best out of the keeper, and they should shoot accordingly.

Coaching Points

As for clock shooting.

Coaching Progressions

Players increase the speed of the practice.

Distributing the Ball

The goalkeeper needs to be able to distribute the ball both by kicking (for distance) and by throwing (for speed and accuracy). He or she must also know when to use the different techniques to set up an attacking move quickly, often by switching play, and when to wait with the ball until team members have moved forward into balanced attacking positions.

Kicking

The goalkeeper should be encouraged to take all goal kicks to relieve other players from this sometimes tiring duty. Perhaps more importantly, the goalkeeper must be expert at the volley kick. (Both kicks are covered in detail in chapter 9.) When volleying, the goalkeeper must also be taught that a kick that produces a ball dropping vertically down is much harder for the forwards to control than a ball with a flatter trajectory. Forwards much prefer balls approaching with flat trajectories, either to control or to play backward behind the defense.

The difference in the trajectory is caused by the way the volleyer places the ball on the foot. Simply tossing the ball into the air and kicking it produces the trajectory shown in Figure 12.23a. Placing the ball down on the instep produces a flatter kick, which results in the trajectory shown in Figure 12.23b.

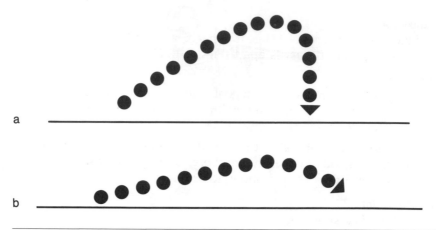

Figure 12.23
A ball that is a) hard and b) easy for the receiver to control.

Distribution by Hand

Goalkeepers can use three popular techniques for throwing: the javelin throw, the overhead throw, and the roll. The roll is very accurate over short distances and is easy for the receiver to control because it has no sidespin. Its weakness is that it can only be used over short distances. The more common techniques are the powerful javelin and overhead throws, which are worth examining in detail.

The Javelin Throw

The javelin throw for soccer is the same kind used in baseball and cricket. The ball is thrown hard and flat, which is achieved when the elbow leads the throwing action. The goalkeeper must practice until he or she can make this throw without imparting sidespin, which complicates the control for the receiving player (Figure 12.24).

The Overhead Throw

The overhead throw is similar to the hook pass in basketball. The goalkeeper stands sideways and uses a long, windmill arm action to achieve sufficient height to clear opposing players (Figure 12.25).

The Goalkeeper Game

The goalkeeper game is an excellent conclusion to this chapter, because it provides an enjoyable practice situation to develop most of the skills

Figure 12.24
Arm position for the javelin throw.

Figure 12.25
Arm position for the overhead throw.

discussed in this chapter, from kicking and throwing to narrowing the angle and dealing with shots (Figure 12.26).

GOALKEEPER GAME

Equipment
    Ample balls; 2 portable goals or sets of flags.

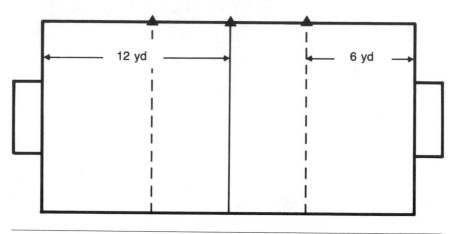

Figure 12.26

Organization

2 goalkeepers practice against each other, protecting 2 opposing goals 20 yards apart, as shown in Figure 12.26.

Instructions

The game starts when one goalkeeper takes a dead ball kick from the 6-yard line and tries to score past his opponent. This kick also restarts the game whenever a shot misses the goal and the ball goes out of play or when there is a dispute of any kind not covered in the rules.

If the receiving goalkeeper catches his opponent's shot, he or she can then shoot back by using a volley or half-volley from the point at which the catch was made. This is a considerable advantage.

If the receiving goalkeeper parries the shot but fails to catch it, then he or she takes a 6-yard kick.

Note: If the ball rebounds over the center line, the goalkeeper loses possession. This encourages the goalkeepers to pounce on any ball they cannot hold.

If a ball rebounds from the goalposts, the goalkeeper takes a 6-yard kick.

The players can set any number of goals as the target or play for a predetermined time.

The goalkeepers can elect to throw at the goal rather than kick.

Note: This game is great fun and is ideal practice for goalkeepers, who can learn to deal with realistic shots and practice their kicking and throwing.

CHAPTER 13

Coaching the Throw-In

Every player must be able to execute a good throw-in; this is the most common way of restarting the game and when done well has great tactical value. Unfortunately, many young players find it a difficult skill to learn, and even professional players make mistakes.

The key to teaching beginners is to have them throw the ball over an obstacle, ideally the goals. By concentrating on height rather than distance and by using a square, two-foot placement, young players will learn the correct throwing action and will not be likely to foul. The key to successful tactics is to encourage players to think quickly and to practice set plays.

The Basic Action

To execute the throw-in, the player must face the field of play, throw the ball with both hands from behind the head, and keep both feet on or behind the touchline and in contact with the ground throughout the throw.

Facing the field and staying behind the line are easily done; releasing a balanced two-handed throw while keeping the feet on the ground is more difficult, especially when trying to achieve a long throw.

Holding the Ball

The player holds the ball on the ends of the fingers with the hands behind the ball in the W formation (Figure 13.1).

Figure 13.1
Correct hand position for the throw-in.

The Throwing Action

The body arches backward and then uncoils in a natural sequence: first the upper body, then the arms, and finally the fingers with an important snap-down action at the moment of release, which helps to generate power (Figure 13.2).

To ensure that the ball is released from behind the head, the beginner should concentrate on releasing the ball with a high trajectory; aiming at the feet of a receiver comes later. As with all throwing actions, a good follow-through is important to achieve accuracy and distance.

Footwork

Keeping both feet on the ground, especially when attempting a long throw, can cause problems even for experienced players. Often the player, quite legitimately, takes a few running steps to gain momentum. But when the ball is thrown, this same momentum causes the back foot to lift off

Figure 13.2
Correct body position for the throw-in.

the ground. To prevent this, I advise that beginners use a square, two-footed (London Bridge) stance. The players can run as fast as they like, but by split-stepping into a square, two-footed stance, they will keep both feet on the ground. However hard players throw, their feet will not leave the ground until the ball has been released.

I recommend teaching beginners to throw the ball to each other over the top of the goals. In this way, players concentrate on height, and a foul throw becomes almost impossible (Figure 13.3).

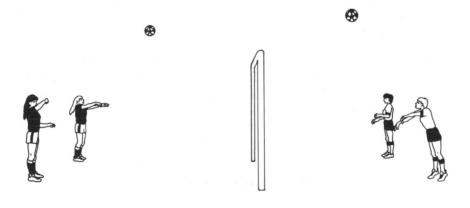

Figure 13.3

OVER THE GOAL

Equipment

1 ball for each 2 players; goals or other barriers.

Organization

Players are in pairs on each side of a barrier, ideally the goals, over which the players can throw.

Instructions

Players throw the ball to their partners, aiming for height before distance.

Coaching Points

Players should face forward, feet shoulder-width apart.

Players should hold the ball in the W formation.

Players should arch back, uncoil their bodies, and release balls above their heads on a high trajectory.

The fingers should snap down as they release the ball.

Coaching Progressions

The distance from the goals increases.

Players try to throw the ball over the goals from the penalty spot and the penalty area line.

Faults and Corrections

The two most common faults (after the foot fault) are throwing the ball with one hand too dominant and releasing the ball too late and thus not from behind the head. Again I can recommend a useful method of overcoming both problems simultaneously.

The player and coach stand as shown in Figure 13.4—one of the coach's hands covering the ball when the player has adopted the ready position. Now, as the player attempts to throw, the coach gently resists the movement at the correct point of release. This gives the player the kinesthetic feel of the correct action (chapter 2).

The Long Throw

The long throw is a very useful tactic and when executed near the opponent's goal line can be almost as good as a corner kick because of the greater accuracy of the throw.

Figure 13.4
A technique for helping a player get the feel of correct positioning.

Drills for Beginners

Players move farther and farther away from the goal, still throwing over the crossbar.

Drills for Intermediates

Intermediates can now add accuracy to distance and try to hit a target (Figure 13.5).

TARGET THROW-IN

Equipment
  1 ball for each 2 players; 3 or 4 flags.

Organization
  Players are in pairs, standing near flags arranged at different distances.

Instructions
  Players take turns trying to hit each flag with the ball.

Coaching Points
  Reinforce the concept of aiming at a target. Be on the watch for a foul throw and for one hand becoming dominant.

Figure 13.5

Coaching Progressions

Players throw from the sideline into the penalty area and then into the goal area.

Drills for Advanced Players

We now move into simple tactics, starting with the following move to exploit a long throw. Now the target becomes the forehead of a player, who tries to back-head the ball (head the ball backward) farther into the goal area (Figure 13.6). The progression for this move is to have a third player waiting for the back-header to try a shot or a head at the goal.

Tactics in Attack

The faster a player thinks, the more likely he or she is to gain a tactical advantage. This advice is especially true with the free kick and the throw-in. Some players do not naturally respond quickly and will need to work to develop this skill. You cannot stress too often the basic tactic for throw-ins, which is to take the throw quickly whenever possible.

The second tactical thought that you should try to develop in the minds of your players is to throw the ball forward. The rules of the game state that a player cannot be given offside (penalized for infringing the offside law) directly from a throw-in. Throwing the ball forward toward the opponent's goal keeps the attacking momentum going and often results in getting a player deep into the opposition's defense. The ''no offside'' rule

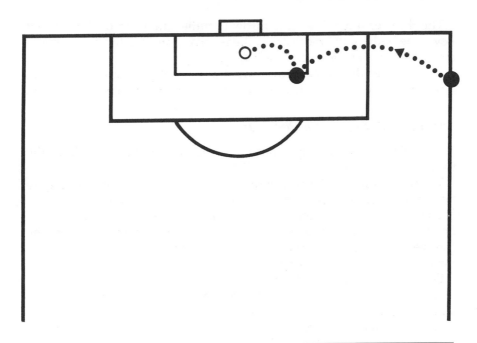

Figure 13.6
Field position for the tactic of passing to a teammate who will head the ball into the goal.

at throw-ins is a tremendous advantage if used correctly; this advantage is often lost if the ball is thrown in square or even backward. Of course, balls are thrown square or backward in professional soccer and resulting plays used to good advantage, but this is seldom the case with young players. Indeed, a ball thrown backward to an inexperienced player, often the fullback, can be disastrous. Nothing is worse for a defender receiving such a throw than the feeling of insecurity that occurs when an attacker rushes in to charge down the kick (bodily block the kick).

Throwing and Receiving—The Basic Duties

Sometimes a quick throw-in is not possible. Therefore, all players must be coached in the basic duties of being a thrower and receiver.

The Basic Duties of the Thrower

The thrower must face the field of play and look for the player who is in the best position (i.e., closest to the opponents' goal or not covered).

The thrower then must catch the attention of that player, either by calling the player's name or by establishing eye contact.

The thrower must direct the throw to either the head or the feet but never the body of the receiver, so the receiver can play the ball immediately without having to control it first.

The thrower then must move onto the field of play and be ready to kick any return pass, ideally directly forward toward the opponent's goal.

The Basic Duties of the Receiver

The receiver must take up a position at least 10 yards away from the thrower.

The receiver must take note of the nearest defender and decide exactly how much time and space he or she has to work within.

The receiver must either control the ball and turn toward the goal (if he or she is not closely covered) or play the ball back immediately to the thrower with the foot or the head. (Very seldom in junior soccer is the thrower covered by a defender.)

Finally, and most importantly, the receiver must accept the responsibility to trigger the throw. The thrower may have the ball, but the quick, signaled reaction of the receiver actually starts the move. Receivers can and must make decoy runs and moves to create opportunities for the thrower. These moves have to be coached and practiced, which takes us on to the next section on positional play.

Players who crowd around the thrower (Figure 13.7) deny themselves the space, and therefore the time, to play the ball. Overcrowding around

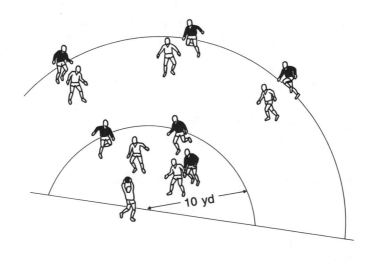

Figure 13.7
Players are too close to the thrower.

the thrower is all too often a feature of poor team coaching of throw-ins, and players cannot be taught too soon how to adopt the much wider, open positions shown in Figure 13.8.

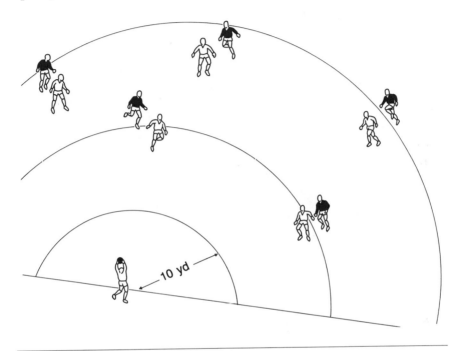

Figure 13.8
Players are well positioned.

The Basic Move in Attack

If the receivers do position themselves 10 yards from the thrower, yet a quick throw to an unmarked player is not possible, the thrower can use a simple but very effective basic move. This move enables the thrower to move onto the field with enough space to kick a long ball forward into the opposition's defense—after, of course, the ball has been skillfully returned to the thrower by a receiver.

The thrower throws to a receiver positioned 10 yards away (Figure 13.9a).

The receiver returns the ball, which ideally rolls gently toward the thrower (Figure 13.9b).

The thrower enters the field of play and either plays the ball forward or dribbles (Figure 13.9c).

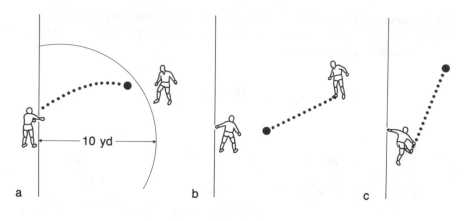

a   b   c

Figure 13.9

*A basic attack move may be practiced where the thrower a) throws to a
receiver, b) waits for the receiver to gently return the ball, and c) plays the
ball forward or dribbles it.*

Drills for Beginners

BASIC THROW-IN

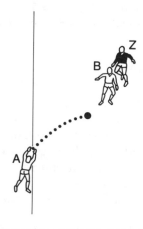

Figure 13.10

Equipment
    1 ball for each 3 players.

Organization

Players are in groups of 3 (2 attackers, 1 defender), standing near a line that represents a sideline (Figure 13.10).

Instructions

The receiver (Player B) triggers the practice by moving.

The thrower (Player A) aims at Player B's head or feet.

Player B plays the ball back using the head or feet.

The defender (Player Z) tries to stop the move.

Coaching Points

Player B should be at least 10 yards from Player A.

Player A must throw to Player B's feet and then move forward onto the field.

Player B should try to make an effective and well-timed move to slip away from the defender and should give a quality return pass to Player A.

Drills for Intermediates

2 VS. 3

Equipment

1 ball for each 5 players.

Instructions

Players are in groups of 5 (3 attackers, 2 defenders) standing near a line that represents a sideline (Figure 13.11). The attackers try to keep possession and make 3 successful passes.

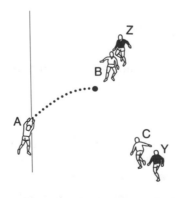

Figure 13.11

Coaching Points

Players B and C should move in relation to each other and Player A.

Drills for Advanced Players

We now develop the 3 vs. 2 situation (Figure 13.12) and introduce more advanced moves such as crossover plays, which create space for other attackers and the direct overhead kick.

CROSSOVER PLAYS

Figure 13.12

Equipment

1 ball for each 5 players.

Organization

Players in groups of 5 (3 attackers, 2 defenders) as shown in Figure 13.12.

Instructions

Player A triggers the move by running directly toward Player B.

Player B reacts by sprinting past Player A and through the vacated space to receive a forward throw from Player C.

Coaching Points

Player A should call and move in a sufficiently convincing manner to deceive Player Y into moving with Player A and thus out of position.

Player B should wait a second before reacting (giving Player Y time to be deceived) and should always run forward on the outside of Player A.

Player C should pretend to throw to Player A but actually delay throwing until Player B is well forward. Player C should then throw the ball beyond Player B for him or her to move toward.

CREATING SPACE FOR OTHERS

In this drill, Player B (the attacker nearest the thrower) moves upfield taking Player Y out of position and creating space and for Player C to move into and execute a move.

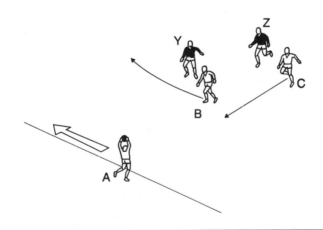

Figure 13.13

Equipment
1 ball for each 5 players.

Organization
Players are in groups of 5 (3 attackers, 2 defenders) as shown in Figure 13.13.

Instructions
Player B triggers the move by moving upfield taking Player Y out of position. (If Player Y fails to react, then Player B will obviously be ideally placed to receive the throw.)

If Player Y does react, Player C moves into the space left by Player B and executes the basic move.

Coaching Points

Player B should make a positive move, because either outcome is successful; as there is no offside from a throw-in, the move gives an additional advantage of creating depth in attack.

Player C should wait a second before reacting.

Player C can also decoy Player Y by pretending to move away from the thrower before actually moving toward him or her.

Player A should watch what is happening and make the most effective response.

Tactics Using a Longer Throw

This next play, which is very successful in games, requires a deep-lying player (usually a fullback) to make a forward run behind those apparently engaged in the throw-in. The thrower simply uses a long throw over the heads of the players to land the ball at the feet of the running player. Naturally this play has to be rehearsed, as do all set play moves.

In Figure 13.14, Players A and B move in close to the thrower as Player C runs down the field behind them.

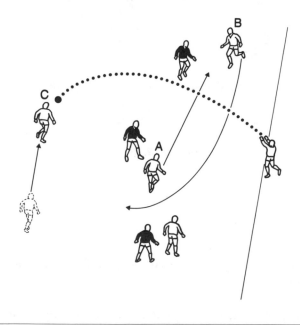

Figure 13.14

A and B move in close to the thrower so that C can move straight down the field behind them.

Tactics in Defense

Organizing defense for throw-ins requires four essential tactics. Time and circumstances may prevent players from achieving all four safeguards on every occasion, but players should aim to achieve them.

One-On-One Marking

First, every potential receiver should be covered on a one-on-one basis. This means that sufficient players must run hard to cover each attacker—this usually involves forwards helping the defense.

Get Goalside

Second, all defenders should position themselves goalside of the attacker they are marking so that each defender can always see the attacker he or she is covering as well as the thrower. This means defenders must move when the attacker moves to avoid being caught out of position.

Cover the Thrower

We have already discussed how attackers can play the ball back to an unmarked thrower, who can then play the ball forward. Accordingly, defensive players must cover the thrower so that the opposition cannot use this move. The best player to cover the thrower is the winger who plays on the same side of the field, especially since he or she can also position halfway between the thrower and the opponents' fullback, who may come forward in support.

Keep a Spare Defender

Finally, a well-organized defense always retains a spare defender behind the area in which the throw-in is taking place. Ideally, this is the fullback on whose side the throw is taken.

A good example of defensive cover at a throw-in is given in Figure 13.15, where all four safeguards are achieved. However, a system of defense is never infallible—it depends upon the defensive skills of the players concerned (chapter 8).

Figure 13.15
Defensive cover where all four safeguards are achieved.

Drills for Defensive Tactics

Watch your team play in a competitive game and observe how many times, if at all, they achieve the four safeguards when it is possible for them to do so. After observing their play, you may need to show them how and where to position themselves to defend at throw-ins. This can be done during "chalk-and-talk" sessions but is more effective on the field in live situations (chapters 17 and 18). In addition to these methods and practices, I suggest two other approaches.

Divide your squad into groups of 4 or 5 players and let each group, independently of you and other groups, design their own attacking moves from a throw-in. Now simply play one group against another and see how well they defend.

Play attack versus defense practices in a full-game situation and coach during play (chapter 18).

You need realistic situations when coaching defense at throw-ins. Observing what players do when they are tired or have to think for themselves is the key to producing successful team responses during a game. To react both individually and collectively in any given situation requires an intelligent understanding of the game of soccer. I hope Part III will provide some of this knowledge.

PART III

TACTICS
AND TEAMWORK

In Part III, I present my ideas on coaching tactics and teamwork. I start by introducing the work of Allen Wade, who first identified 10 general principles applicable to team games. I then provide the reader with a brief history of the way modern systems of play developed, together with an analysis of their strengths and weaknesses. I provide detailed explanations of tactical moves that can be used at set plays, including attacking and defensive free kicks and corner kicks. Finally, I present my ideas on how to coach tactics and teamwork.

CHAPTER 14

Understanding Team Play

One of your main objectives as a coach is to improve team play—but how do you know how well your team is playing? You can't judge simply by the result, because your opponents may have been strong or weak; you can't judge simply by the score, because at any one moment in the game the score might not be a true reflection of how well the teams are playing. You need a measuring stick, a set of permanent criteria against which you can analyze how well or how badly your team is playing. You have to know what to look for; you have to be able to recognize good team play.

This chapter introduces the concepts of team play, which were first identified by Allen Wade in 1967 and which are still in use.

The Three Common Concepts

I start by discussing the three concepts that are common to both attack and defense. These concepts are possession, support, and communication. These concepts are very closely related, but team analysis always starts with the same question: Which team has the ball?

Possession

If your team has possession of the ball, watch to see how well they keep possession. A team that continually gives the ball away or makes haphazard passes cannot be playing well. Keeping possession is very important, and players should only lose possession when they have a shot on goal or attempt a killer pass or dribble. Players should never lose possession in the defending or middle thirds of the field, unless it is a matter of safety.

If your team does not have possession of the ball, look to see how hard the players, both individually and collectively, work to regain possession. If players rush into tackles wildly or do not know how to support and cover each other, then they are playing badly. Even when defending, a team can still put pressure on their opponents by denying them time and space to play the ball.

Your first judgment about successful team play is based upon an analysis of how well players keep or regain possession. You can now examine support and communication to identify why players are or are not successful.

Support

See if your players are making the right decisions and running hard to get into good supporting positions when their team has possession. This feature of good team play is closely associated with the willingness of players to make unselfish runs. Any team in which players stand and watch each other will be playing badly. See Figures 14.1 and 14.2 for examples of poor support and good support. In Figure 14.1, Player A has no support in attack, and Player Z has no support in defense. In Figure 14.2, Players B, C, and D are all supporting Player A.

The principle of support also operates in defense (Figure 14.3). When a player goes into a tackle (we call this player the first defender), he or she should always be supported by a second player (the second defender). In general, the second defender supports at an angle of 45°, protects the most direct pathway to goal, and is never more than 10 yards behind the first defender. Often he or she is much closer than 10 yards, depending upon the circumstances.

Communication

The final common concept is communication. On a soccer field, good communication is achieved by looking, calling, and signaling. Good communication involves talking and calling, not shouting, and for this

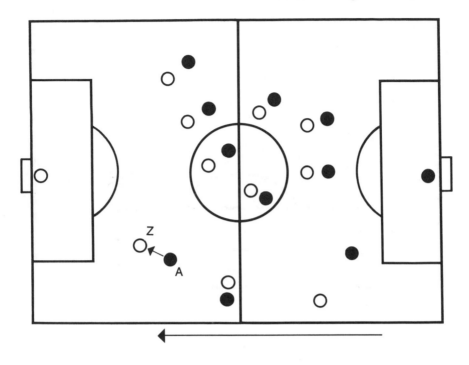

Figure 14.1
Poor support in attack and defense.

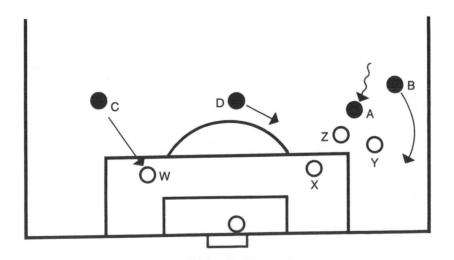

Figure 14.2
Good support in attack.

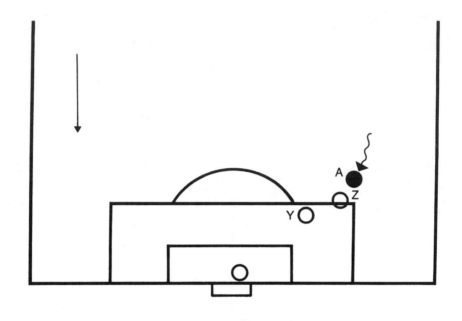

Figure 14.3
Good support in defense.

reason is an advanced aspect of team play. Watch your players carefully to determine the quality of communication between them during play. Also notice how well team members encourage each other, especially when things are going badly and mistakes are being made. Even young players can be quite cruel to each other, so encourage positive communication.

An American psychologist, A.T. Welford, showed that the human ear normally can get the brain to deal with only one message at a time. If several messages or sounds arrive simultaneously, they have to "wait in line." Consider how this law affects a soccer player in possession of the ball. If the player is inundated with shouts from six teammates, he or she hears only the first call; the remaining five are just background noise adding to the confusion. Worse, the six players may all be shouting different advice! (See Figure 14.4.) The player can deal only with the first call, so the first call must be the correct one. You can prompt this by encouraging players to look and think more and to shout less. This will help provide good communication.

"Kick it" →
"Shoot"
"Pass"
"My ball"
"Dribble"
"Hold it"

Figure 14.4
Too many shouts only confuse.

Common Concepts of Attack and Defense

We now consider the concepts of attack and defense. Every attacking strategy corresponds with a defensive strategy. The three major concepts are:

Penetration in attack versus Delay in defense

Width in attack versus Concentration in defense

Mobility in attack versus Balance in defense

Delay in Defense

Delay is important in defense. Slowing the opposition means gaining valuable time for your team to protect its goal. This holds true on both an individual and a team basis.

Individually, players must not rush wildly into tackles. They should remain calm and composed, jockey slowly yet positively, watch the ball, and try not to be beaten by the opponent. If a defender remains goalside of an attacker, preventing a direct shot on goal, then that defender is playing well.

Collectively, two or more players can combine very effectively to prevent direct progress on their goal. If they cannot regain possession they must try to delay the attack by forcing the attackers to play the ball sideways or backward away from the danger area. Defenders should follow two rules of defense.

Rule 1: The nearest defender to the ball (the first defender) must always go forward to meet the ball and stop the direct attack.

Rule 2: The supporting defender (the second defender) must cover the first defender. (The second defender usually stands at an angle of about 45°, never more than 10 yards from the first defender, and blocks the most direct path to goal.)

Penetration in Attack

To counter a delaying tactic, an attacker tries to penetrate defensive territory. Penetration requires fast, direct plays and shots at goal. Again, this can be achieved both individually and collectively.

The First Attacker

Individually, the attacker who receives the ball (the first attacker) should be prepared to turn toward the goal (if necessary), take the ball directly toward the defender, try to outmaneuver the defender, and look for a chance to either shoot at goal or make a killer pass.

The Second Attacker

The second attacker should be prepared to support the first attacker by running past defenders and getting goalside of them while watching out for being caught in an offside trap by the opposition, moving out wide to create more space for the first attacker, and trying to take out defenders by running at them (being careful not to obstruct).

If a team is exhibiting good penetration, players move the ball swiftly and positively toward the opponents' goal and are prepared to shoot, to dribble past defenders, to make killer or lead passes, and to move forward into strike positions. You must encourage all of these qualities and attitudes in your players.

Concentration in Defense

An attacker moving into a crowded penalty area is faced with no room to move forward and not enough space between defenders.

If defenders want to make plays difficult for the attackers, the defenders simply crowd the danger area. This is called concentration, and it is most useful for corner kicks and free kicks in the penalty area when all or nearly all players defend the goal (Figure 14.5).

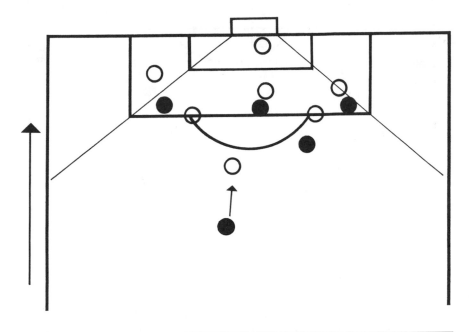

Figure 14.5
Good concentration in defense.

Width in Attack

To overcome concentration, attackers can use width. If a team attacks on a wide front, that team automatically stretches the defense across the field and opens up spaces between defenders, which attackers can exploit (Figure 14.6).

These concepts provide two more permanent features of team play to develop. Does your team concentrate its defense in times of need, and do you have sufficient width in attack to improve your chances of success?

"Honey Pot" Soccer

Let us consider concentration and width in relation to one problem that all coaches of young players experience—the overcrowding of players

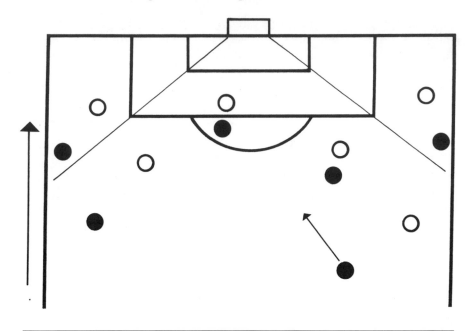

Figure 14.6
Spreading the defense makes attacking easier.

around the ball. This phenomenon of players converging on the ball ''like flies around a honey pot'' and making good play impossible is common in junior soccer (Figure 14.7).

The solution lies partly in the concepts of ''making space'' and ''going wide,'' which are best taught with the small-team games and practices explained in chapters 4 and 5 and the game of shadow soccer, which is shown on p. 307. You can also use concepts of width and concentration to analyze what is happening on the field. When you set up practices to improve your team in any aspect of play, you will rely increasingly upon your knowledge of these concepts.

We now consider the final pair of concepts, mobility and balance.

Mobility in Attack

Perhaps the worst example of team play is two fullbacks who stand rigidly in their own half of the field when everyone else is attacking the other goal. Such a team formation is seldom the fault of the players, who have probably been told to stay back (Figure 14.8).

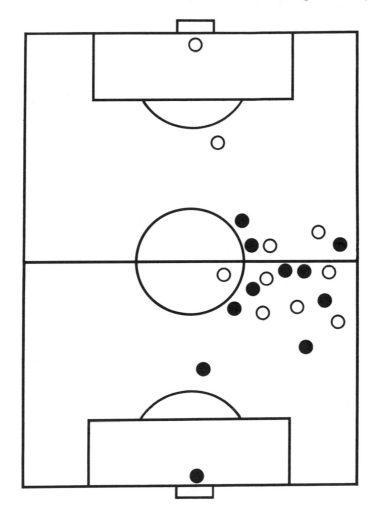

Figure 14.7
"Honey pot" soccer lacks basic principles of width and balance.

This strategy is wrong on two counts. It is wrong in practice because these defenders are too far back to support their halfbacks. The fullbacks can only wait for the ball or for the opposition to arrive, and meanwhile they lose the possible tactical advantage of catching the opposition in the offside trap.

Second, this strategy is wrong in principle. Soccer is a fluid, moving game and can only be played skillfully if all players exercise mobility. They

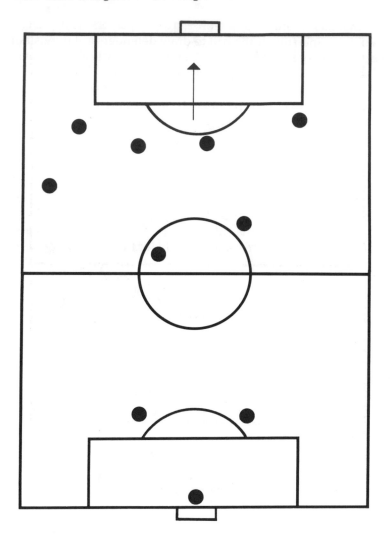

Figure 14.8
Poor defense by the two fullbacks who lack mobility and should have moved forward.

must be allowed the freedom to move anywhere at any time in accordance with their own judgment of the situation. Certainly young players must be taught to make correct judgments about when, where, and how to move; as we have seen, this is not an easy task for the coach. Nevertheless, the coach must undertake this task, because if players cannot make good judgments, a team never will play well.

   Good mobility in attack is demonstrated by players who change positions skillfully and run off the ball to draw defenders out of position and open up passing or shooting opportunities. Mobility is also demonstrated by fullbacks who overlap by moving around and in front of the player with the ball and by midfield players who run forward into the penalty area (from where over 80% of all goals are scored). These are all examples of the successful execution of mobility in attack. The counter strategy in defense is balance.

Balance

Balance is easy to understand if you imagine a child's seesaw. For example, if a winger beats his fullback and all the remaining defenders immediately rush over to his side of the field, then the defense is clearly off balance because nobody is left in the goal area (Figure 14.9).

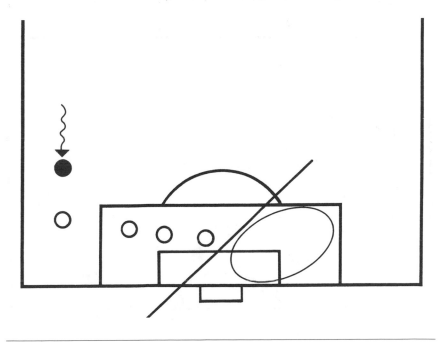

Figure 14.9
Lack of balance resulting from defenders moving over too far.

   In an aerial view of the field, a well-balanced defense would show the formations shown in Figures 14.10a, b, and c, which relate to the different points of attack.

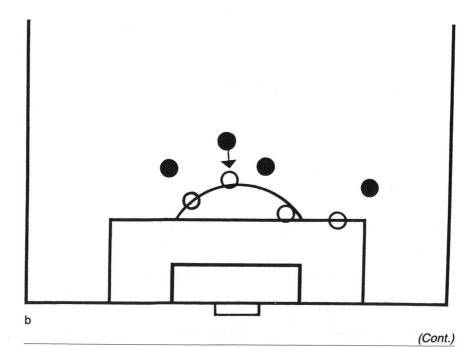

a

b

(Cont.)

Figure 14.10
*Formations for a well-balanced defense for attacks a) from the left and
b) from the front.*

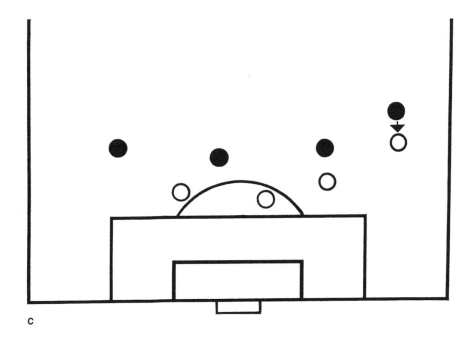

c

Figure 14.10 (Continued)
Formations for a well-balanced defense for attacks c) from the right.

CHAPTER 15

Team Formations and Systems of Play

Every coach must understand the different team formations in order to organize players to the best advantage. Every coach must also understand that a system of play is only as good as the players within it. Players, not team formations, win games. If this were not true, two opposing teams using the same system would always tie!

Every coach must appreciate that systems of play refer to the 11 vs. 11 game. This poses a problem when coaching youngsters, who cannot be expected to play a system successfully until they are mature enough to see what is happening in the entire game and to anticipate how plays are going to develop. Further, they must also be able to kick the ball at least 30 yards. In the absence of these abilities, the 11 vs. 11 game inevitably reduces to 20 youngsters all swarming like bees around the ball. With youngsters, therefore, don't expect too much too soon, and do use the coaching methods set out in this chapter and in chapter 18.

Development of Systems of Play

Before 1870, when the rules of soccer were first standardized, teams played in a 1:2:8 formation (Figure 15.1). There was no passing and no heading, and players dribbled and hacked (tackled) and occasionally shot for goal. Dribbling was the main skill. In 1867, the Queens Park team

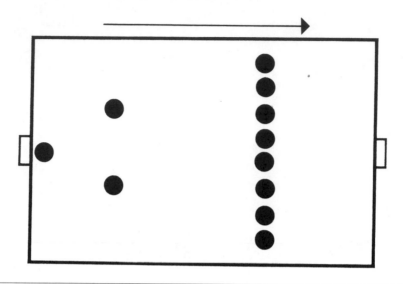

Figure 15.1
The 1:2:8 formation used before soccer rules were standardized.

from Scotland introduced the concept of passing; because of the way long through-passes began to penetrate the defense, the system changed to 1:2:2:6 (Figure 15.2). Incidentally, the Queens Park team played from 1867 to 1874 without having a single goal scored against them.

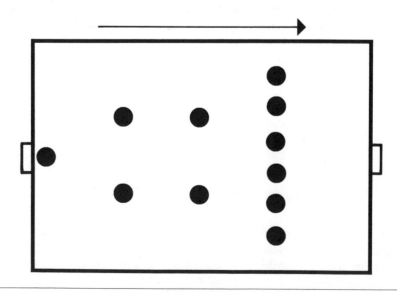

Figure 15.2
The 1:2:2:6 formation used after passing was introduced.

Increasingly, soccer became a game in which team effort was more important than individual talent. As a result, the next system to develop was the attacking center half. This player was the best on the team, and his main duty was to link attack and defense together (Figure 15.3).

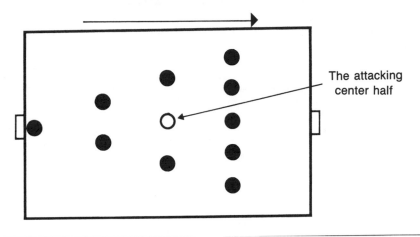

Figure 15.3
The formation using the attacking center half.

In 1925, the new offside law reduced the number of players who had to be between the ball and the goals from 3 to 2. This gave immediate impetus to the attacking game, and to counter it Herbert Chapman of the Arsenal Team in England introduced the stopper center-halfback system (Figure 15.4).

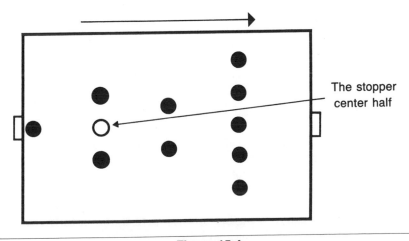

Figure 15.4
The formation using the stopper center half.

The stopper center-halfback system soon led to the invention of the famous WM formation, which reigned supreme for 30 years until Hungary introduced the deep-lying center forward system in 1953. The WM formation was the forerunner of the modern systems and is still a good system to use. It has an excellent balance between attack and defense, provides for good support, maintains depth, and allows players to attack on a wider front. The system is so named because players form a pattern that looks like the letters W and M (Figure 15.5).

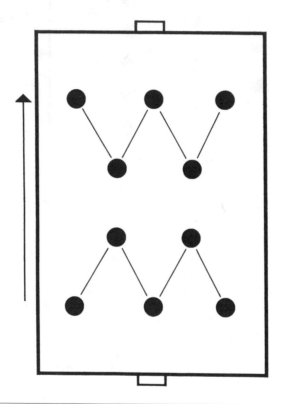

Figure 15.5
The WM system.

This system is a very effective attacking formation, especially if a team has a powerful center forward or striker, two fast wingers, and clever inside forwards and halfbacks. A team must also have a tall, commanding central defender and two mobile fullbacks.

If you play this system, don't let your two wingers become isolated and just stand and watch. If the ball is not reaching them, they must be prepared to leave their positions and look for the ball.

Basic Components of Modern Systems

Modern systems are modified by the ability of the players, the style of the coach, the strength of the opposition, and the state of the game. If you are losing 0-1 with 2 minutes to go, you don't employ a defensive system!

Fundamentally, however, all modern systems are based upon three factors: the dimensions of the field, the phases of the game (attack, defense, and midfield play), and the strengths and weaknesses of the players (Figure 15.6).

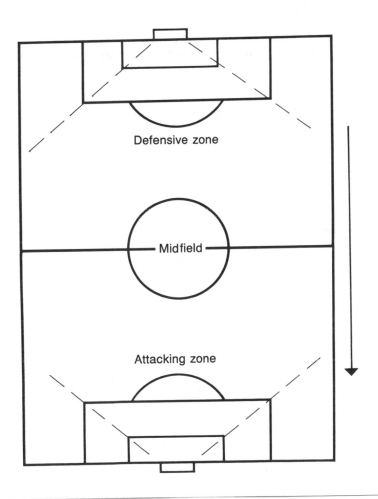

Figure 15.6
The field of play.

The Field of Play

As 90% of goals are scored from inside the shooting zone, it follows that we must both attack and defend these zones. We need players in the middle of the field to link defense to attack, plus we must have a goalkeeper because the rules say so. Therefore, all modern systems, to achieve a balance between attack and defense, involve seven players. Modern systems include two attackers, two midfield players, two defenders, and a goalkeeper.

The Three Phases of the Game

We must now consider how to position the remaining four players. We do this by analyzing the three phases of the game: attack, midfield, and defense. The remaining four players can be used to increase the effectiveness of any of the three phases, but you are always faced with a choice: If you strengthen the defense by allocating extra players to it, then to some extent your attack or your midfield must suffer. The differences are best explained by analyzing the four most common modern systems of play. Fundamentally, these systems are all based on the arrangement of the seven players as shown in Figure 15.7.

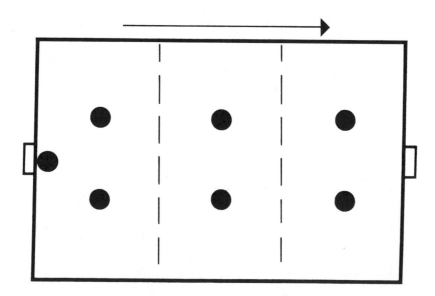

Figure 15.7
A modern system achieves a balance between attack and defense by organizing the field with two attackers, two midfielders, two defenders, and a goalkeeper.

Four Modern Systems of Play

The modern systems are named by the formation in which the players line up or are positioned across the field of play (usually but not always at the start of the game). Thus, for example, the 4:2:4 system has four defenders, two midfield players, and four attackers. Similarly, the 4:3:3 system has four defenders, three midfield players, and three attackers.

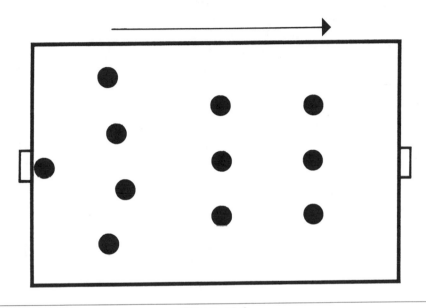

Figure 15.8
The 4:3:3 formation.

The 4:3:3 Formation

This system, shown in Figure 15.8, keeps a strong defense and strengthens the midfield by slightly reducing the attack. It is a well-balanced formation and is very popular. To use the 4:3:3 system you must teach your two wing fullbacks how to overlap. For example, in Figure 15.9, the fullback makes a long, forward overlapping run to meet the ball coming from the middle of the field.

You must also teach the three attackers how to work as a unit. For example, if Player C in Figure 15.10 goes wide with the ball, Players A and B make near- and far-post runs, respectively. Or, Player B might move toward Player C to support.

Finally, you must send players forward (e.g., a center back to center forward) toward the end of any game you are losing and at set plays.

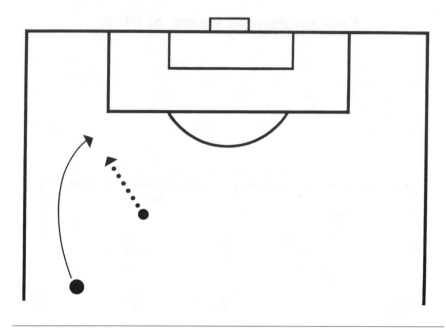

Figure 15.9
Fullbacks must overlap.

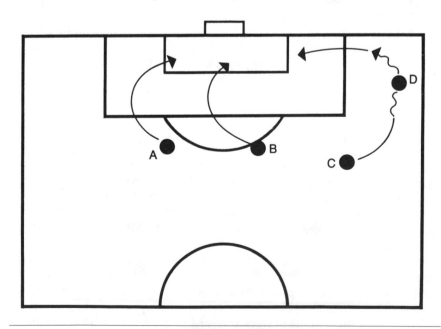

Figure 15.10
The three strikers must play as a unit.

The 4:2:4 Formation

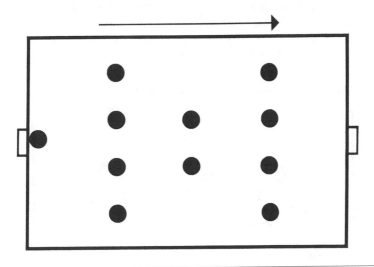

Figure 15.11
The 4:2:4 formation.

The system shown in Figure 15.11 uses four attackers and four defenders. Clearly, this gives good attack and good defense power but leaves a great deal of work for the two midfield players. If you play this system you must have two fit, clever midfield players on your team. You must teach your wing forwards and wing fullbacks to support the midfield player when the ball is on their side of the field (Figure 15.12).

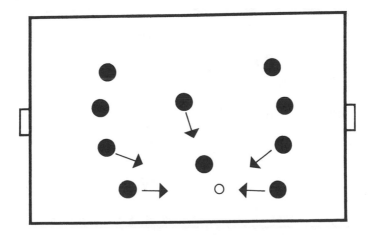

Figure 15.12
Support the midfield when the ball is on your side.

You must also avoid the "squeezebox" problem, when attackers stay up and defenders stay back, leaving the midfield players isolated and out-numbered (Figure 15.13).

Finally, you must not let the opposition dominate the midfield. If you see this happening, you must change the system.

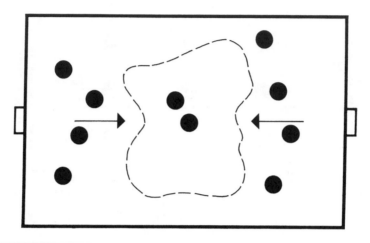

Figure 15.13
Attackers and defenders must work hard to close the midfield gap.

The 3:3:4 Formation

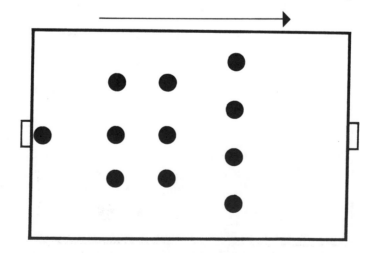

Figure 15.14
The 3:3:4 formation.

This system (Figure 15.14) keeps a strong attack by having two wingers and a strong midfield at the expense of one defender. If you play on a narrow field, this system may be very suitable. The system requires a commanding center fullback, plus you must teach your wing forwards to fall back in defense. Again, you must watch to see that the two wingers do not become isolated.

The 4:4:2 System

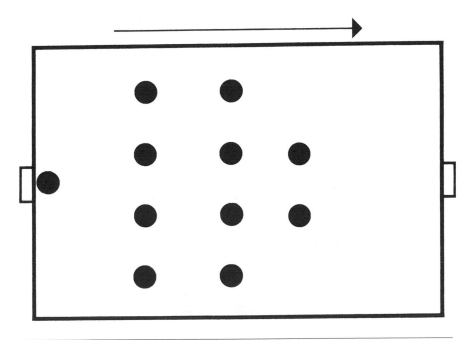

Figure 15.15
The 4:4:2 formation.

With this system (Figure 15.15) you organize your players into a strong, compact defense and midfield, and use two target players in attack. Clearly, defense and midfield are very secure. This system is often used by professional teams playing away from home and seeking a tie rather than a win.

In attack, the system depends largely upon fast breakouts from defense. You need two fast, highly mobile, and very fit strikers. Further, the midfield players must be prepared to move forward as a unit to support the target players, and the outside halfbacks must be prepared to attack on the wings.

Variations of the Basic Systems

We now examine some of the most popular variations of the basic systems, especially the sweeper system of defense and the target player system of attack.

The Sweeper System of Defense

Some European teams play one defender behind a line of three or four defenders. This defender is called the sweeper because he or she must follow and support the defender who is tackling for the ball. (The other defenders can stay close to their own attackers, and the defense is therefore tightly packed.) If you have a fast, tenacious tackler, this system may suit your team, but remember it is a defensive system. Two popular sweeper systems are shown in Figures 15.16a and b. In Figure 15.16a, the sweeper plays behind three defenders. In Figure 15.16b, the sweeper plays behind four defenders.

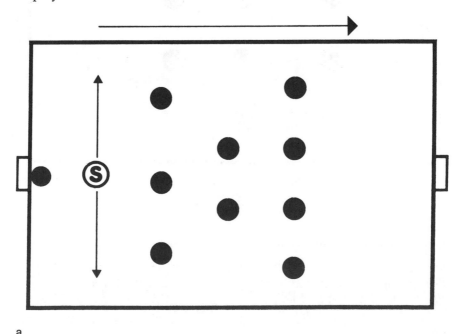

a

(Cont.)

Figure 15.16
The sweeper a) plays behind three defenders.

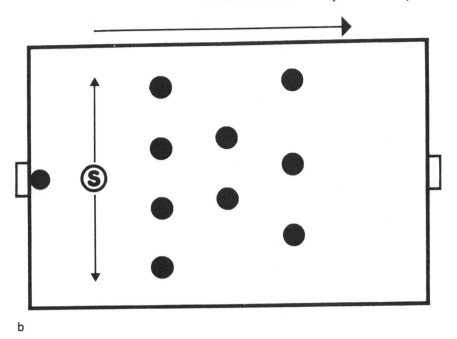

b

Figure 15.16 (Continued)
The sweeper b) plays behind four defenders.

The Target Player

The target player is the player who must get as close as possible to the opponent's goal without moving offside. The target player often stands directly in front of the rearmost defender and by facing his own players presents a target for them (Figure 15.17).

Because the target player stands in front of the rearmost defender (just like postplay in basketball), he or she is obviously in a good strike position. If the ball comes to the target player, it means that most defenders have already been beaten and the attackers have achieved a 1 vs. 1 situation. If a player in such a position can turn with the ball and attack the only remaining defender head to head, then clearly this is good attacking play. It follows that the best tactical advice you can give your target player is, "Turn if you can." If he or she cannot turn, and this is often the case because the ball comes at a very fast pace, the target player should try to "lay off" the ball to a supporting player (Figure 15.18).

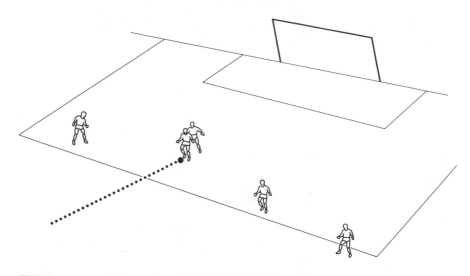

Figure 15.17
A player stands in front of the rearmost defender and presents a target for his or her teammate to aim at.

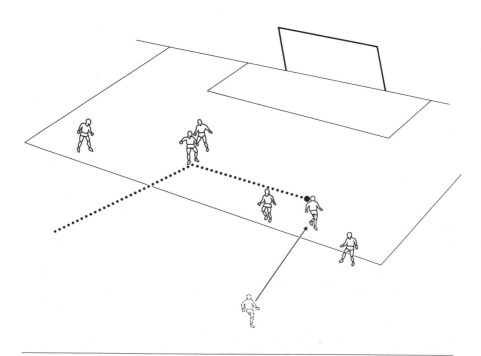

Figure 15.18
The target player lays off the ball behind the defense to a supporting player.

The Counter to the Target Player

If an attacking team uses the target player against your defense, your own players must move forward quickly toward the opponent's goal just before the ball is played to the target player. In this way your defense can either intercept the pass or play the target player offside.

If the ball reaches the target player, your defender must do everything possible to stop the turn, that is, to keep the attacker with his or her back to the goal to prevent the shot.

Selecting a System

One of the most frequently asked questions is, "Which system should I use?" My answer is that only you can answer this question. Certainly I can write about which formations are available, but only you can see how the strengths and weaknesses of individual players can be accommodated, and only you can modify your system to suit different game situations. These are the key factors to have in mind when selecting a system.

The second most frequent question is, "Where shall I play my least able players?"

First, notice that we talk about least able players, not weak or poor players. Accommodating your least able players is an important coaching strategy, particularly for American Youth Soccer Organization coaches, for whom everyone plays. The best answer is to go back to the seven basic positions shown on p. 266. These are the key positions, and they are therefore the positions that call for the highest involvement in the game. You should deploy your most able players in these seven positions. Your least able players should then be placed in the four remaining positions. This also clearly depends upon which system you select.

A word of caution: Don't try to make players fit into set positions until they have tried to play several different positions. You should give your players an opportunity to try different positions as part of their general education.

Individual Duties and Responsibilities

As the success of any system depends upon the manner in which the players make it work, each player must have specific roles and duties to perform. This final section analyzes the fundamental duties that players occupying each position should know and try to practice in the game.

Listed are three basic rules that all players should observe, regardless of their position or of the system.

- When in the defensive zone, think of preventing a goal rather than stealing the ball. Mistakes here can be costly, and it is always better to give away a throw-in or a corner rather than a goal.
- When in the midfield, keep possession. Remember that when developing attacks, there are either fast or slow build-ups. If the opposition is well-organized, you have to be patient and play the ball around; if they are exposed, you have to be quick and direct. But above all, keep possession.
- When in the attacking zone, be prepared to take risks; try to beat the defender and to shoot whenever possible. You don't score unless you shoot!

Responsibilities of Individual Positions

We can now consider the specific duties and responsibilities for each position. In the following sections, I identify important tactical strategies that I think each player should learn.

The Goalkeeper

After gathering the ball safely, the goalkeeper should think only of two things: The goalkeeper should either look for a quick throw to an unmarked colleague to gain an immediate advantage or wait until teammates have moved forward and are ready to receive a long pass.

No matter where the opponents are building up their attack, the goalkeeper should always stay in line with the ball and with the center of his or her goal.

Rather than standing rigidly on the goal line, the goalkeeper should move forward to the edge of the penalty area when the ball is in the opponents' half and should retreat slowly as the opponents attack.

Fullbacks

Fullbacks should try to intercept the ball before it reaches their winger. If the winger gets the ball first, the fullback must try to stop the cross (prevent the winger from centering or crossing the ball into the goal area).

Fullbacks should always position themselves so that if the ball is kicked over their heads or past them, they can always win the race to the ball that is rolling toward their own goal.

When the attack is on the other side of the field, the fullbacks' first duty is to cover across. That means leaving their own wingers to cover the middle of the field.

Central Defenders

Central defenders must decide whether to play the sweeper or the pivot system.

The defenders should always try to keep the attackers facing away from the defenders' goal (i.e., stop the turn).

If the attacker is moving toward the defenders' goal, central defenders should jockey so that their bodies stop the direct shot at goal and should stay on their feet.

Midfield Players

Midfield players should not give square passes unless forced to, because an interception exposes at least two players.

When the opposition has the ball, midfield players must run quickly along their recovery line to get goalside of the ball.

Midfield players must learn when to support in front of the player with the ball and when to support behind that player and keep running.

Wingers

A winger's first duty is to cross the ball.

Wingers should not shoot from the passing zone unless forced to.

When the attack is on the other wing, wingers should move into the shooting zone.

Strikers

Strikers must go for the goal; they can't score unless they shoot at the goal.

Strikers must turn with the ball and attack the defenders whenever possible.

Strikers must watch out for the offside trap and warn teammates of this danger.

CHAPTER 16

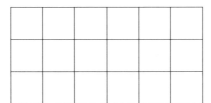

Tactics at Corners and Free Kicks

One of the hallmarks of a good coach is that his or her players know how to organize themselves quickly and efficiently at free kicks and corner kicks. In this chapter I discuss a series of moves and strategies for corners and free kicks and explain ways in which these moves can be taught and built up from basic principles. As many goals are scored directly as a result of set plays, time spent coaching your players in these tactics will be well spent.

The Short Corner

Every player should know how to use a short corner to restart the game quickly and gain a tactical advantage. The short corner kick enables the kicker to get much nearer to goal with a moving ball, which is much easier to kick. This makes for a more dangerous cross when the ball is played, especially on wet grounds. This kick draws defenders out of their defensive positions and frequently causes a general panic in the defense.

The Basic Move

The only way to take a short corner and not get caught offside is shown in Figure 16.1. I describe this as the basic move, and I refer to it again in some of the more advanced plays.

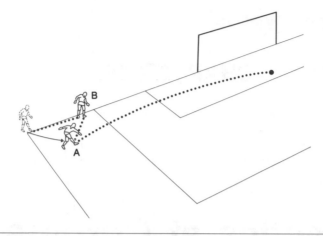

Figure 16.1
Taking a short corner using the basic move.

Player B must stand on the goal line about 6 yards from Player A. (This ensures that Player A can never be caught offside.) Player A plays the ball firmly to Player B after ensuring that the opponents are playing according to the rules and standing at least 10 yards away.

Player B plays the ball gently back to Player A as shown, so that Player A can take two or three strides and kick the moving ball into the goal area. Both players have to practice to ensure that they pass accurately.

If players stand as shown in Figure 16.2, they may get caught offside. The reason for this is that once Player A has played the ball to Player B, then Player A is technically standing in an offside position (i.e., in front of the player with the ball).

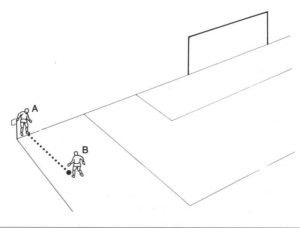

Figure 16.2
Improper set-up in the short corner.

Short Corner Variations

Many variations can be played at a short corner. Two very effective moves involve a third player who moves up from a deep-lying situation to cross the ball. This player can be brought into play by an extension of the basic move, in that instead of crossing the ball the kicker plays the ball back to the deep supporting player who crosses the ball from a different angle. Or the third player can be brought into play when the kicker ignores the basic move and plays the ball directly back to the support player (after the fullback has moved forward unnoticed) (Figures 16.3 and 16.4).

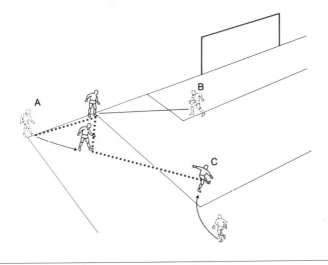

Figure 16.3
Variation 1 on the short corner kick.

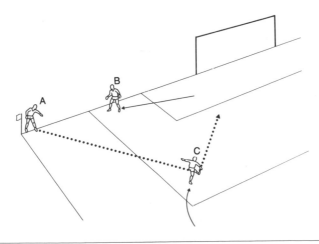

Figure 16.4
Variation 2 on the short corner kick.

In Figure 16.3, Player B comes from the near post; Player A plays the ball into the path of Player C, who moves from a deep position to center the ball. In Figure 16.4, Player B comes from the near post, but Player A kicks the ball to Player C to center.

Another very effective move is played when the player who always supports the kicker for the basic move comes to the corner to prepare for the kick but is then sent back by the kicker who pretends to elect to take a long corner. As the decoy player turns his or her back on the kicker and begins to walk along the goal line back toward the goal, the kicker rolls the ball forward along the goal line for the decoy player to use. This move has the advantage of getting a player with the ball into the penalty area at a position ideal for a pass back to an incoming shooter.

The Long Corner

Only your very best kickers should be allowed to take the long corners. Hold elimination competitions during practice to select those who can kick the ball into the goal area consistently well. Ideally, you want at least one specialist from each side of the field because inswing corner kicks, in which the ball spins dangerously toward the goal, are always more effective than outswing corner kicks, in which the ball spins away from the goal and is usually less dangerous (Figure 16.5). This means that you must cultivate a left-footed kicker to take corner kicks from the right-hand side of the field and vice versa (Figure 16.6).

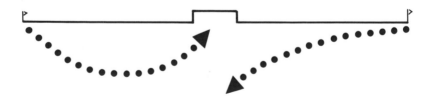

Figure 16.5
The inswing and outswing long corner kick.

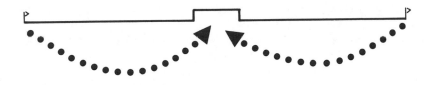

Figure 16.6

Right-footed players take the corner to get an inswing from the left side of the field. Left-footed players take the corner to get an inswing from the right side of the field.

Attack at Long Corners

Use seven attacking players (plus one kicker) and teach them to make the formation shown in Figure 16.7. With younger players, each player can have a landmark to stand on. These landmarks are carefully detailed and should be memorized by the players.

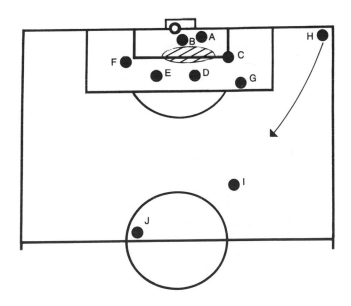

Figure 16.7
Attacking positions at corners.

The Landmarks

Take your players to the exact spot on which you want them to stand and give them the following directions.

Player A is just in front of the goalpost nearest the kicker.

Player B is just in front of the goalkeeper (but must not touch or try to interfere with the goalkeeper).

Player C is at the corner of the 6-yard area nearest the kicker.

Players D and E are in line with the penalty spot opposite to the left and right goalposts, respectively.

Player F is at the corner of the 6-yard area furthest from the kicker but moves in as the kick is taken.

Player G is on the penalty area line opposite the 6-yard line nearest the kicker.

In this formation, players can attack the goal and the shaded area, take advantage of any rebounds or knockdowns, collect any semicleared corners, and get possession of any corner kick that a teammate kicks inaccurately. The kicker, Player H, should run directly back toward his or her own half of the field regardless of the accuracy of the kick. Many inexperienced players simply stand and watch what happens! Tell your kicker to kick and run back. Players I and J stay back as shown to defend against a fast break.

Tactical Variations for Long Corners

Tactical variations at long corners are of two types: near-post plays (in which the target area is the goalpost nearest the kicker) and far-post plays (in which the target area is the goalpost furthest from the kicker).

Near-Post Plays

Near-post plays have two main variations. The target player, who is positioned in or moves into the near-post area (Player A in Figure 16.8), either tries a direct strike on goal, usually by heading the ball, or back-heads the ball into the area in front of goal, hopefully into the path of the three converging attackers or to the player in front of the goalkeeper or any attacker who positions in front of the goalkeeper. In Figure 16.9, Player A heads directly into the goal or tries to flick the ball toward Players B, C, or D.

Far-Post Plays

Here the kicker aims to land the ball in the area at the far side of the goal. Ideally this target area is outside the reach of the goalkeeper (at least 6 yards from the goal) but close enough to the goal to enable an incoming player to achieve a direct strike on goal, usually by heading the ball. A target landing area 8 to 10 yards from the goal line is ideal. In Figure 16.9, Player A runs forward to draw opponents to the near post, but the corner is played long for other forwards coming in.

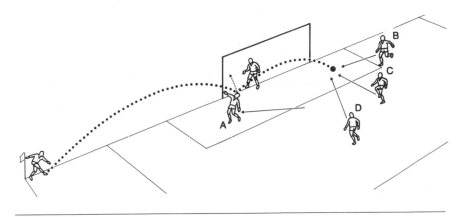

Figure 16.8
Player A heads the ball directly into the goal or tries to flick the ball to the far post for players B, C, or D coming in.

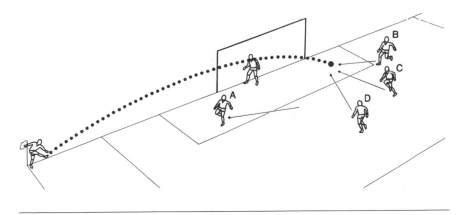

Figure 16.9
Player A runs forward to draw opponents to the near post, but the corner is played long for other forwards coming in.

Give a Signal

Attackers can confuse defenders by making decoy runs and executing tactics from either the long or the short corner moves. Such moves, of course, must be rehearsed and signaled for maximum benefit. All players must understand that only the player taking the kick can signal the move.

The Same Starting Move

The reader may have noticed that one player (Player A in Figures 16.8 and 16.9) makes the same starting move regardless of whether it is a near-post or a far-post move. This kind of consistency is an important advantage to your team, as players gain confidence by rehearsing and executing tactical moves.

Defense at Corners

Professional teams normally use a combination of two defensive systems, which cover both the danger areas (zone marking) and the danger players individually (one-on-one). For younger players, this is too complicated. A simpler method involves assigning each player a zone with instructions to be the first to the ball if it comes into that zone.

Organization

Figure 16.10 shows the organization of eight players plus one goalkeeper. During critical moments in the game (e.g., you are winning 1-0 with a minute to play), bring all 11 players back into defense. Note that Players I and J, the two forwards, should stay upfield in wide positions and try to attract at least three defenders by moving about.

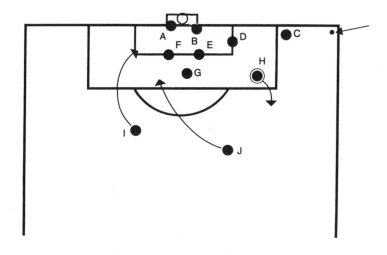

Figure 16.10
Defensive positions at corners.

Landmarks

Again, place your players on the exact spot, and then give them their landmarks.

The goalkeeper is in the center of the goal line, facing at a 45° angle to the field.

Player A is on the goal line behind the goalkeeper.

Player B is just outside and just ahead of the post nearest the kicker.

Player C is 10 yards from the kicker and in line with the intended line of the kick.

Player D is in the middle of the 6-yard line.

Player E is on the 6-yard line opposite the near post.

Player F is on the 6-yard line opposite the far post.

Player G is on the penalty spot.

Player H is in the corner of the penalty area. This player is also in the best position to break away because most corners are defended on the same side.

Players I and J remain upfield unless needed in a crisis situation.

The Perfect Clearance

Encourage your defenders to clear the ball away for height, width, and distance.

Height gains time, width gets the ball away from the shooting zone, and distance relieves the pressure. The perfect clearance from a corner kick has height, width, and distance and reaches one of your own players!

The Attacking Free Kick

One of the most effective of all the free kicks at goal is the direct shot, especially the curved or swerved shot, which can bend around the defensive wall. The second most effective play is one that involves two players. Three or more players who combine in a rehearsed move must spend a great deal of time in practice. Such moves are difficult for young players to master and are not recommended.

One-Player Moves

The most effective and spectacular move at a direct free kick involves your best kicker taking a direct shot (often a swerved or banana kick) at goal. Such moves improve if other players make decoy runs, but these moves basically depend upon your kicker, who must practice.

The Direct or Swerve Shot

We have already covered the technique of swerving the ball (p. 162). Select your best two or three players and let them practice shooting around a wall made up of two corner posts and a piece of string positioned at different places in the penalty area. Use a kicking tee at first to encourage the swerve shot (Figure 16.11). In Figure 16.11, players swerve the ball around the wall aiming for the top corners of the goal.

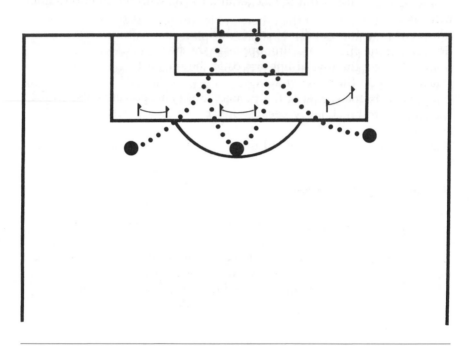

Figure 16.11
A safe way to practice the swerve shot at goals is to shoot from different positions.

Two-Player Moves

A player can either play the ball over the wall or around it. With two-player moves, the kicker passes the ball sideways for a colleague to shoot, or the kicker lofts the ball over the wall for other attackers to head or shoot at goal.

Passing the Ball Sideways

Several moves can be successful when the ball is simply played sideways to open up a space at the side of the wall through which the ball can be aimed. The kicker can play the ball either way, left or right, but it is usually better to play the ball toward the center of the goal because this improves the size of the target (the goal).

Again the kicker must signal his intention in some way, and the designated shooter should always allow at least 5 yards to move forward to make the shot. Younger players usually need this amount of space to prepare (balance) themselves for the instep drive.

In a useful variation of the sideways pass, two players face each other, feet wide apart. From this position, either player can play the ball sideways through the legs of the other. In Figure 16.12, Players A and B are on the ball, facing each other. Player A plays the ball through the legs of Player B for Player C to shoot. Note that Player C remains at least 5 yards behind the point at which the ball is actually kicked so that he or she can balance and time the approach run to the ball. For this reason the players concerned must practice. Note that the pass is made toward the center of the goal.

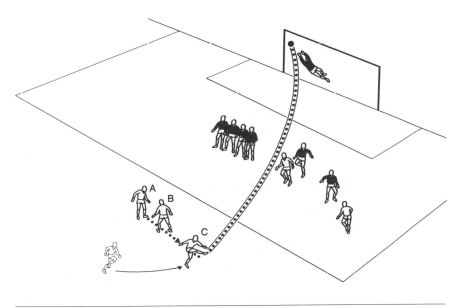

Figure 16.12
A variation of the sideways pass.

Crossing the Ball

This is a very simple but dangerous alternative move at a set free kick. It is like a corner kick and can be played to the near or far post (usually the far-post area). The kicker simply lofts the ball over the defensive line into the path of designated attackers converging on goal. In Figure 16.13,

Player A plays the ball long over the wall to the near post so Player B can head for goal. This is a simple move but must be practiced to ensure that Player B times the run correctly.

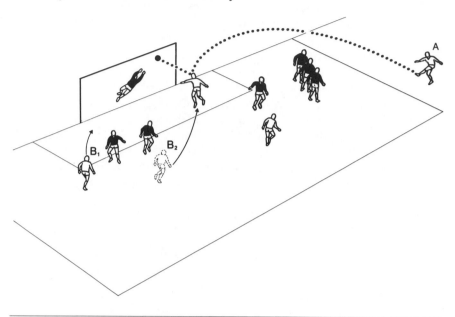

Figure 16.13
A technique for crossing the ball at a set free kick.

Tactical Variations at Free Kicks

Free kicks have many effective variations, and every good coach will enjoy creating his or her own moves. Among the standard moves are those that involve putting one of your own players into or at the end of the defensive wall; at the last moment that player moves out and away from the wall, leaving a space through which the shooter aims. Such a tactic is unlikely to be effective against a well-organized defense, however, because players will simply re-form behind the player.

The attacker-in-the-wall theme has two effective variations. The attacker in the defensive wall can move forward to the kicker and play the ball sideways for the shooter, or that player can turn behind the wall and shoot a chipped pass over the wall.

In Figure 16.14, Player A stands in the wall. As Player B kicks, Player A moves forward and passes to Player C, who shoots. In Figure 16.15, Player B stands in the wall. As Player A chips, Player B turns, collects the chip, and shoots.

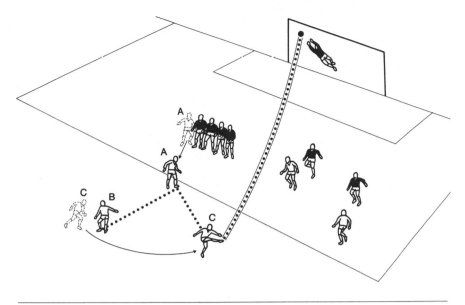

Figure 16.14
Variation 1 of the attacker in the wall.

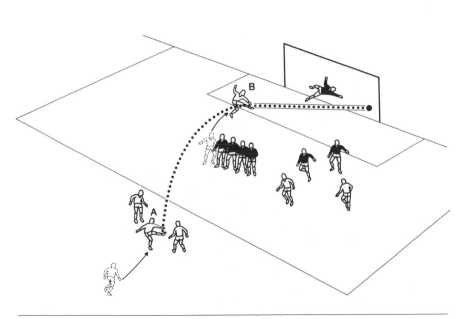

Figure 16.15
Variation 2 of the attacker in the wall.

Ignoring the Wall

A very effective alternative is to ignore the wall altogether and simply get one of your players to the goal line, from which position a shot, or more likely a cross, can be made. In Figure 16.16, Player A runs behind the wall, making sure he or she is not offside, in order to take Player X out of position. Player B runs from the rear into the space behind the wall. He or she can now shoot or cross the ball.

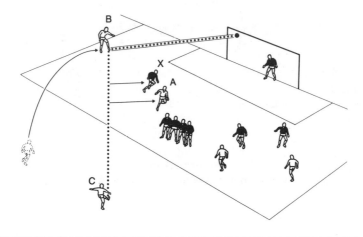

Figure 16.16
In Variation 3 the attacker ignores the wall.

Playing the Ball Behind the Wall

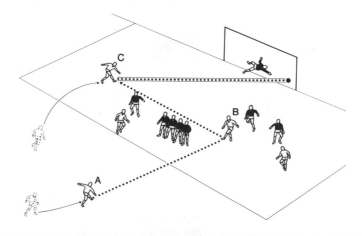

Figure 16.17
In Variation 4 the attackers play the ball behind the wall.

In this move, as shown in Figure 16.17, Player B positions behind and to the side of the wall. Player A plays the ball to Player B so Player B can play the ball behind the line to Player C, who runs from a deep position to shoot. Note that in this move, Player A has to play the ball to Player B's left foot so that Player B can make an accurate, flowing pass. If the move is on the other side of the penalty area, the pass is made by Player B's right foot.

Defense of Free Kicks

All 10 outfield players must be prepared to defend at free kicks, either by joining the defensive wall or by occupying key positions around it. The first decision—how many players in the wall—should be made by the goalkeeper according to the position of the kick.

The number of players is determined by the position of the ball (Figure 16.18). In Area 2, you need two players because of the acute angle. In Area 3, you need three players. (In extreme cases of an indirect free kick inside the goal area, all 10 players would be positioned in the wall.)

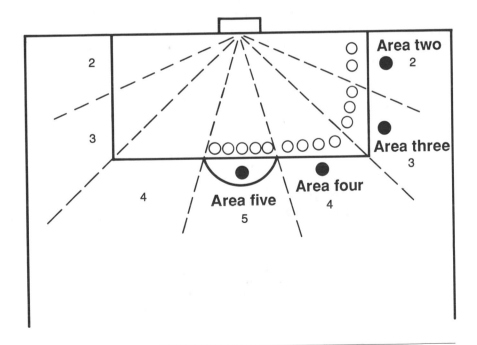

Figure 16.18
The number of players needed in the defensive wall is determined by the area of the field where the ball is.

Making a Wall

Figure 16.19
The key player in this wall is the one to the far left.

The key player in the wall is the one who has the goalpost directly behind his or her head (Figure 16.19). When players are in this position, the goalkeeper can cover the remaining half of the goal because few junior players can swerve the ball around the key player. However, if you think that the opposition does have such a player, position your defenders so that the post is directly behind the head of the second player (Figure 16.20). This makes the wall very safe from the outside curve, but increases the risk of an inside curve shot.

Figure 16.20
This set-up helps defend the goal from the outside curve.

How to Stand on the Wall

Boys can stand facing the kick with their hands held in front. Girls should stand sideways to the kick, looking over their shoulders at the ball. The end girl faces the opposite way that the rest are facing (Figure 16.21).

Figure 16.21
Girls should stand sideways to the kick for protection.

Positioning Around the Wall

The players who are left after the wall has been formed must be positioned to stop or reduce the success of the opposition's attacking moves. In particular, the remaining players must cover the area into which a sideways pass might penetrate and the area into which a lofted kick might be directed.

Figure 16.22 shows a typical way defending players might be positioned against a free kick requiring four players in the wall. Players A, B, C, and D are the wall. Players E and F stop the side pass; Players G, H, and I stop the high cross; and Player J stops the wing move.

Figure 16.22
A typical defense at free kicks.

The Goalkeeper

Having decided on the size of the wall, the goalkeeper should not control how it is positioned. This role must be undertaken by a nominated outfield player so the goalkeeper can watch for a quickly taken kick or shot at goal.

The goalkeeper's position on the goal line is determined by two priorities: The goalkeeper must be able to see the ball and must be on the most vulnerable side, which is the one not covered by the wall. However, the goalkeeper must not stand too far from the center of the goal line because of the danger of the swerve shot. The best compromise is to stand where the ball can be seen and as near to the center of the goal line as possible.

Coaching Set Plays

Because of their importance, tactical moves from corners, throw-ins, and free kicks have to be rehearsed many times, as during the heat of the moment even experienced players can forget or ignore what they have practiced.

First, you should appoint a player to mastermind your set plays and advise the other players which move is to be attempted. You will have more than one player capable of fulfilling this role, and you may have different players for different plays.

Second, you must set aside practice time for coaching and rehearsing set plays. Because set plays usually involve small numbers of players, you can often work with just these units so the players not involved in the play won't be inactive while the others practice. If you have an assistant coach, divide the team into attacking and defensive units for practice and then bring the two together in attack versus defense situations directed toward creating set play situations.

Third, have a simple playbook that contains the moves you have practiced and identifies players' roles. These plays can be revised during chalk-and-talk sessions and studied by the players on their own time.

One of the hallmarks of a good coach is that his or her players know exactly how to organize themselves for set plays and how to use these plays successfully in games. Set plays represent the only point in the game when you have possession of the ball, the opposition must allow you 10 yards of space to execute your move, and they do not know what to expect. You must take advantage of these conditions by being well prepared.

CHAPTER 17

Coaching Tactics and Teamwork—Methods

Coaching in game situations is not easy, especially in an 11 vs. 11 match, because so much is going on and the players don't really want to be stopped and coached. As a result, coaching often is reduced to refereeing or watching or, worse still, to a verbal commentary to which players don't listen.

The best way to approach the problem is to ask three questions: What do I want to coach, where is the best part of the field to coach, and what methods shall I use?

What Do I Coach?

First, you should always have a theme in mind. This will be based on how your team played in the last match, how you hope they will play in the next match, and your long-term program and system of play.

Second, you will normally choose from one of five themes.

1. How to play when your team has possession of the ball
2. How to play when the opposition has the ball
3. What to do at the moment the ball changes possession—the breakdown point
4. What to do at restarts and set plays
5. How to encourage players to help each other

Where Do I Coach?

Always set up your coaching practice in the area of the field where such play normally takes place (e.g., coach the goalkeeper in the goal, the winger on the wing).

You must always be on the field of play yourself, close to the center of action but never inside it where you will only get in the way of the players.

How Do I Coach?

I have found five methods most helpful: game conditioning, silent soccer, advance calling, the playback system, and videotaping.

Game Conditioning

The first method, game conditioning, can improve teamwork. For example, if you are unhappy about the way your players ran to support each other in their last game, you might play two-touch soccer. If your defenders watch where the ball goes rather than where their opponent goes, you might play one-on-one marking. You can also invent special rules. For example, blowing the whistle twice in succession might mean that the team in possession has given away an indirect free kick against themselves. You can now watch to see how quickly players react at the breakdown point when the ball changes hands. Similarly, three quick blasts on the whistle might indicate a direct free kick. You can now see how well your players form a defensive wall or use a rehearsed set play.

Silent Soccer

One of the best conditioned games to encourage good team play is silent soccer. In this game, no player is allowed to call out or even whisper for any reason. The penalty for doing so is a direct free kick. Players quickly realize that they have to think and act entirely for themselves. Because no one tells them what to do or how to play, their actions are entirely the result of their own thoughts. You can see what they are thinking. Further, because the players are quiet, it is much easier to communicate with them, and you won't finish the practice with a headache or a sore throat!

Use silent soccer for limited periods, and hear and see the difference. This is a boon for coaches of the noisy young, and it is much enjoyed by the more sensitive players who for once are not continually shouted at by teammates. Silent soccer is a thinking and acting game—the essence of good soccer.

Advance Calling

With this method the coach thinks ahead for the players, for example, "Kelly, make a through pass to Chris." Because the coach is not actually playing, he or she can more easily think ahead; by talking to the players, the coach can help them develop tactical appreciation.

This method keeps the game flowing, and the players learn while playing. It is most important when introducing new players to plays, especially set plays such as free kicks.

The Playback System

This method is the most important of all coaching methods. Here you reconstruct or play back what has happened so that you can demonstrate not only what happened but why. Further, you can then show players what should have happened, which is always the most effective way of communicating good tactical play.

This method has six stages:

- Arrange and start the practice.
- Watch and wait.
- Stop the practice and move to the focal point.
- Rearrange the players.
- Replay the move correctly.
- Restart play.

Stage 1—Arrange and Start the Practice

Imagine that you play a 4:2:4 system and that you want to coach the four defenders, who did not cover each other very well in the previous game. In this case, you would choose an attack versus defense practice (p. 305) and position yourself behind and to the side of the defenders (Figure 17.1). To get a realistic start you might kick the ball forward over the heads of your defenders to one of the attacking players.

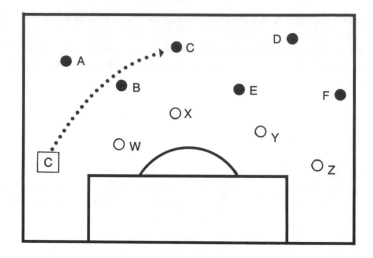

Figure 17.1
Stage 1—A realistic start.

Stage 2—Watch and Wait

Now, simply watch and wait until one of your defenders either covers a colleague particularly well or makes a bad mistake. Try to select a good example because, as discussed in chapter 2, this will give you a double positive effect. In Figure 17.2, Player F cannot outmaneuver Player Z, so Player F passes to Player E. Player Y fails to react.

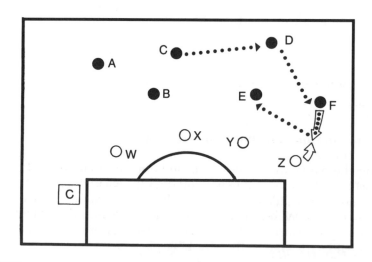

Figure 17.2
Stage 2—Player Y fails to react.

Stages 3—Stop the Practice and Move to the Focal Point

Stop the play by using a clear command like "freeze" or "stop" rather than with your whistle. Then move quickly to the key player, the one who you want to coach or use as your example (Player Y in Figure 17.3).

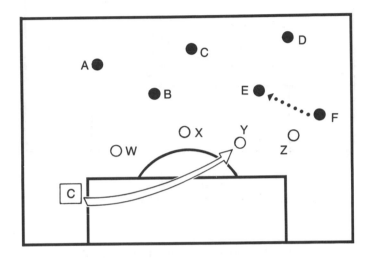

Figure 17.3
Stage 3—Coach moves to the focal point.

Stage 4—Rearrange the Players

Stand by the key player and rearrange the other players into the positions they held at the start of the play. Make sure that everyone can see and hear you.

Stage 5—Replay the Move Correctly

Replay the move to show and explain to the players what happened and what should have happened.

Don't talk too much; if you can, use the question-and-answer technique (chapter 2) to increase player participation. You now replay the move showing the players what should have happened (Figure 17.4).

Show Player Y the correct move, restating the rule, "Nearest defender goes to meet the ball."

Be sure Players W and X also know how they should react.

Stage 6—Restart Play

Put everyone back into their original positions, tell Player F to pass to Player E, and shout "play on." The defenders should now react correctly.

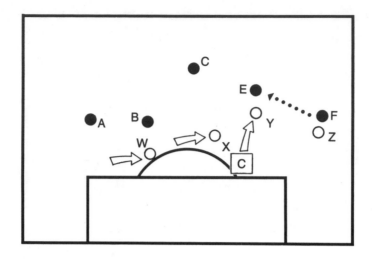

Figure 17.4
Stage 5—Defenders react correctly.

Move away to the side and watch for the next point.

If possible, restart the game with the correct move. It is not always possible, but it does reinforce what you have just explained. The game now continues until you are ready to make your next coaching point.

Videotaping

Videotaping is becoming increasingly popular at all levels of soccer and is particularly valuable for analyzing set plays. It is also very useful for concentrating on individual players, especially the goalkeeper.

I spent two weeks during a world hockey championship in Pakistan recording the moves of selected individual players in order to quantify work rate and design game-related fitness training programs. If you have time or know a friendly parent who can help, why not try something like this yourself? I can offer you some suggestions about filming techniques and the best way to show tapes to players.

Filming Techniques

With hand-held cameras it is very difficult to film wide-angle shots that will make good viewing. Unless you can position yourself high above play, wide-angle shots to capture technical moves are unlikely to be helpful to players. For these reasons, hand-held video cameras are best used in small areas of play. For example, you can videotape the goal area effectively, focus on set moves, and film throw-ins and short corners. You can also, as I did in Pakistan, focus on individual players at least for limited periods of the game. If you do this, however, don't stop your camera when the game stops. Keep the film running, because how a player moves into position while the game is stopped might be significant.

If you have access to a high flat roof or window in an adjacent building and use a tripod, then you can make very good tapes. Alternatively, and only if the authorities allow it, you can get quite good wide-angle shots from a tripod positioned on top of a truck. Much depends upon your local circumstances.

Showing and Using Your Videotape

Having made your tapes, beware! You are now entering what is potentially the greatest time-wasting aspect of coaching. Let me offer some lessons I have learned over the years.

- Never show an unedited tape to your players.
- Having selected the key passages you want to show, prepare your comments either by using a voice-over on the tape itself or by preparing notes.
- Discuss key points or plays as they occur. Don't run the tape through and then ask players to remember or recall events—comment during or immediately after the events.
- Don't allow videotapes to replace your regular field practice. If you have some valuable material, use it to supplement your field coaching. Ideally, have your players arrive early, and show the film before your practice sessions. In this way you will have a wealth of visual references to reinforce your field practices.
- Don't let the length of the tape dictate the length of your viewing session; be very selective and limit your viewing time to effective material.
- Let your players have copies of the edited tape to take home and watch during their leisure time.

Remember that video tapes are very useful coaching devices. However, you must use them correctly for your players to get the maximum benefit.

CHAPTER 18

Coaching Tactics and Teamwork— Practice Situations

The coaching methods described in chapter 17 can be applied in game situations involving up to 22 players. Very often, however, you will want to coach tactics and teamwork with a smaller squad, perhaps 15 or 16 players. Indeed, this is the most common situation for most club coaches. In this chapter I explain three practices designed specifically for such situations, and I also offer ideas on how to encourage players to make good decisions.

Attack Versus Defense Practices

This practice is designed to accommodate a regular team squad of 15 or 16 players. It can also be used with larger groups, but you will have to divide your defenders or attackers into two or three units and coach them on a rotation basis—we call this using wave attacks.

Organization

The practice takes place on one half of a soccer field, each attack starting from the halfway line.

Figure 18.1 shows how to organize your players. Defenders play their normal positions, and forwards attack them. Midfield players can be used in defense or attack, depending upon the theme of your practice.

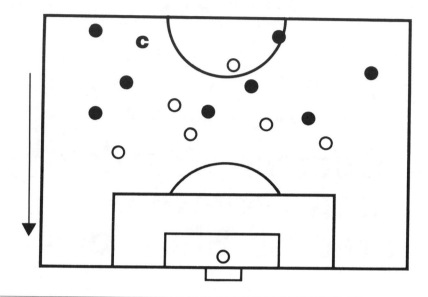

Figure 18.1
Organization of players on a 15- or 16-member squad for practice.

Starting the Practice

First, the defenders must move upfield and stay clear of the penalty area. Second, you start each attack with a realistic pass to a different player so that a variety of moves develop. Ideally, dribble the ball before you pass, because this gets all the players thinking and moving as they would in a game. An alternative way of starting the practice is for the goalkeeper to distribute the ball to an attacker.

Instructions to Players

Give the players the following general instructions.

Attackers: Try to score. If the attack breaks down, give immediate chase to put the defenders under pressure; mark tightly on your side of the field; or run hard to get goalside of the ball if the first two tactics don't work.

Defenders: Try to win possession. Then, play the ball directly to a target player (often the coach, who can then start the next practice); play the ball to the goalkeeper and move out as in a game; interpass and play the ball forward; or in an emergency, clear your lines by playing the ball up-field or over the sideline or even by giving away a corner.

Coaching Progressions

You can develop this practice in four ways.

1. Coach a theme (e.g., accuracy of passing or good support play).
2. Select a small group of players (e.g., the back four defenders, the midfield players, or the strikers), and coach them as a unit. This is the most common way of using the practice and might include, for example, showing the defenders how to cover or showing the forwards and midfield players how to combine in a target player drill.
3. Select an individual player for special coaching. Here you work closely with one player and by giving quiet instructions and advice help him or her to develop tactical awareness. In essence, you see the game through the eyes of the player and try to make decisions with and for that player. Done well, this is a rewarding practice and a great confidence builder.
4. Referee the game, observe what is happening, but say nothing. After a period of time, call the players in to discuss what you have seen.

Shadow Soccer

This practice gets its name from the fact that you start by playing your full team against an imaginary team. This is one of the best ways of teaching players how to combine as a team. Furthermore, when you introduce defenders, it becomes a very realistic and physically demanding practice. (I once watched the Belgian professional team, Liege, complete a 1-hour, nonstop game of shadow soccer, and it was a most impressive workout. Every attack finished with a strike at goal, and both keepers were very active.)

Organization

The practice takes place on a full-size field. Arrange 10 players in their regular team positions with a goalkeeper at each end (Figure 18.2).

One goalkeeper starts the practice with a pass to a defender. The team then builds an attack just as if in a game, finishing with a shot from outside the penalty area or a header at goal from a cross.

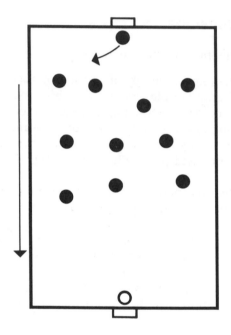

Figure 18.2
Starting to practice shadow soccer.

Immediately after the attack is completed, the practice reverses. Forwards become defenders, defenders become attackers, and midfield players stay where they are; the team now attacks the other goal. This is a popular change for the defenders, who rarely get the opportunity to demonstrate their attacking skills.

Coaching Progressions

Once the players understand the idea of practice without opposition, introduce up to four defenders, positioned as shown in Figure 18.3. Initially, these players must remain in the third of the field in which they are placed, although later they are not restricted.

As the practice develops, allow the defenders to move into an adjacent zone. The attackers will now be faced with two and possibly three defenders in each zone. Finally, allow your defenders to tackle anywhere.

Every time the defenders spoil an attack it counts as a goal for them. Because defending is very exhausting, this last condition is a great motivator.

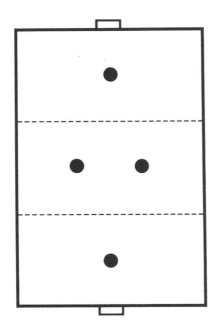

Figure 18.3
Introducing opposition.

Positional Practices for Individuals

Positional practices help individual players learn more about the tactics of their regular position. Occasionally you can coach two players together (e.g., central defenders or twin strikers), but mostly you are concerned with a single player. You must remember two main points.

First, to coach an individual player to improve tactical awareness or develop a particular skill, you should develop the chosen activity in stages. In this way you can introduce the player to the activity in simple, straightforward steps that allow you to make your coaching points and at the same time encourage the player to develop confidence. For example, you can start by working with the individual player and gradually introduce defending and attacking players. As the players improve, you can then move into set plays, attack versus defense situations, or even a full game.

Second, remember that the most important factor is that the player makes or tries to make the right decisions. Good execution is important, but of greater concern at this time are the player's thought processes.

The following example shows how positional practices are developed through a series of progressions.

Coaching the Target Player in Attack

Imagine that your center forward or one of your strikers never seems to play well when receiving a pass with his or her back toward the opponents' goal. For example, the player is reluctant to try to control the ball, turn with it, attack the defense, and shoot for goal. The following discussion demonstrates how a progressive practice could be developed to help this player; remember that this method is applicable to any position or player.

Stage 1

Position the player on the part of the field that is most realistic for practice—in our case the D area outside the penalty area, with the player's back toward goal. Have a supporting player stand 10 to 15 yards away and feed in a number of realistic passes for the target player to bring under control (Figure 18.4).

Stage 2

Encourage the target player to not only control the ball but to turn with it, look at the goal, and shoot. The shot should be released from just inside or on the edge of the penalty area. During these practices you can check on the techniques that the target player uses for controlling, turning, and shooting, and you can begin to implant the sequence of events in the player's mind. At this stage you might also ask the server to play the ball in at different heights and speeds, thus posing additional control factors for the target player. Remember to encourage a shot at goal.

Stage 3

At this stage, introduce additional players and begin to increase the realism of the practice (Figure 18.5).

First introduce a defender positioned immediately behind the target player, as in a real game. This defender might initially be passive but

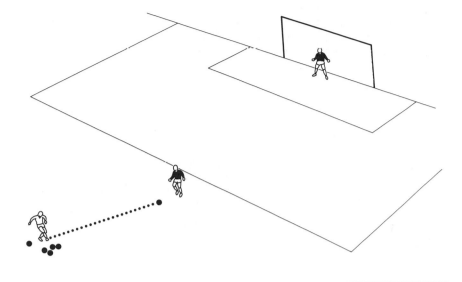

Figure 18.4

The first step in coaching the target player in attack is to recreate the starting position.

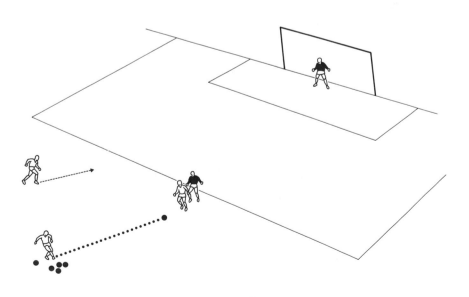

Figure 18.5

Introduce the opposition.

increasingly becomes more and more active, thus presenting a realistic challenge. If the target player can control the ball, turn, and release a shot on goal under these conditions, he or she is doing quite well.

Stage 4

Next, introduce a second attacking player, which will present the target player with an alternative strategy. The target player can now screen the ball from the defender and pass to the supporting player, who shoots for goal. Providing an alternative to the target player creates a decision-making situation similar to that experienced in the game. The player should by now have developed the confidence to either beat the defender or screen the ball and then pass it to the supporting attacker. Indeed, if the target player is prepared to screen, take a pass, and then try again to turn and beat the defender, then he or she is playing very well.

Stage 5

Now make the practice more realistic and more complicated by introducing a second defender and a third attacker (Figure 18.6). Immediately the number of alternatives for the target player increases. Encourage the target player to make his or her own decisions. Coach as necessary, but let the player think independently. The server starts the practice by playing the ball to the target player.

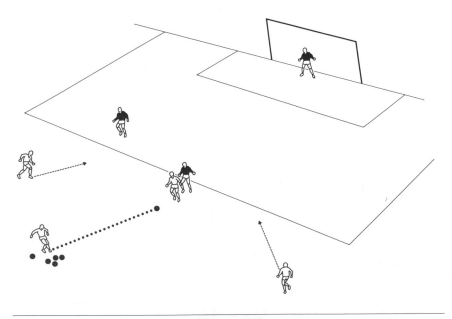

Figure 18.6
Increase realism.

Stage 6

The final stage is to play attack versus defense (chapter 18) or to play a full game and coach the target player during the game. In either case, you ease the player back into the game situation, but he or she is now more knowledgeable about what to do and how to do it.

Good Decision Making

You will observe four kinds of decision-making situations when you are coaching, each of which requires a different coaching strategy. The four situations are

- correct decision–successful execution,
- correct decision–unsuccessful execution,
- incorrect decision–successful execution, and
- incorrect decision–unsuccessful execution.

These alternatives are arranged in Table 18.1, which offers appropriate coaching strategies.

Table 18.1 Decision Making

Decision	Execution	Your reaction	Reason
Correct decision	Successful execution	"Great. Good decision and good execution—well done."	This is a double positive situation—everyone wins. Now make the task a little harder!
Correct decision	Unsuccessful execution	"Good try. You made the right decision, and this is what matters."	Reinforce the fact that the decision was correct. Repeat the practice until the execution improves.

(Cont.)

Table 18.1   (Continued)

Decision	Execution	Your reaction	Reason
Incorrect decision	Successful execution (e.g., player gets away with an incorrect pass)	"O.K. The pass/shot/head was a good one, but tactically you could have . . . It would have been better to . . ."	Don't overreact. Acknowledge what was right, but then focus on the decision.
Incorrect decision	Unsuccessful execution	"That wasn't very good, was it? Don't worry about what happened to the ball. Let's question what you tried to do and why."	Don't over-criticize—nobody makes a mistake on purpose. Focus on the intent.

PART IV

TEAM MANAGEMENT

In Part IV, I present my ideas on team management. I explain the activities I use to prepare my teams for competitive games, my approach to mental preparation and tactics talks, my methods for handling difficult players (including the problem of dropping a player), and the activities I recommend for fitness training.

CHAPTER 19

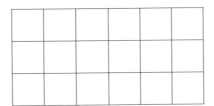

Physical and Mental Preparation for Games

You must consider two aspects, the physical and the mental, when preparing your team for competition. However, do not think that because I present mental and physical aspects separately I believe that they are separate things, that there is a simple distinction between mind and body. Nothing could be further from the truth. Throughout this book I have tried to promote the holistic concept of the person.

Physical Preparation

Proper physical preparation for a match is essential if your players are to perform their best. Proper physical preparation also reduces the chances of players being injured while playing.

Warm-Up Program

In soccer, most injuries occur during the first 15 minutes of the game because of insufficient warm-up and during the last 15 minutes because of fatigue. Thus you should try to get your players as fit as possible and always give them a thorough warm-up before play starts. For young players, who seldom pull muscles, warm-up activities may include some drills with the ball, but for older players, especially adults, I recommend a set program.

Initial Warm-Up

Many people start their warm-up by stretching; this is wrong. Muscles respond best when they are warm, so the correct way to start a warm-up is with general body exercises that increase the heart rate and the breathing rate. For safety, these general body movements must also be low impact activities, that is, they must not expose the muscles to violent or sudden stretching to the full extent of their range.

Ideal starting exercises include running in place or skipping; the best practice is to gently run backward and forward across the field six times. The first two runs should be gentle and loose, the movements free and relaxed. The third and fourth runs can include sideways and backward movements. The final two runs should be at increased tempo and should consist of four phases—jog, stride, accelerate, and slow down—each phase covering about 15 yards. In cold or inclement weather, players should wear warm-up suits.

After the starting exercise, players are ready to begin progressive stretching. The stretches must concentrate on the front, back, insides of the thighs, and on the spine. Goalkeepers must also include gently rolling and springing movements as well as shoulder mobility exercises. All stretches should be static stretches, that is, the muscle should be gently extended into a stretch position and held for 10 seconds. Don't let your players bounce up and down using ballistic movements, as such actions are dangerous. When static stretching is over, the players should then move into ball drills.

WARM-UP SEQUENCE FOR SOCCER

Engage in running activities as described previously.

Stand, hold ankle, and stretch the thigh backwards; alternate legs (Figure 19.1).

Figure 19.1

Cross feet. Static stretch the hamstrings by letting the body and arms hang down. Do not bounce up and down. Change feet and repeat (Figure 19.2).

Figure 19.2

Shake and loosen arms and legs.

Open groin muscles (adductors) by stretching the inside of the legs gently (Figure 19.3).

Figure 19.3

Raise knee and turn leg 90° sideways. This opens the groin in a second direction or plane. Place hand on the raised knee for balance (Figure 19.4).

Figure 19.4

Shake and loosen arms and legs.

Stretch arms above head. Bend slowly backward as if preparing to throw the ball. Gently simulate the throwing action a few times (Figure 19.5).

Figure 19.5

Finish with a 5-second run in place or short sprints across the field, then move into ball skills preparation.

Note: A stretching session is an ideal time for final tactics talks and mental preparation.

Ball Skills Preparation

All players need time to prepare their ball skills before the game. I always advise that they carry out a prearranged series of activities in small groups (Figure 19.6). Some examples follow.

Goalkeeper.   The substitutes prepare the goalkeeper by volleying balls to him or her from short range. This gives the goalkeeper the feel of the ball. The substitutes should then play a variety of balls from just inside the penalty area to give their goalkeeper practice at dealing with shots and crosses from both wings. Younger players should kick crosses from their hands to get height and accuracy. If the sun is out, the goalkeeper should practice while facing the sun to get used to this condition.

Defenders.   The defenders work together in pairs (e.g., two fullbacks and two center backs). They should practice dealing with high dropping balls and, like the goalkeeper, must practice against weather elements like the sun and wind. They must also practice long kicking, quick turning, and defensive heading.

Midfield Players.   These players practice in their own group, using lots of short passing for accuracy. They must get the feel of the ball on the surface. Older players should practice chipping the ball, dribbling, and turning.

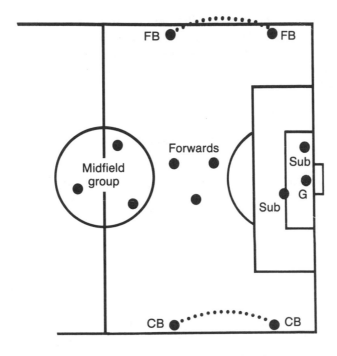

Figure 19.6
Pregame skills practice organization.

Forwards.   These players do not go straight to the goal to practice shooting. They need to practice lots of short passing with each other, such as one-two passes and wall passes. They must also practice dribbling, attacking heading skills, and corner kicks. When the goalkeeper has finished his or her preparation, the forwards should practice shooting at the goal. When they shoot, they should build up the power of the shot—too hard too soon can be dangerous. The specialist penalty kicker should also have a few practice penalty kicks.

Substitutes.   Keep your substitutes warm and give them at least 5 minutes notice before asking them to play. Warming up before the game does not keep them warmed up throughout! On the contrary, they cool off quite quickly and should keep active by running and stretching every 10 minutes or so and by doing ball work.

Cooling Down

If your players are in a tournament, they need at least 10 minutes of cooling down activities after the game. This helps to disperse lactic acid and clear the muscles. The ideal activities are the running and stretching activities you gave to the players before the game. This should be moderate work starting with jogging and strides and gradually slowing to stretches. You will find that the only way to get a good cooling down session is to conduct it yourself.

Mental Preparation

In sports, mental preparation is just as important as physical preparation. Coaches need to carefully prepare athletes mentally for competition. Poor mental readiness can be more detrimental to performance than poor physical readiness.

Pregame Talks

Overly dramatic talks in the locker room can be counterproductive. A well-known psychological law—the Yerkes Dodson Law—says that when performing skillful activities players have an optimum level of arousal or excitement. If you try to motivate some players too much, especially introverts, you can actually reduce their performance of skillful tasks because they become too emotional and excited. For example, you might make a sensitive goalkeeper too anxious to catch the ball properly or make a young center forward unable to stay composed in the penalty area. Even an experienced player can have these problems, and you don't want to contribute to them.

To make players competitive, you have to get your psychology right. This means recognizing that any team contains a mixture of personalities. You must handle players individually and be careful when using prematch talks to psych up the whole team at the same time. Young players often need calming down more than psyching up. Emotions such as frustration, anger, fear, and jealousy usually interfere with performance. Successful players are competitive but not overanxious. They can retain their composure and stay cool under pressure. The strategies I use to try to achieve and sustain this ideal are as follows.

The Positive Approach

When I give pregame tactics talks I always try to use positive reinforcement. I continually reinforce the good, rather than the bad, by referring to movements, styles, or skills that have been successful. I do this so players will form mental images of the good plays they have made in

After the Game

After the game, I thank the referee and the coach of the opposing team. They are (or should be) friendly colleagues seeking to encourage the same goals as you are, and they have the same emotions! When I talk to players after the game, I use one of four strategies, which depend upon the result of the game and the manner in which the team played. The latter point is more important in determining what I say and how I say it. The four strategies are as follows:

1. **The team played well but lost.**

   Approach: "Well done! You played well today and should feel no disgrace in losing."

   Reason: A track and field athlete who achieves a personal best may not win the event but will gain satisfaction from having performed well. Similarly, if your team really did play well, players should not feel despondent because the result went against them. The best team doesn't always win.

2. **The team played well and won.**

   Approach: "Well done! You played well, and you deserved to win."

   Reason: Let your players enjoy victory, and enjoy it with them. At the same time try to get your players to associate winning with playing well. The best team doesn't always win, but it usually does!

3. **The team played badly and lost.**

   Approach: "Well, we didn't play very well today, so we didn't win. We'll work it out at practice.

   Reason: If the team didn't play well there is no point in disguising the fact, but remember that nobody plays badly on purpose. Don't dwell on failure and don't criticize your players when they are down.

4. **The team played badly but won.**

   Approach: "We didn't play very well today, but at least we still won! See you at practice."

   Reason: You want your players to enjoy having won, but you know that it was a poor performance and that at the next coaching session you will be working hard to improve their play.

These four strategies provide the basis of what you need to say to the whole team after the game. I try to leave the "winning is everything" philosophy to the professionals, and I try not to overreact to either victory or defeat. As Rudyard Kipling advised, "Treat those two impostors [success and disaster] just the same!"

A coach of young players must try to ensure that the players love playing soccer regardless of the result. With young players, I try to promote the importance of the intrinsic satisfaction of playing well over the extrinsic reward of winning.

CHAPTER 20

Handling Problem Players

Every coach has to deal with problem players, from violent or argumenta-tive players to those who simply arrive late for practice every week. Coaches must deal with so many different kinds of problems that any ''solutions'' are at best little more than suggestions about how to approach a problem. Nevertheless, many problems have a familiar pattern or cause and I feel it is worthwhile to identify these problems and to consider ways in which they might be resolved.

This chapter begins with prevention, because I feel that many of the problems I have had to face could have been avoided with better manage-ment! Problems very often develop as a direct result of your own person-ality or the manner in which you approach a situation.

Prevention, Not Cure

Have you ever considered that players only become difficult when they behave in a manner that conflicts with your personal views about what should be done, about what you think is right? Players who conform to the coach's expectations rarely cause a problem; the nonconformists are more difficult! For this reason, I always make sure that players under-stand my general expectations. I also let them know that my expectations are accepted by parents and assistant coaches. For example, I tell players my views about punctuality, about giving notice if a player cannot attend practice or has to leave early, and about the attitudes I expect my players to demonstrate toward officials, opponents, and teammates. In this way I try to establish with my players an agreed-upon code of practice that will ensure that everyone knows what is expected.

Second, I try not to take good behavior for granted. I make a point of reinforcing the code of practice from time to time by rewarding behaviors ranging from shaking hands after the game to never arguing with the referee.

Third, I try to be consistent. Consistency is one of the hallmarks of a good leader. Players should be able to anticipate how you will react in given situations, and they should be able to model their behavior after yours. For example, you cannot tell your players not to argue with the referee if you yourself enter into a public argument with the same official. Similarly, you must react consistently with different players and offer no special privileges for your best players.

Fourth, I always try to be optimistic that any problem can be resolved. This approach is a challenge to my initiative and usually elicits a better response from players. Imagine the reaction of a player to a coach who said, ''Oh dear! I don't think I can help you improve.''

Fifth, and perhaps most importantly, I have learned that it doesn't always pay to try to find an immediate solution. Certainly, some situations do require an immediate, almost instinctive, reaction (e.g., a sharp word of caution to a player who is about to start an argument). Most of the problems examined in this chapter, however, are more deep-seated and will test both your knowledge and your management skills. With many of the more serious problems, the player must first accept that he or she really does have a problem. As I shall argue, finding out that you cause other people a problem can be an embarrassing or hurtful experience. Spending time preparing your strategy will often pay off in the long run.

Finally, please remember that the way to handle a problem player might be to enlist outside help, for example, another player, a friend, a parent, or a doctor. What matters most is that the problem is solved, not who solves it.

The Ball Hog

Ball hogs are usually skillful dribblers because they get so much practice with the ball, and they often mature into good adult players. Certainly they believe that by keeping possession they are acting in the best interests of the team because they will eventually produce a game-winning play. Generally, however, they hold the ball too long, lose possession, and frustrate teammates, especially those who have worked hard to get into good supporting positions. Worse still, other team members might even stop running to support them or be reluctant to pass the ball to them.

Solutions

Start with a question to the player: "Do you realize that on occasion you hold the ball too long and that this is hindering our team play?" Depending upon the answer you receive, and given that the player cannot correct the problem alone, you can use any or all of the following strategies.

In Practice

Explain to the player that for set periods of time, he or she will be conditioned to play two-touch (or even one-touch) soccer. This forces the player to release the ball quickly and requires the player to run hard to get into good supporting positions. This will demonstrate to him or her just how frustrating it is to run into good positions but not receive a pass.

If the player shows improvement you can begin to relax this condition (e.g., he or she can play normally when in the opponents' penalty area).

Also, supplement team practices with 1 vs. 1 dribbling competitions so that the ball hog and others can practice their dribbling skills. This is most important as it provides the ball hog a legitimate stage upon which to demonstrate prowess.

On Match Days

Give special reminders to the players during pregame talks; for example, "Be content to beat one defender," or "Remember that it is dangerous to dribble in your own penalty area."

Set targets; for example, "Last week you were caught in possession of the ball four times. Can you improve on that today?"

Include in your match analysis a record of how many times a player destroyed team play as a result of trying to dribble too much.

Finally, give the ball hog special responsibilities during set plays to help encourage the spirit of unselfish teamwork. For example, put the ball hog in charge of set moves that require the player to make the decoy run.

The Violent Player

There are two different kinds of violent players: the hothead who is guilty of frequent, short outbursts and the player who demonstrates a less frequent but more deep-seated problem.

The Hothead

Hot-tempered outbursts can usually be traced to specific triggering moments such as a hard tackle or a bad call by an official. Some solutions are as follows.

Prevention

In your pregame talks, remind hotheaded players that soccer is a body contact game that involves hard physical knocks.

Remind such players that officials will make mistakes and that players' reactions to such mistakes must always be tactical, not emotional. When a bad call is made, every player should concentrate on getting on with the game so that no one is surprised by a quick counterattack. The player who argues or reacts emotionally loses concentration on the game and temporarily becomes a liability.

Reinforce your points by giving players a model to follow. For example, illustrate your pregame talk with a reference to a fine professional player, preferably a soccer player.

Correction

If preventive measures fail, you must employ correction or punishment of some kind. In order of severity, these include the following.

- Be prepared to substitute the player for a cooling-off period, even though the referee might let an incident pass. If short penalties fail to have an effect, substitute the player for the remaining period of the game.
- Do not include the player in your starting line-up. This will emphasize that playing on your team is a privilege too valuable to sacrifice for a momentary lapse of control.
- If the player does not respond to other measures, you will probably have to suspend the player for a set number of games. Hopefully, your hotheaded player will eventually realize that staying cool means staying in the game!

The Deep-Seated Problem

Players do exist who deliberately inflict pain and suffering on others. This kind of violence is characterized by deliberate kicking, late tackles, tackling over the ball, and fouling when the referee's line of sight is obstructed. There are three solutions.

Expulsion

You can simply expel the player from your team. By doing so you will undoubtedly earn the gratitude and respect of many of your players who know that such behavior is degrading to them by association. Because they are members of the same team, such behavior reflects badly upon them; worse, they may also resort to violence.

Reeducation

Alternatively, you can try to reeducate violent players. In effect, you will be using soccer as a vehicle for socializing the player, because this kind of problem is not caused by soccer but is brought to the game by the player. You can try the following strategies.

- In practice games let the problem player referee; this may help to develop a soccer ethic. Talk to the player privately, pointing out that violence on the soccer field is just as bad as any other violence because it violates one of the most important ethical principles—respect for other persons. State your views on violence at team talks. You need not necessarily mention individuals by name, but you must make your views public and so reinforce your code of practice.
- In competitive games, substitute the player immediately after you see a violent act, especially if the referee fails to see the foul or take action. Or, suspend the player for a fixed number of games.

Outside Help

Seeking outside help is not acknowledgment of failure on your part; on the contrary, it is an example of detached, objective thinking. Such help requires the knowledge and consent of parents or guardians, which reinforces the point that not all problems have an immediate or easy solution. Solving serious problems takes time and thought!

If all these solutions fail, then you must expel the player from your team. You must retain your own integrity as well as the integrity of your team and of the game of soccer. If you take this step, explain your reasons to the player (even if you have to write to him or her) and offer your help if the player wants to try again. This gives the player the opportunity to reflect upon his or her behavior and leaves the door open to try again.

The Timid or Frightened Player

The player who "chickens out" of a tackle or a 1 vs. 1 duel is in many ways more difficult to handle than the violent or aggressive player. You can always command the latter from the field, but you cannot always command the timid player to be brave. A player must want to win the ball, and players who lack this inner drive are difficult to coach. Some young players, for example, will go to great lengths to avoid heading the ball. Even among professional players are those who can be intimidated. Such players will develop a high degree of subterfuge and become adept at arriving at the ball a fraction too late, jumping out of the way to avoid a tackle, or kicking the ball away too hastily. Such avoidance tactics do not happen by chance; players employ these tactics out of fear of being injured.

Solutions

One recognized procedure to overcome fear or anxiety that is very popular with swimming coaches is called counterconditioning. With this technique the player is first removed from the stressful situation and then reintroduced to it in small stages. For example, the frightened nonswimmer is reintroduced to the water through an "anxiety hierarchy" of sitting by the pool followed by gentle, confidence-building activities. When applying this technique to soccer we can approach the problem in two ways.

In Practice

You can give the player special coaching in four key soccer skills, all of which involve a positive act by the player. These are moving to the ball, tackling, shooting practice, and heading.

In each of these practices you should carefully explain the progressions, using the following procedure.

Reintroduce the player to the anxiety-provoking skill in small stages. Make sure that at each stage you allow the player time to enjoy success and thus gain renewed confidence. Give the player your individual personal attention. If you cannot join in the practices as an active performer, choose your helpers wisely and make sure that they are fully informed about what you are trying to do. Use positive reinforcement and, above all, be patient.

In Games

In competitive or even practice games it is more difficult to give your problem player direct help because the other players control the situation. However, you can reward and reinforce successful actions and keep a match analysis.

Use a pregame talk to remind the player to think and act positively and to avoid undue worry about the possibility of injury. Remind the player of successful practice experiences. Keep a record, and encourage the player to keep a personal diary of the number of successful plays during each game. Ideally, the number will increase during the season and thus encourage the player. Positively reinforce every occasion during the game in which the player acts courageously, and use these as examples in future tactics talks. Finally, place your timid player in a position on the field that reduces the possibility of body contact and gives increased room to maneuver. For example, place the player first as a winger; then as the player's confidence grows put him or her into more physically demanding positions. You can also play the timid player short periods of time and by careful substitution reward increasing determination with longer periods of play.

Above all, be patient. You might on occasion successfully force a positive response from a player by loud verbal encouragement, perhaps even mild bullying. But use this approach carefully with sensitive, possibly introverted players, as this approach may inhibit, not improve, performance.

The Dictator

The dictator thinks and acts for everyone, gives a constant stream of commands, and dominates all around, including the weak referee and sometimes the coach. A well-meaning dictator is a problem; a dictator who is also a bully is a much more serious problem. Two such players on one team will cause conflict and other players may take sides to the detriment of the entire team.

Solutions

There are two starting points for dealing with a dictator. First, in your team talks and during practical coaching sessions stress the importance of a good first call. You do not have to explain the single-channel hypothesis (p. 249); a simple practical demonstration of the confusion caused when several players all shout at the same time will make the point.

Second, players must clearly understand the difference between shouting and talking to colleagues. Emphasize that only two types of calls are helpful to the player with the ball. These are "time" (which means the player has time to look up and play the ball) and "player-on" (which is a signal that a challenge is imminent).

Make sure that all your players, including the dictator, are fully aware of what is meant by good communication. Then try the following strategies.

In Practice

In practice, play silent soccer (p. 298), conditioning the dictator to silence. In this way you will demonstrate that other players can think and act for themselves and will emphasize that successful teamwork depends upon thinking for oneself. The dictator must realize that excessive shouting can reduce team effectiveness.

In Games

If the dictator is a good player and is well liked, then he or she may make a good captain. Appointing the dictator captain allows this player to talk to other players during the game. If you use this strategy, you must initiate the dictator into the skills of leadership. For example, teach the player to use encouragement rather than negative criticism, to recognize good plays, and to lead by example.

If your dictator does not possess leadership qualities or is too unpopular to appoint as captain, then you need another strategy. In pregame talks, remind him or her of the continuing need to recognize the difference between shouting and calling; and use goals to work toward behavior change (e.g., the player tries to go 20 minutes without shouting at teammates or tries to save calls for those moments in the game when they can be really useful).

If all of these solutions fail, then short periods of substitution following an incident will help to get the message across.

The Poor Tactician

The poor tactician persistently makes the same kind of mistake during a game and as a result either ruins a good play or exposes the defense unnecessarily. Typical examples include the attacker who continually runs offside; the defender who rushes in and commits himself or herself unnecessarily; and the midfield player who makes too many inaccurate or poorly planned passes.

Such "unthinking" actions are not done deliberately, but they have to be minimized if a team is to be successful. The coach can use two methods to improve tactical awareness. The first method is described in chapters 6 and 7, which established the importance of using small-team games to develop tactical appreciation, and in chapters 17 and 18, which discuss several ways of coaching better teamwork (e.g., attack versus defense, individual positional plays, and coaching in the game).

The second method, which is useful for the coach who has a particularly difficult problem to resolve, is based on recent thinking in the field of behavior modification psychology. The method involves a careful analysis of the problem followed by the construction of a checklist that is used to monitor progress. I will explain the method using the example of a player who continually runs offside, but keep in mind that the method is the same whatever the problem.

The Offside Problem

• Sit down with the player and analyze all the possible reasons for being caught offside. This will inform the player as well as provide information for your checklist. The causes can be divided into two groups, those for which the player is personally responsible and those over which he or she has no control.

The player is not responsible when the referee gives a bad call or when a teammate delays the pass too long. The player is responsible when he or she falls for a deliberate offside trap played by the opposition; runs too soon out of anxiety to gain the advantage; fails to look both ways along the line of the defense; turns his or her back on the passer and runs away; or forgets the rules and stands in line with the defenders.

• Arrange the factors that the player can control into a grid (Figure 20.1).

• Each time the player gets caught offside, the coach records the reason why.

• Behavior modification theory does the rest, with a little help from you! Now the player is personally involved, is able to analyze and evaluate the reasons for the mistakes, and becomes both more knowledgeable and more coachable.

Reason   **Date**

Caught in an offside trap

Ran too soon

Failed to look both ways

Turned and ran away from passer

Didn't know the rules

Figure 20.1
Offside checklist.

Dropping a Player

Every time you select a team you are in danger of losing a friend! Those you don't select are going to be disappointed, and their self-esteem will take a beating. How can you drop a player and still retain his or her respect and allegiance to the team? My advice is as follows.

Be sure that the player being dropped is the first to know; don't let him or her find out second hand. Tell the player personally. This is a responsibility that you cannot delegate to others. Give the player an honest reason. If it is a matter of tactics (e.g., you want to play a different system) or if it is for reasons such as injury, which are not related to loss of form, then the task of informing players is easier. The difficulty comes when the player has lost form and is playing badly.

I seldom drop a player because of one bad game. First, this would be an admission of poor selection on my part. Second, a player can have a poor game for a variety of reasons, such as very superior opposition, poor support from colleagues, or personal reasons.

Third, the player will probably realize that he or she had a bad game and will seek to improve on the next occasion. In all these cases, a coach can do much between games.

When a sequence of poor games occurs, I still only drop a player when I have a replacement or can implement a change in tactics that is likely to improve performance. I don't drop a player unless I have an alternative strategy.

Finally, I try never to drop a player from the team in one move. I prefer to use the substitutes' bench as a platform both onto and off the team, unless I have a second or lower team on which an immediate place is available.

Talking to the Player You Have Dropped

The above strategies are all related to one objective—a concern for the self-esteem of the player. It is easy to hurt the pride of a young player and, worse, turn him or her away from soccer. When you discuss the reasons that resulted in the player being dropped, try to do so in a manner that focuses on the way the player acted, not one that makes a judgment on the player as a person. For example, consider a player who continually avoids going into a tackle. To bluntly tell the player that he or she is "chicken" would be to attack the player as a person. Such an opinion might be true, but it would probably hurt the player's feelings considerably. A better way would be to highlight two or three examples during the game when the player's judgment or decision not to move into the tackle was wrong and exposed the team in a way that cannot be allowed to continue. This puts the focus on the poor judgment of the player, not on his or her character. From this kind of base it is much easier to rehabilitate the player and eventually restore him or her to the team. At the very least, the player has something concrete to practice and knows exactly what you expect in improvement.

CHAPTER 21

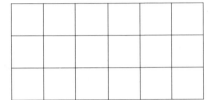

Fitness for Soccer

Fitness training is a complex subject that embraces many different elements. This chapter includes those elements that are directly relevant to soccer and that can be addressed by any coach who has access to a field, a stopwatch, a tape measure, and some markers. Of course, muscular strength and mobility are important, but the coach who is limited to a few coaching sessions a week must give priority to the major fitness element in soccer—the ability to run.

The drills in this chapter require a minimum of equipment, and I hope they will provide every coach with practical advice that can be applied in all circumstances. I have developed and used this unique battery of tests over many years. For each of the tests I provide the standards achieved by international and Olympic players and include some useful data for boys (I do not yet have any data for girls or women).

Fitness training is, by definition, demanding. It is your duty to check the physical condition of your players and keep record of their condition. It is also your responsibility to ensure that training is progressive. Give your players time to improve, always give them a thorough warm-up, and cater to individual differences. It is also your responsibility to have first aid equipment available and to be able to use it.

Five Strategies for Fitness Training

Fitness training for soccer can be based on five ideas. First, study and identify the fitness requirements that are unique to the sport and the different positions within the team. In soccer, for example, every player needs to develop the kicking muscles, but wingers are more likely to benefit from concentrating on speed and acceleration while midfield players need endurance training.

Second, train players in one fitness component at a time. Of course all of the components are related, but each one requires a different training regime. I always target a specific goal and conduct my program accordingly.

Third, keep in mind that a soccer team comprises 11 individuals with varying physiques. A training method that works with one player may not work with another. The skillful coach designs an individual program for each player that can be facilitated by employing the methods I recommend later. Individual programs are much more effective than giving everyone the same exercises, and the tests I have designed really do enable you to train individuals in a group system.

Fourth, keep records so you can analyze the success or failure of your program. Careful records enable you to compare performances over a number of seasons and between different teams. Indeed, with select teams you can even set minimum qualifying standards similar to those used in other athletics, and you can easily compare performances of players within your squad.

Finally, strive to motivate players so they will want to train hard. Good supervision and extrinsic motivation are important, but far more important is the intrinsic, self-motivating drive of wanting to improve. Training should never be a punishment. I try to add enjoyment to activities through carefully graded handicap situations, which are easily arranged.

To get players fit you must understand how the body releases energy and how it responds to exercise. Fortunately, the necessary physiological information can be reduced to a small number of easily remembered facts, which are included at the beginning of each section.

Let us again take note of the potential dangers of fitness training. Players need time to improve, so make your work progressive. Players are different, so try to accommodate these differences and don't expect everyone to do the same amount. Things can go wrong, so make sure that you have a first aid kit available and that you can attend to simple accidents.

Cardiorespiratory Fitness

Like a car, the body has two kinds of energy. The car has a battery for starting and gas for sustained running. The body uses the glycogen in the muscles to start activity, but it needs a supply of oxygen to continue. An activity that does not use oxygen is anaerobic; one that does use oxygen is aerobic. Soccer players need both aerobic and anaerobic fitness. They use short bursts of energy and yet continue to play for up to 90 minutes or longer.

Aerobic Fitness

To improve aerobic fitness, young players have to run continuously for 20 to 30 minutes. They have to run at a pace fast enough to elevate their heart rate to over 130 beats per minute, and they must do this three times a week. This means that you will have to encourage your players to run on days when you do not have team practice, because running uses too much practice time.

Testing Aerobic Fitness

The most famous and the best field test of aerobic fitness is Dr. Kenneth Cooper's 12-minute run/walk test. Ask your players to run or walk for 12 minutes, and measure how far they travel. A fit youngster will cover 1-1/4 to 1-1/2 miles depending on age and sex. A very fit youngster will cover up to 2 miles. However, aerobic fitness is related to body weight, so make allowances for heavy players (and try to help them slim down). Fortunately, just playing soccer helps children to develop aerobic fitness, and this is one of the benefits of the game.

Anaerobic Fitness

Soccer calls for repeated bursts of strenuous activity, and this kind of fitness is developed through interval training, which varies the ratios of work and rest. It is important to get these ratios right to avoid a by-product of exercise called lactic acid, which begins to accumulate after 30 seconds of hard exercise. I therefore recommend that you either work players for less than 30 seconds and give them a rest of 60 seconds between runs, or keep them working for 60 seconds or more but then give them a longer rest (e.g., 4 or 5 minutes).

When assigning repetitions for interval training, start small and increase gradually. You should determine the number of repetitions by the age and level of fitness of the players. I believe that three repetitions are enough for children under 12, even those who are very fit. Players should not attempt five repetitions unless they are very fit and are over the age of 16. I never give adults more than six repetitions because the players begin to pace themselves and this detracts from the training effect. I feel it is better to have quality work.

Testing Anaerobic Fitness

The timed shuttle-run test is an excellent field test of anaerobic fitness. It is reliable and easy to understand and is very hard work, but the standards are related only to men and boys. Coaches of girls' and women's teams should collect their own data.

THE TIMED SHUTTLE RUN TEST

The shuttle run is a well-used but rather boring form of training that with a simple modification became one of my most successful activities for both testing and training. It reflects very well the soccer pattern of running, stopping, turning, and accelerating.

You should use this test after a warm-up and should not follow with any other tests, as players will need several minutes to recover from lactic acid build-up. If you are using the activity for general training, I advise you to do so at the end of your coaching session.

Equipment

1 stopwatch.

Organization

A total of 6 chalk lines are drawn at 5-yard intervals. The player stands at the start line.

Instructions

On the command "go," the player sprints to the 5-yard line, touching it with one foot, and returns to the starting line, touching that line with one foot. Without stopping, the player follows the same procedure with the other lines: 10-yard, 15-yard, 20-yard, and 25-yard lines (Figure 21.1). The time for each run is recorded and the total time calculated.

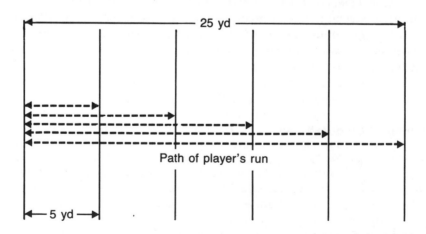

Figure 21.1
The shuttle run.

Table 21.1   Typical Scores for Youth Players Who Complete 3 Shuttles With a 60-Second Rest Between Runs

Age (years)	9	10	11	12	13	14	15	16
Average (seconds)	120	117	114	111	108	105	102	99

Typical Scores for International Adult Players Who Complete 6 Shuttles With a 35-Second Rest Between Runs

International soccer and hockey players average 30 seconds per run for 6 runs with a 35-second rest period between runs. Very fit players will beat 180 seconds total.

Note: It is very important to time the rest period between runs just as carefully as the runs themselves. When engaged in serious testing, I always use two sets of timekeepers with their own watches. The person who times the rest period gives the command to start the next run.

Training Activities for Anaerobic Fitness

Shuttle Run

The shuttle run is an excellent training activity in addition to being a valid anaerobic test. Providing you make your grid lines long enough, you can put several players on the run at the same time. They will compete against each other, which helps motivation. You can use handicap shuttles, in which you give the slower players a 5-yard or even a 10-yard start. Or, you can pair players for partner work. As one player finishes a run, his or her partner takes over. The object is to be the first pair to complete a given number of runs. By pairing your fastest and slowest players together you can get a better competition.

Training With a Ball

All forms of training are enlivened if you can introduce a ball as an incentive. A ball, however, is a variable you cannot always control, which can detract from the serious effort that is required to stress the system. In the following activities I provide several suggestions about how to use a ball with a minimum of interference. In every case you must still set the working period to either 35 or 60 seconds and adjust the rest period appropriately. Please note that while these activities appear quite simple, properly conducted they provide excellent endurance training and the basic information you need to design your own drills.

PASS AND RUN

Equipment
2 balls for each 3 players; ample cones or flags.

Organization
Players are in teams of 3 (teams of 4 for younger players). Chalk lines are drawn 25 yards apart, with 2 additional markers placed 5 yards from the end lines as shown in Figure 21.2.

Instructions
In turn, each player makes a set number of runs. As the runner comes to the 5-yard marker, the server passes to the runner who immediately passes the ball back to the server.

The runner then turns and sprints back across the area to the other 5-yard marker, where the passing sequence is repeated with the next server. A useful challenge is to see how many passes players can make in a given amount of time.

Coaching Progressions
The runner starts with the ball. As the runner approaches a marker, he or she passes to the waiting server, who returns the ball. The runner then dribbles to the other end and repeats with the other waiting server (Figure 21.2).

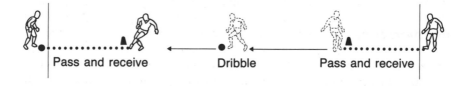

Pass and receive   Dribble   Pass and receive

Figure 21.2

The runner must head the ball back to the server. The pattern of running remains the same as do the number of repetitions and the rest period given (Figure 21.3).

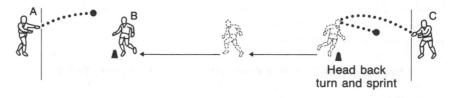

Head back
turn and sprint

Figure 21.3

The active player receives a thrown ball, controls it, passes back to the server, turns, and sprints across to the other side. Again the quality of service from the thrower must be supportive (Figure 21.4).

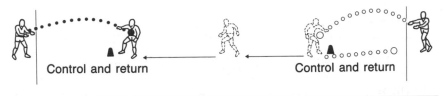

Control and return   Control and return

Figure 21.4

Designing Your Own Activities

These drills are simple to design using a basic process. You must measure the distance the player has to cover, record the time taken to complete the drill, and control the rest period between repetitions as well as the number of repetitions players complete. Review my recommendations about the severity of the workload to prescribe for young players. If you have fit adult males, give them six 40-second repetitions with a 40-second rest as a starting activity and see how they respond. Now that you know how to control the variables, the drill is in your hands!

Acceleration

The ability to accelerate is priceless in soccer, and you must try to improve this ability in all your players including the goalkeeper. Acceleration is a result of three things: mental alertness, strong muscles, and practice. Practice is the most important of all with young players because the body literally must learn how to accelerate. The muscles have to establish movements, and the brain has to lay down what are called cell assemblies, which are little groups of brain cells that control the actions. Players must keep speed work to less than 10 seconds duration, which reduces the possibility of lactic acid accumulation. Such training is called anaerobic alactic training.

The two best tests for speed of acceleration are the Hargreaves 4-second acceleration test, which I designed, and the zigzag test, which is a modified version of the old Illinois agility test.

THE HARGREAVES 4-SECOND ACCELERATION TEST

Equipment
10 markers; 1 stopwatch.

Organization

Players are in groups of 12 or more (1 runner, 1 timekeeper, 10 judges). Markers are placed at the following distances from a start line: 24, 25, 26, 27, 28, 29, 30, 31, and 32 yards.

Instructions

The runner stands with his or her back to the direction of the sprint and with both heels on the line.

On the command "go," the runner turns and sprints past as many markers as possible in 4 seconds.

The timekeeper starts the watch on the command "go" and then concentrates on the second hand. When the hand reaches 4 he or she shouts "now." The timekeeper has to be accurate. An error of 0.1 is allowed either way (i.e., 3.9 or 4.1), but outside this margin the test is invalid. With practice, a good timekeeper can achieve a high degree of accuracy, especially if a digital watch is available.

To count the number of markers passed, use players who have already run or are waiting for their turn.

Players must wear cleats and the test must be done on flat, firm grass (Figure 21.5).

Figure 21.5

Table 21.2 Standards for Young Players

Age (years)	9	10	11	12	13	14	15	16
Distance (yards)	19	20	21	22	23	24	25	26

How Do Your Players Measure Up to International Players?
The average distance covered by professional players and Olympic hockey players is 30 yards. The record is 32 yards.

Using the Test as Training

Measure how far your players run in 4 seconds and then reverse the practice. Start them at their best distance and let them sprint back to the start.

By putting 2, 3, or 4 players against each other, you make each run into a race and provide competition. Players of different speeds can compete because of the handicap difference. The back runner can see those in front and will try to catch them; the front player runs as fast as possible to avoid being caught. This is good motivation and good fun.

For an elimination activity, follow the same organization but this time the winner in each heat is eliminated. Those left try again until only 2 players are left. Of course, you will also organize "winners' races" while the main group is resting to ensure that everyone runs the same number of sprints during the session. In this way you will soon identify which are the fastest and the slowest sprinters and you can then train them accordingly.

ACCELERATION ACTIVITIES

Select players of equal ability and organize the following activities:

Through the Legs

Figure 21.6

A has the ball.

B faces A with legs wide apart.

A passes the ball through the legs of B who has to turn, accelerate, and stop the ball as quickly as possible (Figure 21.6).

Progression

Arrange a marker between 5 and 10 yards away. Player A now has to pass the ball just hard enough to permit B to stop it before it reaches the marker.

This practice depends upon how well A judges the force of the pass. Too soft makes the challenge too easy; too hard and player B will not even try to accelerate because he or she will see that the task is impossible. Given time to practice, all players will quickly improve because the challenge to both players is infectious.

Turn and Go

Figure 21.7

Two players stand back to back and at equal distance from the ball. On command they turn and accelerate. The first to *touch* the ball wins. No tackling is allowed (Figure 21.7).

Turn and Tackle

Players stand back to back. B has the ball.

On command, B dribbles forward, while A has to turn and chase (Figure 21.8).

Figure 21.8

Backing Off and Turning—For Defenders

Figure 21.9

Players face each other. A runs gently forward causing B to back-off. A now accelerates past B, either left or right. B has to turn and stop A from getting by (Figure 21.9).

Do this several times across the field and then change positions.

Resistance Running

Figure 21.10

A and B hold the towel while C tries to sprint (Figure 21.10).

This practice is well-known to sprinters and is excellent for conditioning the leg muscles which accelerate the body forward. However, make sure the towel is in good condition and warn players not to let go of the towel.

THE ZIGZAG TEST

This test is based on the Illinois agility test. Five posts are arranged in the shape of an X. The distances between the markers in the rectangle are 16 feet and 8 feet. The center marker is placed where the diagonals intersect. The player must wear cleats, and the grass must be firm and flat. The test range should be positioned on spare ground because the constant turning quickly damages the turf. The flags must be at least 4 feet tall to prevent the player leaning as he or she turns. The player runs in a figure eight pattern (Figure 21.11).

Table 21.3 Standards for Young Players

Age (years)	9	10	11	12	13	14	15	16
Average speed (seconds) 1 run	8.4	8.2	8.0	7.8	7.5	7.3	7.1	6.9
3 runs		27	26.3	25.6	24.9	24.2	23.5	22.8	22.1

How Do Your Players Measure Up to International Players?
Professionals can complete one run in less than 6 seconds, and 3 runs in 18 to 19 seconds.

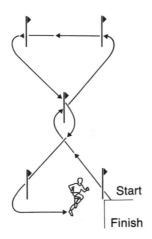

Start

Finish

Figure 21.11

ZIGZAG COMPETITION

Arrange 3 or more sets of posts as shown in Fig. 21.12. Start 3 players simultaneously and let them compete against each other, or you can arrange elimination and handicap events. It is important to also run the players in the reverse direction around the makers. In this way, you ensure that they practice turning to the left and the right in equal proportion.

1

Figure 21.12

Speed

Speed and acceleration are closely related. In soccer we are more concerned with acceleration because a player seldom sprints more than 30 yards at a time. However, players must also practice sprinting distances between 30 and 40 yards. In this way they will improve acceleration and be able to sustain speed when they are involved in a race for the ball.

In track and field sprinting, running style is important. The body leans forward, the head is kept still, the arms pump forward and backward in a straight line, and the knees are raised high to increase stride length and drive the athlete forward in a series of explosive bounds. The whole motion is elegant, balanced, and controlled. In soccer the player enjoys few of these opportunities, and for this reason running style is less important. Indeed, the arms are usually carried low and moved across the body, the head is moved about to watch the ball and other players, the body remains upright, and the stride length is much shorter because the player must prepare to arrive at the ball or change direction.

For all these reasons, speed training in soccer should always be done on grass, in soccer shoes, and if possible in competition with someone of similar ability. Don't worry about style; let your players practice what they do naturally and simply emphasize the basics—using the arms and driving the legs. As with acceleration, what matters is that you give the players the opportunity to practice the act of sprinting.

Testing for Speed

There are many tests of speed. The following speed test enables you to evaluate a whole team very quickly and without any help.

THE HARGREAVES 50-YARD FLYING START TEST

Equipment
   3 markers; 1 stopwatch.

Organization
   The players are in a group of unlimited number on a field marked as follows.

   Measure 50 yards along the sideline with the halfway line as the midpoint. Then measure 50 yards into the field along the halfway line, and mark all three points with a corner flag or post.

   The players stand 15 yards from the starting point because they need this distance to reach maximum speed as they start the timed section. The timekeeper looks along the line of the posts and both starts and stops the watch as the player breaks the line of the posts (Figure 21.13).

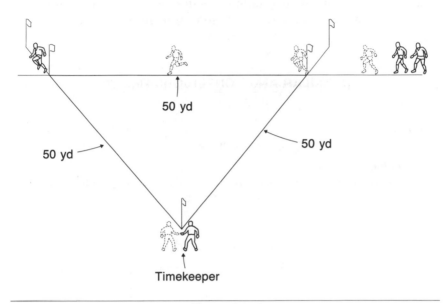

50 yd

50 yd

50 yd

Timekeeper

Figure 21.13

Instructions

Players normally have 2 attempts with only the fastest time being recorded. Players have at least 5 minutes rest between trials. This is needed to let the players walk back to the start and to recover. Players wear cleats and soccer clothing. The grass should be flat and level and firm. Wet or soft conditions will reduce performance times. Players must be properly warmed up.

Table 21.4 Standards for Young Players

Age (years)	9	10	11	12	13	14	15	16
Average (seconds)	9.0	8.6	8.2	7.8	7.4	7.0	6.6	6.2

How Do Your Players Measure Up to International Players?

Professional soccer players and Olympic hockey players average between 5 and 5.5 seconds. Very fast players achieve 4.8 seconds. Slow players take up to 6.0 seconds.

Speed Training Activities

The following three training activities are both popular and effective. They make an excellent finale to a training session or can be used before you move into game practices. All are based on team competitions.

CIRCULAR AND CONTINUOUS RELAY

Equipment
> 6 corner posts; 1 relay baton or stick.

Organization
> Players are in groups of 7; two players are at the starting post, the other 5 are as shown in Figure 21.14.

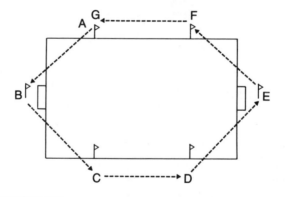

Figure 21.14

Instructions
> The coach gives a starting signal. The relay continues until Player G has completed his or her 6th run and everyone else is now back in their starting positions.

Coaching Progressions
> Two teams race against each other but in the opposite direction. This is highly motivating because the players cannot easily judge who is winning until the final two runners converge on and cross the finish line.

> Two teams race. You record the difference in time between them and handicap the winning team by that amount for a second race.

SHUTTLE RELAY 1

Equipment

    2 markers for each 4 players.

Organization

    Players are in teams of 4 between 2 markers fixed 30 yards apart; players stand as shown in Figure 21.15.

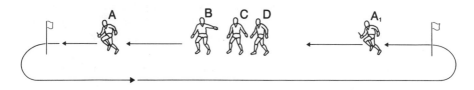

Figure 21.15

Instructions

    Players exchange the baton as in a normal track and field relay (e.g., Player A passes to Player B). Each player sprints in turn until all 4 have finished.

    By timing each team, you can introduce handicap races (e.g., the slowest team starts).

SHUTTLE RELAY 2

Equipment

    2 markers for each 6 players.

Organization

    Players are in teams of 6 positioned near 2 markers placed 50 yards apart (or less if you want to use this practice for acceleration) as shown in Figure 21.16.

Figure 21.16

Instructions

The incoming player runs to the left of the marker. The receiving player holds his or her hand behind the marker to receive the baton. This prevents any cheating by starting too soon.

Pressure Training

Pressure training is fun and is a very effective training method. It involves selecting one player and normally one skill such as heading or collecting the ball. You then serve the player balls in a continuing stream, starting slowly and then increasing the tempo as the player becomes accustomed to the practice. The drill becomes harder and harder for the player, who has to try to maintain a high skill level even when tired—hence the name pressure training.

Organizing pressure practices is quite simple. You either provide one server with a plentiful supply of soccer balls and some helpers to replenish the stock or provide several players with balls who serve in turn to the player under pressure.

For example, to practice heading, have three players stand in a triangle with a ball each (Figure 21.17). One player stands in the middle. Each server throws the ball in turn, and the header has to return the ball to each server in sequence. The speed of the throws depends upon the ability of the header.

Figure 21.17
Practicing heading the ball.

Figure 21.18
Diving heading practice.

To practice diving heading one player kneels down and receives a continuous service from one or two servers (Figure 21.18). The rate of service depends upon the skill and response of the header, and the ability of the servers to recover any misdirected returns. Provide the servers with an ample number of soccer balls. With advanced players, the service can be directed to either the left or right of the receiver, who responds with extended diving movements similar to those used in the full-game situation when attacking the goal.

Skill Circuits

The final way to increase players' fitness in an interesting and enjoyable way is to design a skill circuit. To do this you plan a series of soccer skills in a sequence and let the players take turns competing against each other or against the clock (Figure 21.19). With imagination and some equipment you can play any number of skill circuits, even with only a few markers available.

Start the stopwatch and the first player simultaneously. Start all the other players at 15-second intervals, letting the watch run. When each player finishes, deduct the starting time from the finishing time to see how long it took to complete the circuit (performance time). A sample record is shown in Table 21.5.

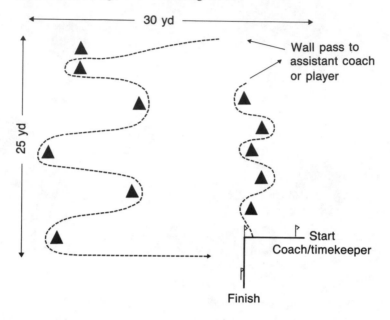

Figure 21.19
A field set up for skill circuits.

Table 21.5   Circuit Results

Player	Time started (sec)	Time finished (sec)	Performance time (sec)	Rank order for positions
A	0	64	64	5th (tie)
B	15	75	60	3rd
C	30	92	62	4th
D	45	109	64	5th (tie)
E	60	119	59	2nd
F	75	145	70	7th
G	90	147	57	1st

For variation, start the players at different points on the circuit and let them try to catch the player in front. In this game the practice would be continuous but you would set a time limit (e.g., 3 minutes). Set out two identical circuits with a common starting and finishing point. The player who completes the circuit first is the winner.

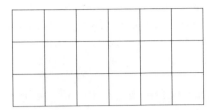

Glossary

aerobic—Exercise that uses oxygen.

anaerobic—Exercise that does not use oxygen and that produces lactic acid.

angle, narrowing the—Moving toward the player with the ball; especially applied to goalkeepers.

angle of passing—Direction of pass in relation to either the defending or supporting players.

angle of run—Direction a player runs in relation to a specific situation.

angle, widening the—Movement of the receiving players into usually safer receiving positions; also describes the movement of the player in possession of the ball who may adjust position in order to create better passing angles.

back door—See *blind side*.

back four—Conventional defensive line comprising right back, two center backs, and left back.

ball—Alternative term for pass (e.g., good ball).

ball watching—Attending to the position of the ball but failing to see the tactical situation that is developing or the movement of a specific player.

blind side—The side or direction on the side of the ball opposite the defender. Also called *back door*.

block tackle—Committed frontal tackle done in an attempt to win the ball.

box—Penalty area.

calling—Verbal help between teammates.

center—See *cross*.

closing down—Advancing to restrict space in front of an opponent while covering his or her path to goal.

come off your man—Avoid the player covering you in order to create space in which to receive the ball.

commit the defender—See *defender, commiting the*.

control, cushion—Control of the ball by withdrawing on impact the surface in contact with the ball (e.g., the thigh).

control, platform—Control of the ball with the use of any flat surface of the body.

control, wedge—Control of the ball with the use of a rigid surface (e.g., the sole of the shoe).

cover—To stand behind a teammate who is challenging the player with the ball. In team terms, having enough players goalside of the ball to defend adequately.

cross—A long pass played, often diagonally, into the center of the field. Also called *center*.

cross, far-post—A cross aimed toward the goalpost farthest from the kicker.

cross, near-post—A cross aimed toward the goalpost nearest the kicker.

crossover—When a player running without the ball crosses the path of the player who has the ball. Also called *scissors*.

decoy run—Movement in which a player runs into a position to pull defenders away from certain parts of the field so a more effective pass can be made to a teammate filling the resulting space.

defense, back of the—The area between the rearmost defenders and their goalkeeper.

defender, committing the—Moving toward or past a defender, with or without the ball, in such a way as to attract the attention of that defender, allowing him or her no opportunity to observe other attackers or tactical development.

disguise—See *feint*.

dribble—Close, skillful control of the ball, especially when seeking to beat a defender.

dummy, selling the—Successful attempt to trick or unbalance and therefore gain advantage over a defender.

early ball—Pass played at the first possible opportunity, usually into space for a teammate to move into.

eye contact—Method of nonverbal communication particularly to initiate rehearsed moves.

feint—Action that attempts to confuse or trick the defenders. Also called *disguise*.

flank—Area of the field up to approximately 15 yards of the touch lines.

flight, line of—Flight path of the ball.

give and go—See *push and run*.

goalside of the ball—Position between the ball and the goal one is defending.

half-volley—Volley in which contact is made with the ball immediately after it hits the ground (i.e., on the fly).

instep—Upper surface of the foot or shoe (i.e., the laces).

inswerve—Path of a ball that curls in toward a target.

jockeying—Holding up or delaying the advance of an opponent who has the ball, usually by trying to force him or her toward or along the touch line.

killer pass—Through pass that splits the defense.

late tackle—Challenge that, whether intentional or accidental, makes unfair contact with the player after he or she has played the ball.

line of recovery—Path a defender takes when running back toward the goal to get goalside of the ball.

lofted drive—Powerful kick with the instep through the bottom half of the ball.

mark—To cover a player closely to prevent the opponent from receiving the ball.

marking, one-on-one—A system of defense in which all defenders mark their own particular opponent (e.g., at a throw-in).

narrowing the angle—Moving nearer to an opponent in order to reduce his or her passing or shooting opportunities.

offside trap—Play in which a defensive player or unit, usually acting on a call or signal, moves forward in such a way as to catch at least one opponent in an offside position.

off the ball—Movement away from the area around the player who has the ball.

one-touch play—Play in which the player passes the ball immediately after receiving it.

one-two pass—A pass involving an immediate return ball.

on the ball—When an individual player is in possession of the ball.

outswerve—Path of a ball curling away from a target.

pass, chip—Pass made by a stabbing action of the kicking foot to the bottom part of the ball to achieve a steep trajectory and heavy backspin on the ball.

pass, half-volley—Pass made by the kicking foot contacting the ball at the moment after the ball touches the ground (i.e., on the fly).

pass, push—Pass made with the inside of the kicking foot.

pass, swerve—Pass made by imparting spin to the ball, causing it to swerve. Which way the ball swerves depends on whether contact with the ball is made with the outside or the inside of the kicking foot, and on which side the ball is kicked.

pass, volley—Pass made before the ball touches the ground.

penetration—Principle of play used to assess a team's ability to break through the opposition's defense.

peripheral vision—Outer part of the field of vision.

pitch—Field of play.

play, conditioned—Play to which an artificial restriction has been applied (e.g., all players must pass the ball on the first touch).

play, crossover—Play in which two attacking players move in opposite directions past each other. These movements are usually made with the ball but can also be made without it.

play, shadow—Method of coaching that allows players to create movements without opposition.

player, covering—A defending player who supports the first defender by adopting a position that will enable the covering player to challenge if the first defender is beaten.

player, supporting—An attacking player who is positioned to receive a pass from the player in possession of the ball.

pressure training—Method of training players in rapid succession for a limited period.

push and run—Play in which a player plays a short ball to a teammate and immediately runs, often for the return pass. Also called *give and go*.

run, blindside—Run by an attacker on the side of the ball opposite the defender.

run, overlap—Movement of an attacking player from a position behind the ball to a position ahead of the ball.

running off the ball—Tactical run to support a teammate who has the ball.

run with the ball—To move with the ball without dribbling past an opponent.

scissors—See *crossover*.

screening the ball—See *shielding*.

selling oneself—Overcommitting oneself to a challenge for a ball and being beaten.

set piece—Restart after an infringement or when the ball goes out of play (i.e., goal kicks, throw-ins, corners, indirect free kicks, and direct free kicks, including penalties).

set plays—Moves worked out in training to exploit set pieces.

shadow marking—Assigning one player to mark a dangerous opponent closely for the whole match.

shadow play—Training technique in which players create movements without opposition.

shielding—Maintaining control and possession of the ball by keeping one's body between the ball and the challenging opponent. Also called *screening the ball*.

showing oneself—Making it obvious to the player with the ball that one is available for the pass.

sliding tackle—Tackle made by sliding one's supporting leg along the ground.

space, creating—Increasing the distance from opponents.

square ball—Any pass made across the field that is approximately parallel to the goal lines (at right angles to the touch line).

square defense—Defense spread in a line across the field. Such a defense is lacking depth and is vulnerable to the killer pass, and is thus said to be caught square.

stretched defense—Defense that is spread out and has no cover.

support play—Assisting the passer by moving into positions which increase his or her passing opportunities.

support, wide angled—Support at an angle wide enough to give the greatest possibility for passing the ball forward.

sweeper—Defender who plays behind and covers the rest of the defense.

swerve—See *inswerve* and *outswerve*.

switching the play—Changing the point of the attack, notably with a crossfield ball.

tackle—A challenge, using the foot, to win the ball.

taking a player on—Trying to beat a defender by dribbling past him or her.

target man—Front player who presents himself or herself as a target for midfielders' passes.

thirds of the field—Areas roughly 35 yards in length signifying the defending, the middle, and the attacking thirds of the field.

through pass—A pass played between two defenders into the space behind them, into which a teammate runs.

top roll—Forward rotation on the ball, in a straight line, which causes the ball to hug the ground.

turning one's opponent—Causing an opponent to turn, usually by playing the ball past or by moving past him or her.

turning with the ball—Receiving the ball when facing one's goal and turning, with the ball under control, to face the opponent's goal.

volley—Kicking the ball before it lands.

wall—Line of players forming human barrier against a free kick near goal.

wall pass—A pass between two attacking players, in which the player acting as the wall plays the ball the first time, at a similar angle to which the player received the ball. The pass is usually made behind an opponent.

wall player—Player acting as the wall in a wall pass.

weight of the pass—Pace or force of a pass.

wide player—Front runner or attacking midfielder who plays near the touch line, not necessarily a winger.

winger—Attacking player whose main role is to play out wide, get to the goal line, and supply crosses to teammates in the central areas.

work-rate—Player's overall physical contribution to the team effort, particularly running off the ball and covering.

wrong side—The side of an opponent that allows the opponent to get between a defender and the goal.

zonal defense—Defensive system in which each member has an approximate area or zone and is responsible for covering any opponent who enters that zone.

About the Author

Alan Hargreaves, MA, MEd, played for Lancashire, Loughborough Colleges and English Universities. A fully qualified Football Association coach, he directed national residential coaching courses for players up to 18 years of age and co-directed the Soccer Academy for Young Players in California. He was head coach for the British Colleges soccer team and coached professional soccer for five years—two years with Stoke City and three years with Crewe Alexandra. He has conducted numerous coaches and players courses in England and California and is a consultant in Fitness Training for soccer and hockey.

Formerly chairman of the Madeley School of Graduate Physical Education, Alan directed the fitness training program for the 1980 and 1984 British Olympic Men's Field Hockey Team. He has also worked extensively in universities, soccer coaching clinics, and residential camps, many for the American Youth Soccer Organization.

In his leisure time, he enjoys golf and traveling.